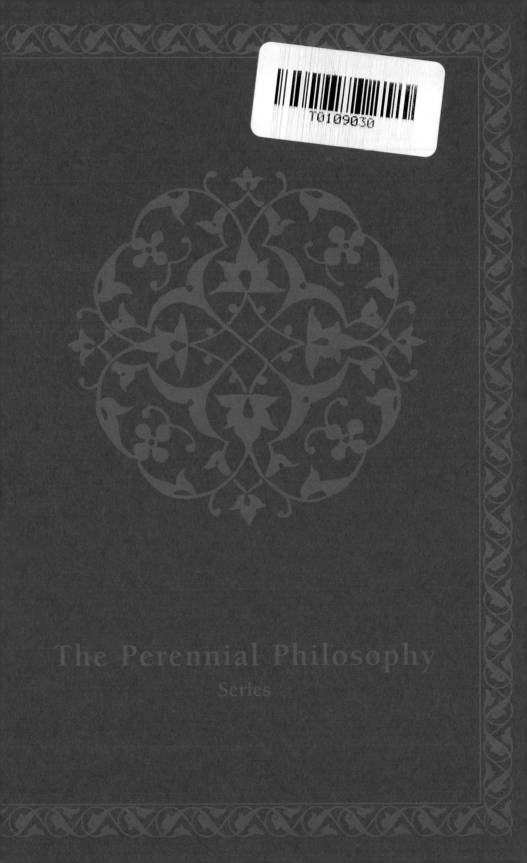

The Perennial Philosophy

Series

World Wisdom
The Library of Perennial Philosophy

The Library of Perennial Philosophy is dedicated to the exposition of the timeless Truth underlying the diverse religions. This Truth, often referred to as the *Sophia Perennis*—or Perennial Wisdom—finds its expression in the revealed Scriptures as well as the writings of the great sages and the artistic creations of the traditional worlds.

The Perennial Philosophy provides the intellectual principles capable of explaining both the formal contradictions and the transcendent unity of the great religions.

Ranging from the writings of the great sages of the past, to the perennialist authors of our time, each series of our Library has a different focus. As a whole, they express the inner unanimity, transforming radiance, and irreplaceable values of the great spiritual traditions.

Returning to the Essential: Selected Writings of Jean Biès appears as one of our selections in the Perennial Philosophy series.

The Perennial Philosophy Series

In the beginning of the Twentieth Century, a school of thought arose which has focused on the enunciation and explanation of the Perennial Philosophy. Deeply rooted in the sense of the sacred, the writings of its leading exponents establish an indispensable foundation for understanding the timeless Truth and spiritual practices which live in the heart of all religions. Some of these titles are companion volumes to the Treasures of the World's Religions series, which allows a comparison of the writings of the great sages of the past with the perennialist authors of our time.

Cover Reference:
"En-no-Gyoja, the Friend of the Travelers,"
painting by Nicholas Roerich, 1925.

JEAN BIÈS

Returning to the Essential

SELECTED WRITINGS
OF
JEAN BIÈS

TRANSLATED FROM THE FRENCH
BY DEBORAH WEISS-DUTILH

Introduction by Patrick Laude

World Wisdom

Returning to the Essential: Selected Writings of Jean Biès
© 2004 World Wisdom, Inc.

For complete bibliographic information on the articles
in this anthology, please see the List of Extracts
at the end of the volume, p. 266.

Library of Congress Cataloging-in-Publication Data

Biès, Jean.
 [Retour à l'essentiel. English]
 Returning to the essential : selected writings of Jean Biès /
translated from the French by Deborah Weiss-Dutilh ; introduction by
Patrick Laude.
     p. cm. – (The perennial philosophy series)
 Includes bibliographical references (p. 267) and index.
 ISBN 0-941532-63-1 (pbk. : alk. paper)
 1. Spirituality. I. Title. II. Series.
 BL624.B4913 2004
 204–dc22

                                                    2004015867

Printed on acid-free paper in Canada

For information address World Wisdom, Inc.
P.O. Box 2682, Bloomington, Indiana 47402-2682

www.worldwisdom.com

TABLE OF CONTENTS

V PHILOSOPHIA PERENNIS

INTRODUCTION

In the last few decades, the family of thought that has come to be known in the English-speaking world as the "perennialist school" has generally been designated in the French-speaking world by the two adjectives *traditionnel* and *traditionaliste*. These latter two terms have had the important merit of underlining a deeper and richer understanding of the devaluated and flattened word "tradition," highlighting both its sacred and integral implications by contrast with the all too common view that equates tradition with stifling custom and lack of imagination. One of the signal contributions of this school has been to introduce contemporary readers to a definition of Tradition that is indissociable from its divine and supernatural origin, and which emphasizes the imperative need of the sacred means that it provides in view of returning to the Essential. On the other hand, it must be acknowledged that these two terms—especially *traditionaliste*—can be somewhat ambiguous or even misleading since they also routinely refer, at least in France, to that portion of the Catholic Church that has radically rejected the dogmatic and liturgical innovations of the Council of Vatican II.[1]

Be that as it may, while the perennialist school has often been characterized in the Anglophone world as stemming from a triad of philosophical fathers comprised of René Guénon, Ananda K. Coomaraswamy and Frithjof Schuon, the *école traditionaliste* has tended to be more emphatically and exclusively considered, in the Francophone world, as springing forth from René Guénon's seminal works alone. This holds true for a variety of reasons, all more or less related to Guénon's privilege of anteriority, and to the specifically French modality of the mindset through which he distilled universal principles. As has sometimes been implied, Guénon's work has the somewhat paradoxical characteristic of expressing the substance of Shankaracharya's teachings in the language of René Descartes, a language that has been associated—for better or worse—with a sense of rational clarity which is particularly fit for metaphysical and philosophical exposition.

---

[1] Perennialist *traditionalistes* undoubtedly agree with *Catholiques traditionalistes* in their diagnosis of the Church's maladies; it is obvious, however, that the concept of tradition, or rather Tradition, which they foster is much deeper and more all-encompassing than the tradition of the latter.

René Guénon's work first appeared in a country[2] that had just
passed from the celebrated status of "eldest daughter" of the
Roman Catholic Church to that of a land undergoing radical and
vehement laicization, as evidenced in the Law of 1905 mandating
the separation of Church and State—and this, following more than
twelve centuries of quasi-constant union between the two. In the
early twentieth century, the new "gospel" of the French Republic
was disseminated through the secular and anti-clerical "seminaries,"
the *Ecoles Normales,* in which schoolteachers were trained to become
the apostles of the new values that were to substitute the previously
pervasive ones of the Catholic Church in matters of mind and soul.
If the French Revolution was the end of what had remained of traditional France *politically,* the Third Republic—which lasted almost
seventy years, till the beginning of the Second World War—put an
end both *socially* and *culturally* to what had still managed to survive
this revolutionary onslaught, the industrial revolution, and the
ascent of the *bourgeoisie.* The fact that France is today one of the
most non-religious countries in the world is primarily a consequence of the ideological effectiveness of the Third Republic and
its transformation of a whole society. It is indeed an irony of history—and no doubt also a compensation—that the initial steps of the
perennialist school, or *le courant traditionaliste*—a current of thought
that was to articulate the most radical critique ever of the modern
world—were taken in the very country that had shown itself to be
arguably the most anti-traditional in the world, through its inaugu-
ration of both the intellectual Enlightenment—the *Lumières* of the
Encyclopédistes—and the French Revolution of 1789. Guénon himself came from a Catholic lineage that was representative of what
remained of the social and cultural *Ancien Régime,* and his antago-
nistic relationship with the French academic structure and milieu
was in a sense symptomatic of the opposition between two worlds.
Be that as it may, it is all too rarely mentioned that the country of
Voltaire is also that of Guénon, although it is obviously less often
recognized as the latter than as the former.

In the wake of Guénon's work, the publication of which spanned
over thirty years until his death in Cairo in 1951, a large segment of

[2] Guénon was born in 1886. His first work, *Introduction générale à l'étude des doctrines
hindoues* (*Introduction to the Study of the Hindu Doctrines*), was published in 1921.

traditional works were published in French, and in France in particular. Most of this production issued from collaborators of Guénon or from individuals who were profoundly marked by his writings, and who often had connections with him in the form of personal relationships or correspondence. The works of Frithjof Schuon, Titus Burckhardt, Leo Schaya, Michel Valsân, Jean Borella, Jean Canteins, Jean Hani, Jean-Louis Michon, and others, were, with a very few exceptions, written in the same language as Guénon. They were, moreover, made available by French publishing houses such as Gallimard, Editions Traditionnelles, or Dervy. Among these works, only Schuon's and Burckhardt's, and to a much lesser extent Schaya's and Borella's, have been made available in English translations in print. The works of Jean Biès are situated in this intellectual lineage. He belongs to what could be called the second generation of traditionalist writers, the generation of Seyyed Hossein Nasr, Jean Borella and those others who were born between the two world wars. This generation makes the link between the generation of the "fathers" of the movement, who grew up in a world that still conserved some residual traces of traditional principles, and the generation of those who were born after the Second World War, in a world that had already become almost completely topsy-turvy.

Jean Biès was born in Bordeaux, but spent the first years of his life in Algeria, which he left when he was just twenty-four. The years of his youth in Algeria marked his first contact with the world of Tradition, in the context of an Islamic tradition that was then still relatively alive. Jean Biès' biography reflects a simple life that has revolved around writing, teaching, and meeting with remarkable men and women and many individuals in search of spiritual light; this has been punctuated by some essential intellectual discoveries and spiritual encounters (Guénon in 1951, Schuon in 1967, Mary-Madeleine Davy in 1981), as well as some inspiring voyages (Greece in 1958, India in 1973). Biès is an erudite scholar, and he was an inspiring teacher—some of his former students, who have remained in contact with him throughout the years, have become well-known figures, such as the former French Minister of Education François Bayrou—but he has always remained a very "independent scholar," shunning the academic establishment and ideological cliques.

Jean Biès' works remain unknown in the English-speaking world and this situation calls for some words of explanation. Less pro-

fusely speculative—in the highest sense of the term—than those of
Leo Schaya and Jean Canteins, less technically initiatic than those of
Michel Valsân, less philosophical than those of Georges Vallin and
Jean Borella, and less focused on a given tradition than those of
Jean Hani and Jean-Louis Michon, Jean Biès' works have a room of
their own in the house of traditionalist thought, and a voice of their
own in the concert of perennialist works written in French.
Compared with the aforementioned works, Jean Biès' opus is both
more diverse, without in any way lacking essential unity, as well as
more literary, without attaching to this term any aestheticist
nuance. There is a mercurial mobility and diversity about Biès' writing, as well as a particular lightness of touch in dealing with topics
of metaphysical and spiritual weight. Even when touching upon
substantial matters of doctrine, Biès is never pedantic or cumbersome. One would be tempted to say that his is an understanding of
literature as *lîlâ*, a divine play that enlivens and enlightens. He
shapes his aphorisms and formulae with a nimble brio that pertains
to joy and grace; he does not disdain to play on words, as a contemporary adept of *nirukta*, in order to suggest subtle analogies and
crystallize spiritual allusions.

He is a writer just as one is an artist or a craftsman. It is not only
that Biès writes; the truth is that his pursuit of Reality and Beauty
takes place through writing. He is a writer who treats of metaphysical and spiritual topics rather than a metaphysician or a sage who
writes in order to disseminate traditional principles and ideas. This,
perhaps, has been his main distinctive feature among French traditionalist writers. In a sense this concern for literary form has also
been, by his own admission, something of a hindrance to the full
dissemination of his works. It certainly makes their translation a
more arduous task, and the current English translation of excerpts
from his oeuvre, under the title *Returning to the Essential*, must be
saluted as a very successful and meritorious labor of love. Still, the
fact is that those who love literature as an art form tend to read his
books because they are attracted by their poetic and stylistic qualities, while those who are in quest of spiritual knowledge will tend to
bypass this aspect, and look for the doctrinal substance that they
provide. As a consequence, the latter may sometimes have a tendency to belittle the importance of his works because of the concern they display for aesthetic form, whereas the former may well
enjoy the inviting beauty of Biès' pages without paying sufficient

attention to the urgent message that they transmit. This is not to say that Biès would claim a kind of symmetry, or equivalence, between the form of his writings and the ideas that they convey. Principles and ideas obviously form the essential core, to which he invites his readers to turn, but he does not feel in the least guilty to join *l'a-gréable à l'utile,* to reverse a French expression—*joindre l'utile à l'a-gréable*—that means joining the useful to the pleasant.

While there is no greater priority than the truth, writing is also a spiritual discipline that is akin to other kinds of qualitative creation, involving both the production of a beautiful object and the beautification of the soul. As with other forms of art, writing involves a form and an essence. The form is the material: the paper, the pen, the table, the physical posture, and so on. There is a certain qualitative aspect to the very act of writing, a quality that most of us have unfortunately lost sight of in an age of word-processors. Jean Biès holds fast to this dimension of his art. It is related to the equilibriating influence of nature and the normal pace of human activity. True writing, both as an act and a product of this act, involves a harmonious blend of meaning and beauty. One cannot reduce the words to the function of mere vehicles; they have to engage our sense of beauty, harmony, and music. This beauty is nowhere more accessible to a writer such as Biès than in and through nature. Nature distills the essences that are like the fragrances emanating from the Divine; and it is certainly not by chance that the catalyst for writing is, for him, none other than the contact he has with the peaceful landscape of the foothills of the Western Pyrenees, a landscape that has the gentleness of its green slopes but also a promise of the peaks outlined on the horizon. Biès' writing is akin to this gentle landscape that leads to metaphysical and spiritual summits. The daily contact of the writer with nature is more than the source of an inspiration as it was for tormented Romantic poets. It forms an integral context that balances and shapes the soul, predisposing her to the expression of Truth. Saint-Michel-la-Grange, the farm in which Biès has lived for over forty years, was first built in the seventeenth century and is a contemplative space that has become for him a creative haven; it exudes the very ambience in which his written work has come to being.

The literary output of Jean Biès is, according to his own indications, three-fold. There is, first of all, a doctrinal and speculative fold that consists in a series of essays in which Biès, like other perennialist authors, aims at transmitting traditional principles while introducing contemporary readers to the treasury of metaphysical, esoteric, and spiritual teachings and sacred sources. This segment of Biès' work is itself to be divided between academic studies devoted to particular figures or movements, such as *Empédocle d'Agrigente—Essai sur la philosophie présocratique* (1969) and *Littérature française et pensée hindoue: Des origines à 1950* (1973), and works of exposition of traditional principles as a response to the spiritual crisis of modern man, among which one must mention *Passeports pour des temps nouveaux* (1982), *Retour à l'Essentiel: Quelle spiritualité pour l'homme d'aujourd'hui?* (1986), and *Sagesses de la Terre: Pour une écologie spirituelle* (1997).

The second grouping is comprised of more "experiential" works that may take the form of travel accounts, memories, and personal testimonies. The first work to be mentioned in this category is *Athos: la Montagne transfigurée* (1997), a mystical and poetic account of Biès' journey to Mount Athos, full of the pristine light of the Mediterranean sun as a terrestrial reflection of the Byzantine Christ's glory. Then comes *La Porte de l'appartement des femmes* (1991), a more personal, but in a sense no less universal, book devoted to the spiritual presence and influence of women in the author's life, a kind of autobiographical celebration of the Eternal Feminine that highlights the function of women as manifestations of the creative energy. Finally, what is, in my opinion, the most beautiful and perhaps the richest of Biès' books, *Les Chemins de la ferveur: Voyage en Inde* (1995). This book highlights the spiritual treasures of India as the author encountered them along his itinerary in Vrindavan, Madurai, Tiruvannamalai, and Benares. It is the literary outcome of an authentic spiritual journey, the delicious and substantive fruit of a rare encounter between the author's profound familiarity with Indian metaphysics and his keen ability to *see* the essential in the most daily experiences. Biès' doctrinal knowledge of India is brought to life in and through his aesthetic and spiritual encounter with the motherly land of Bharata, which prompted Jean Herbert, one of the foremost European specialists of Indian spirituality, to write: "[*Les Chemins de la ferveur*] is the best work on India that I know."

The third grouping of Biès' work is perhaps the least well known, yet it is the most essential to the author himself. Jean Biès is first and foremost a poet: he considers poetry to be the most essential sector of literature, in that it is the very essence of language. In Biès' own words, "poetry is certainly the last enclave of the sacred." Although real poets are rarely known as such in our day and age, Biès' poetry has not remained inconspicuous to those who have an ear for the lyre and a heart for the truth. He received the prestigious High Prize of the Society of French Poets in 1970 and he was saluted by the Catholic philosopher Jean Borella as "one of the great and most authentic poets of our time." As a poet, Jean Biès distances himself from two of the most prevalent features of contemporary poetry: the rejection of rhythmic and harmonic forms, and the cultivation of the ego. These two tendencies share, in fact, in the same error; they sin out of an egocentric presumption and a lack of sensitivity to the normative message of nature and our true Self. The respect for formal imperatives is, in poetry, a kind of "metric reconstitution of the Self," to use Biès' well-inspired phrase. It is therefore part and parcel of the spiritual work to which it calls. Moreover, the mode of operation of poetry is akin to that of "magic," understood here in its broadest sense of a transformation by means of forms; and this is enough to say that words have to be carved and bound together so as to obey an invocatory, suggestive, or evocative music that is the secret of their ability to touch the heart. Although some of Biès' best poetry is personal in the highest sense, expressing the vibrations of the soul in contact with the mysteries of nature, eroticism, and above all, God's presence, Biès is too traditional to conceive of poetry as a kind of amorous cultivation of one's idiosyncrasies; far from that: he simply considers his poetic work as a humble attempt at "versifying the *philosophia perennis.*"

If I had to highlight two among Biès' intellectual and literary gifts, I would opt firstly for his poetical sense, and then for the conceptual and linguistic precision of his language. These two qualities are illustrated by the frequent dual structure of his titles, the first part being suggestive, and the second explicative. Biès wants to suggest, but he also wants first of all to be understood. Precision stems from a respect for language, and for the reader. It is, as it were, a manifestation of the sense of the sacred with regard to language. But precision does not mean dryness or formal perfectionism. In fact, Biès' mode of exposition alternates between his ideal of rational clarity and his affinity with the musicality and the nuances of reality. He has himself acknowledged a certain development or evolution in this respect. His first books bear very clearly the mark of Guénon's rigorous style, while his later books manifest a greater fluidity and subtlety—as if his pen had been touched by a Taoist fairy. This is not only a matter of style but also a matter of substance. It is undeniable that, without compromising any aspect of the essential, the experiences of life and meditation on the most profound truths cannot but make supple, and subtilize, the heart and mind. The latest writings of Biès express a high sensibility to the unfathomable share of the Real, and to the somewhat irreducible complexity of human existence. However, what makes these writings so precious is their consistent rooting in the inexhaustible soil of the *philosophia perennis*: the language of the Essential to which this book invites us, inspiringly, to return.

PATRICK LAUDE
Georgetown University

I

Autobiography

———— ❦ ————

1. GOD'S BOOKSHOP[*]

I had looted the bookshop.

I had stopped purchasing books a long time ago. Tarini let me borrow them; I neglected to return them. It had taken only a few readings for the existence of an entire strange, baroque, and disconcerting society to be revealed to me, one that went unnoticed by those around me and that had risen from the depths of the world: nude ascetics amidst glowing embers, pilgrims bowing down at every step, hermits on their pillars, others, isolated in grottos, turned into masters of the "driving forces" and the "waves of energy." A new vision of things, no longer one of middle-class reason but entirely symbolic, taught me that a mountain was less a mountain than an arch between heaven and earth, a wheel was less a wheel than a rotatory movement of the universal future, and fabric was less a fabric than the texture of the world, where the chain of taut threads represents the immutable axis, and the weave, which is subject to the sliding movement of the loom's shuttle, the impermanent element.

Everything that seemed essential according to us: material comfort, systematic doubt, the belief in progress, gradually lost its consistency, frayed at the edges, and collapsed in entire parts, to be supplanted by the thrill of extremes, by proven facts, or by the wonder of a childlike state nourished by secular knowledge. Moreover, these discoveries determined what would be the nature of my relationships, my trials in life, my journeys, and even the books I would write. I am still astonished at the decisive and definitive impact of everything I received over those three years, still unable to suspect that nearly everything I would be destined to accomplish here below would come from the readings, would come my way from the trailblazer who would recommend them to me.

I read pell-mell the Tibetans, the Hindus, the Persians, Taoist wise men, Zen poets, all of the spiritual writings one would expect to find on the shelves of the One who is the real author.

[*] From *Tarini, Pioneer of Awakening*, V.

I read *Song Offerings* by Rabindranath Tagore:

> O Master, sitting at your feet, may my life be some-
> thing simple and straight,
> like a reed flute that You can fill up with music....

One spoke of the dust on the road where the poet was anxiously on the look-out for the return of the Friend, of the clay lamp burning while he watched for His footsteps in his home, and of the storm clouds announcing the rumor of His banners.

Now this yearning was mine. I, too, could have asked:

> Let only this bit of me live on so that I can call You
> my whole!

This flute, I heard in the garden when old Tâhar was collecting dewdrops. This tufaceous road, which led to our house, I knew as well as I knew the evening lamp encircled by fire-flies or the clouds at twilight scored by the palm trees and the bamboo. From its floor to its ceilings engraved with maxims from the Koran, the Turkish style house that I lived in had mogul airs that I would recognize at the edges of the Jamuna, and was every bit as much a book as was this poetry. In moments of solitude, in the suffocating summer heat, it did more than suggest to me the same atmosphere of anxious expectation penetrated with sacredness.

I read Ibn Arabi, whose *Wisdom of the Prophets* taught me that "existence is continuous perplexity," that "there is no movement in the cosmos that is not a movement of love," and that "the contemplation of God in women is the most intense and the most perfect" because the beauty of a woman is what most resembles God.

The magnificent verses of the *Khamriyya* impressed me with their scintillations: "In memory of the Beloved we drank a Wine that made us drunk before the creation of the vine"; this Wine praised by the "Sultan of Lovers," "is a limpidity, and it is not water, a light without fire, a spirit without body"; this Wine is nothing other than God's Love, drunk by the Lovers in the tavern of the heart, whose only unhappiness is in mixing it with something other than the breath of God.

I read the *Diwan* of al-Hallaj, who in his mystic folly dared to proclaim himself God:

When I wanted to drink to quench my thirst, it is
You that I saw in the shadow of the goblet.

As he had predicted himself: "I will die by the supreme judgment of the cross," the Christ of Islam died crucified. But his head suspended from the placard continued to murmur: "It is enough for the enraptured that the One reduces it to Oneness."

One day Tarini said to me, "Jean, you must meet the Sufis. They've invited me to their festival again. I'll take you. It's a rare occasion. Your parents have to agree."

The previous year she had gone to the *Ihtifel* and had been the only woman, the only French person among three thousand Muslims. I couldn't go with her to the Hoggars; I would follow her to Tigditt.

In a huge sacred space, they danced the *imarah*. They danced for three days and three nights. Circles of initiates in multi-colored caftans danced the *imarah* under the sun and the stars while holding hands and rhythmically bending their knees, chanting the name of Allah for hours on end in awe-inspiring psalmody. The voices of three thousand men uttered the Name of God; the earth shook beneath their feet as the tide of their expirations ardently unfurled until it reached the banks of Fulfillment. Those who faltered or fainted were replaced by others to run the same race toward enlightenment.

Men danced, hours passed. The rhythm became breathless while cheeks reddened, eyes shut and were sealed with tears, voices became hoarse and turbans came undone, faces lit up.

"He who does not dance in memory of the Friend, has no friends...."

Already, spellbound by the divine Fervor, the dancers had become the intimate friends of Truth, more by blending in with it than by forcing their way. Paradise is restored, the lightest and lithest dancers once again become birds and leaves.

How long have they been dancing? The evening hugs us with stars and ecstatic roaring. How many dancers are there? A thousand, some will say. Ten thousand, will say the others.

They are ONE, says Love.

So, I am indebted to Tarini not only for the discovery of mystic literature in that same year when we seriously studied Fontenelle, who shows that religion and poetry are lies because reason can account neither for the oracles of one nor for the charms of the other; I am also indebted to her for the privilege of having been included in the intimacy of that festival of God's Embrace.

I am even indebted to you, O Tarini!—have I ever confessed it to you?—for having scented my name. It is by your doing at this same time that I saw my work published for the first time. To *Les Amis de l'Islam*, the review that you founded, I gave nothing less than a description of the "divine Folly" and an exegesis of a verse from the Koran: "Follow God very closely!" (It would only be much later, while rereading one and the other that I would come to realize how little one doubts at twenty!)

Have you ever suspected the emotion a young writer feels when, for the first time in his life, he reads his name printed on the first page, and goes dizzy sniffing the ink whose particular invigorating odor announces that something astonishing has just happened somewhere in the world?

*
* *

I am indebted to Tarini—is there anything for which I am not indebted to her?—for having heard about Eastern Christianity for the first time while discussing Jacques Lacarière's latest book of photographs of the monasteries of Mount Athos and their tall monks with coiled hair and gray beards. On this occasion I learned the strange word "iconostasis" which designates the wooden partition decorated with icons that separates the bema from the nave and at the same time the sacred from the profane.

It is observations of this kind which lead me to suspect that in Orthodoxy there was a very different Christianity than the one we knew, and would make me decide to go to the Holy Mountain.

From the very beginning of *The Way of a Pilgrim*, I felt as if I were wrapped in an Edenic coolness. The author, an anonymous Russian peasant, had traveled through woods and over plains, armed only with his rosary and his continuous prayer. The more he prayed in the Name of Christ, the more he wanted to pray; and finally his ardor spread to me, who had never before prayed! He even prayed in his sleep, his heartbeat substituting for his lips. With each repetition of the Name, a compassionate gentleness for all creatures grew within him and put him into a state of continuous exultation.

Transfigured, the universe appeared to him as being drenched with the joy of Easter, and in his eyes simple cabins shone like palaces.

> Everything beckoned me [he wrote] to love and praise God: men, trees, plants, beasts, everything seemed familiar to me, and everywhere I found the image of the Name of Jesus Christ. Sometimes, I felt so light that I believed I no longer had a body and could softly float on air....

Reading these lines, I had the feeling that I, too, was floating and the world surrounding me was bedecked with the same splendor. The view of olive trees trembling in the wind, the airy performance of the clouds over the terraces, and the full wind rising from the Berber sea transported me, in an undoubtedly different decor, to a paroxysm of gladness that gave me the desire to embrace passers-by and incited me all the more willingly to kneel before the beauty of the world, youth that likes itself to be mystical with its easy ecstasy. Even the tiny laborious populations in the garden that I had previously exterminated could now count on me as a defender and friend.

The Fool for Christ reminded me of Swami Ramdas, author of *In Quest of God*, which I had finished reading, and who, with childlike candor, gave into the hazards of roaming and taking trains whose destination he ignored. Secretly I would have liked doing what they did and asked myself: "Why, why complicate everything? Why burden life with chores, unbearable work and useless obligations when, in its true nature, all it really aspires to is the simplicity of the heart and the essence of being? Why were all these systems, dialectics, prohibitions, and curses invented? Why all the rivalry, all the tests, all the reciprocal surveillance and the hardening of a world rebelling against all transparency, when the main activity of man should be walking in the country while honoring the Divine Name?"

Even less comprehensible to me than the Western obsession with sin was this accommodating attitude that life is tragic. How much more I preferred the Pantocrator, glorious victor over death, to Jesus agonizing until the end of the world! Western Christianity offered the spectacle of a bleeding God committed to his dereliction and that of theological confrontations between flesh and spirit, reason and faith, nature and mercy. Concerning modern atheism, it reduced man to the state of a sociological animal possessed by property and to a deserter of the being; it deified History, and had enough contempt for man to justify and organize totalitarianism which ended up destroying him.

That nothing of this tragic dimension was to be found in the East, be it Christian or not, pleased me. Tarini explained to me that the East neither affirmed nor raised the ego in front of the Absolute—an ego shaped by ignorance and illusion didn't even exist in relation to itself—but taught that our real life is nothing other than the Absolute. The ego didn't have to fight or rebel against something of which it was a part; it had to become once again what it was. This absence of duality eliminated all opposition and contradiction, therefore, all conflict, and consequently, suffering and its multiple tragedies. It was up to the ego to rediscover and recover its true identity.

We were reading *The Plague* by Camus, from which our professors derived the idea of the non-existence of God because the innocent perished like the guilty. From the Orient, I learned that the death of the innocent was not a revolting scandal because there was no innocent existence. There was only man's *karma* that either had or didn't have enough time to come forth. A man's ego was not the real man; that which was truly real could neither suffer nor be destroyed. Man always had the freedom to reunite with his real being, this universal dimension from which, in fact, he has never been separated and that is known as the Self.

I have not forgotten how blunt these considerations and others of the same type could be for a young man who opened himself up to the meaning of life and worked at understanding himself when "himself" was nothing more than an accumulation of impressions and changing impregnations, superficial and contradictory emotions, and factitious identifications. How elegant this invitation to die so that I could live! Intellectually, however, I adhered to this interpretation of things not so much by my personal experience of its truthfulness but because the truths that had been imposed upon me elsewhere seemed overwhelmingly false.

No more than I, did Tarini appreciate this propensity for the tragic and this is undoubtedly why she had little liking for European music, whereas Eastern music with its pronounced cadences didn't betray any anguish; its rhythm took priority over the melody and proclaimed the gladness of creatures who were not yet separated from their essence.

This music of good spirits was introduced to me by Tarini with the record, *Folk Music of India*, which had taken a year to reach her by going the wrong way around the world. An ample Introduction spoke of the *raga* of dawn and dusk and told of Tan Sen who, having had to play a night *raga* in the middle of the day, made the darkness grow little by little. The amusing names of *gubgubi* and *ghunghur* came along to dance in my ears, one designating a cord drawn across a drum, the other a cluster of tiny bells.

Now, what was revealed to me after the slow preludes where the musician searched for his notes, played hooky from the music, delighted in delaying the moment of departure for parabolical trips to far-off adventures, for gigantic digressions and the descents of vertiginous scales, were the games of joy with flashing ballets of sound, acrobatic variations, crackling arabesques, garlands of cheerfulness draped around the shoulders of existence. And where the nasal *sehnai* winked at the *kartal,* where the *tabla* ran behind, feigning, racing with the *sitar*'s metallic rain, galloping frantically to the roll of drums resounding so rapidly that they were becoming simultaneous, to finish with an accelerated rhythm and an orgiastic delirium that provoked the explosion of layers of unknown consciousness deep within me, reducing any forces that might have made me run through a fire, before falling to the ground, panting in amazement.

*

*   *

I gulped down the nectar of the *Upanishads*, the ones about the Clan of the Toad and the Clan of the Quail, the one about the Sage with a white mule, and even the Great Upanishad of the Forest.

They cast me directly onto the shores of a world clad with impenetrable jungles and wild rivers woven from a still transparent heavenly sky; a world where the eyes of astonished creatures reflected the brightness of dawn; a world exempt from any malignant pollution, from any neurotic unpleasant smell, where being religious spontaneously and regularly was as normal as drinking or walking; a world that was short of any rigid organization, of any clerical control, of any hypocrisy as well as any grief.

Sitting in a circle in the glade near straw-roofed huts, surrounded by ascetic children and tame gazelles, noble brahmans with slender hands, always content, always joyous, talked tirelessly about the birth of the gods, those friendly companions encountered on the road, and gave into oratorical jousting over the number of spokes on the wheels of the chariot of the soul. The winner was rewarded with a thousand zebus. Then they broke out laughing as if they had tricked the gods or had made fun of their own claims to having spoken the language of men. Present were the Lords Bharadvaja Satyavaha and Jayantiputra of Mandukayaniputra as well as the Blessed Medhyatithi, disciple of Kauva, guardian of men, and the venerable Pravahana Jaivali, authority on the umbilical centrality of the earth; many others whose names escape me at the moment were also there.

These long-haired ascetics, these eloquent speakers who had returned from long journeys to their inner souls, compared their discoveries, conversed about the lotus they had seen in the depths of their subtle bodies and about what its petals carried: magic syllables, an elephant with several trunks, a black antelope, sitting or dancing divinities. They spoke about the moon and the wind, the sun, "the honey of the gods." They argued about offerings reserved for departed spirits and about blissful ambrosia.

I was totally *Upanishadded* and went about improvising sublime incantations:

> I am Zenith and Nadir, I am Ether. I am an eleven-syllable meter. I am the altar's brick. I am Luminescence. I am the subtlety of the subtle. I am the auroral Cow. I am the harnessed Wind, the Arrow sharpened by the homage to….

In the Kurukshetra field, I stood near Arjuna, under the blasting of the war horns and the pearl colored shells, among the heroes, "kidnappers of victories." I listened to Krishna teach the art of becoming God by massacring the enemies within: by becoming master of one's senses and thoughts. I aspired to resembling the "fervent disciple" who never shows any hostility toward others, who is always kind and compassionate, fair and serene: "That disciple there is dear to Me." Uprightness, purity and austerity when simply expressed seemed supremely desirable. The absence of any indiscrete willingness to convince—all of this glistened with evidence—

emphasized the benefits of these virtues, the reality of invisible things, the presence of fellow divinities. I suspected the voluptuous pleasures of good, felt wrought by the demon of self-denial.

Can one imagine any greater joy than the joy of feeling certain that God exists, sees us, loves us, that he is not just a terrifying master with deciding powers, but perhaps a friend, a fellow player, a child held in your arms or a faithful confidant, and in knowing that the smallest gesture carried out under his gaze, the smallest memory of Him is a benefit for eternity? The Swami reminded me of Ramakrishna's words: "When man takes one step toward God, God takes one hundred steps toward man." Can one imagine any greater joy than the joy born from the certainty that we will never again be alone, never again be unhappy, never again be abandoned?

It was almost as if I had already made all the requested sacrifices when I hadn't made any. Yet I was ready to agree to them with the enthusiasm and sincerity of a twenty-year old. Did I have so much to do, was I so far from my goal, if it is true at that age, that the sum of actions and their motives scarcely affect or compromise the best of our virtualities? Didn't the *Bhagavad Gita* assure that:

> the one who, full of faith, has simply listened to these secret conversations with kindness obtains the radiant worlds of the just?

Perhaps the true source of this gladness was in the recent meeting of an exceptional being; a meeting that I knew to be decisive, and equal to the Great Being, had "the splendor of a thousand suns." The separation from the joy that I felt at having caught a glimpse of God and that which I felt at having set eyes upon Tarini was difficult to distinguish: their duplicate currents were too intimately mingled for me to sort them out at the confluence in my heart.

Be that as it may, and under the effect of so much consistent stimulation, there was no question that now more than ever I put into practice what had been taught to me with books and with words. I realized this when my grandfather died at this time. In spite of the great affection there had been between us and even though I understood how much I had lost by losing him, I was surprised to see how little I was afflicted by my grief, feeling relieved by the reading of verses such as this:

In truth, sages cry neither for the dead nor for the living.... The sage does not rejoice in pleasure nor does he grieve over displeasure.... He remains equal in pleasure and in pain.

And as if to better dissipate any inclination towards sadness, I have the memory of something like a mysterious sign being sent to the cemetery. Among the mourners, I spotted the woman holding power of attorney for my grandfather, whose physical resemblance to Tarini was so striking that from a distance they would have been easily confused. It was as if Tarini had discreetly come with me, or had wanted to deliver a message to me through another person, a message whose content was something like this: "Jean, I want you to know that in this time of sadness, I'm here with you."

*

* *

Of all the personalities presiding at the time of the Lotus, it goes without question that the most important one was and always will be Sri Ramakrishna. Very quickly, this priest from Kali knew how to move me and bewilder me, replacing within several hours every one of my childhood heroes.

First of all there was his face, his loving gaze, his smile partially hidden in his short beard (with that little space between his two upper incisors); there was the face of this man who could barely write his name, who had never read a book and who knew more than the scholars, of this man living both at the threshold of "relative consciousness" and in the consciousness of the Absolute, sharing the fears of the most humble as well as plunging into the depths of transcendence. There was this man who saw into the soul of his visitors and in the presence of an impure being felt as if he had been bitten by a cobra; this man, who when very young, rolled on the ground in pain when the Holy Mother did not appear to him, and whose back bled along with the savagely beaten buffalo; this man, who one night with his long hair, swept the floor of a pariah's house and even when his throat was burning with cancer said that a day when no one needed him caused even greater suffering.

He had spent more than half of his life in *samadhi*: in an ecstatic union with the Absolute, in this ultimate level of consciousness beyond the ego, of time and space which accompany the stopping of the heart and of breathing, and wherein every yogi dies after several days. He no longer felt anything, even when serpents slid across his body and when birds pecked his hair for grains of rice that had fallen there during worship. However, beneath the shape of a huge luminous triangle giving birth to the worlds, beneath the ocean of unlimited Consciousness whose dazzling waves unfurled over him with terrifying noise, ready to engulf him in ineffable bliss, this sublime corpse contemplated the Supreme Cause of the universe. To Naren, who asked him if he had seen God, he replied:

"I see him like I see you, but more clearly."

One night he had heard the Holy Mother—another name for cosmic Energy—go up to the top floor of the temple with the lightness of a little girl, her anklets jingling. He saw her standing, her hair floating around her shoulders, her dark silhouette at the top of the terrace standing against the nocturnal sky. Soon, every woman would appear to him with the same traits as the Holy Mother; he would surprise her even in a prostitute and prostrate himself before her in the middle of the street.

I was pleased by the abundance of familiar details brought back to his place; however, with regard to Christ, the Evangelist is happy with a meager portion of his sayings and doings. We possessed his words in his own language, Bengali, when nothing subsisted in the Aramaean teachings. We had several photographs of him; we could visit his village, his house. In short, as much as the unverified affirmations concerning Christ kept our skepticism in tact, the irrefutable proof of the existence of a man such as Bhagavan accredited that of Christ. And since the "Great Royal Swan" had had similar striking experiences which witnesses still remembered, we couldn't see why others would not have also known, and firstly, Christ in person.

Thus, when Ramakrishna said of him, that he was "Love incarnated, in eternal oneness with God," I believed him more easily than when I heard it said in empathetic or formal sermons given by preachers who were no doubt sincere but who, as opposed to the sage of Dakshinesvar, were satisfied with repeating what they had been taught.

I owe my discovery of something in Christianity that is much more important than most Christians suspect, as well as the beginning of my interest in my own religion with all the attention and reverence it required, to India and to Ramakrishna. Better yet, I have become indifferent to the lack of precise documents about the Son of God, which in my opinion seems to contribute to his greatness. The fact that barely any traces of his passage remain is persuasion to seek him within; without a portrait of him his face is closer to the ideal model, stylizing him in an icon; ignorance of the exact terms he used confines his language to silence, at the same time leaving us to translation; such scant knowledge of his actions exalts him in the deepest mystery, arousing the desire to know him.

It would only be much later that I would come to all this.

2. SHARING THE FIRE[*]

Lande-Helene's[1] vocation had been confirmed long ago in her herbarium of dreams. Several times, her dreams showed her handing out little envelopes tied with a red ribbon to passers-by, intended to convert them to life; she was the "decolonized soul" who had kissed a man's burns: every bit of skin she had kissed healed. Someone having assured her that her washing machine was repaired—"I don't have one," she answered.

"Here's one!"

"But I don't have anything to wash."

"Then you can wash the world."

She even saw herself—prodigal!—rising completely naked from an egg with her hair blowing in the wind and winged arms, ready to speak to the crowds.

There was also the dream about the lady in purple.

"I was coming down the stairs of a great monument when I saw a beautiful woman with an enchanting smile approach me. She was wearing a purple dress—the color of crocus. She was carrying an umbrella that could have protected thirty people. The entire circumference of the umbrella, which was also purple, quivered like a foamy fringe. In a swinging stride she came up the stairs toward me, seeming to float above the ground. I was mesmerized by this vision."

Without a doubt, the stairs resembled the ladder of dreams, just like the color of colchicum brought about a conciliation of colors; it suggested Colchide, the country of Golden Fleece that still remains to be conquered and confers the light of Knowledge. This umbrella closely resembled a pledge of safety, a canopy representing the sky and at the same time protection from its violence. Thirty was the numeral of the child born of the father (one) and of the mother (two), of man and woman reunited in oneness, the zero added on as a sign of completeness. The sea foam was a reminder that Alchemy is the "Sea of the Sages," from where, like Aphrodite, the woman emerged, and in a personification of this royal science,

[*] From *Tarini, Pioneer of Awakening,* XVIII.
[1] Translator's Note: Lande-Helene is Tarini's French name.

she reproduced celestial apparitions by floating over the ground with her willowy airy step.

This conclusive dream confirmed the project that had for so long been unacknowledged: of reaching out to castaways, of helping them through purifying hardships to become fulfilled in a different way. Once again, Lande-Helene was in the middle of a passage, helping others ford a river.

"When destiny calls," she said, "you follow it, even if you'd rather back out. Everything works out and falls into place for the best. There is even a law that forbids keeping the secrets of spiritual life to ourselves: we must share them or else run the risk of having them turn against us or crush us. Personal fulfillment doesn't mean possessing a certain enlightenment; it means establishing a network of communications that will diffuse it. Others need us to awaken them; but we need them to avoid falling asleep. The one who has accumulated too much unused psychic energy will eventually be consumed by it; it has to circulate, to be distributed. When we are alleviated of a certain knowledge, our unconscious is no longer encumbered by images and submerged by emotions; it avoids the inflation of the ego. We don't have the right to egotistically keep such a treasure: when we've received so much, we need to know how to give a lot."

That is what is said in the *Bhagavad Gita*: "He who does not respond to a gift by giving is a thief."

As a matter of fact, even in Heaven, we wouldn't be happy knowing there are so many who are unhappy. Many times Lande-Helene had assured me that our happiness would crumble if we confined it exclusively to possessiveness and didn't respond to some of these intimidated or silent requests that surrounded newly born understanding. Taking care of the weak and the unfortunate, or simply those, who for the moment, are encountering some of life's setbacks, would protect us more than any barricade we could build.

*

*　　*

Over the years, the gestation became an exchange. A golden thread involuntarily wove one heart to other hearts. First one cry was heard coming from the thick of the coppice of suffering, then another and yet another. Then, like the night sky studded with lights, each moment was a distress call. We simply had to agree to look to discover that they were countless. And they were not at the antipodes, but here, there, nearby, desperately calling with breathless flickering.

Lande-Helene set to work: helping leaded hearts become hearts of gold. And thus was born a new *Lotus d'Or*, but a *Lotus d'Or* that did field work.

One would have thought that the same complaining voices heard in Algiers had returned without having aged at all. The oldest of them even appeared to have grown younger by four or five lustrums, starting all over again, persisting with their moaning processions as if magnetically attracted to the one who would know how to listen without condemning, to give unconditionally; animated by the guarantee that they would be accepted, received, and loved just as they were.

Nevertheless, their mood appeared to have slightly deteriorated over the past thirty years; more anxious, more defeated than the regulars who had come to the *Lotus*. Thirty years—wasn't that symbolized by the thirty people gathered under the umbrella?— seemed sufficient to destroy the ultimate remnants of resistance to deterioration, the last couples still holding out, the last pillars to lean on in the corruption of an era. The Iron Age had definitely worked, not wasting any time in doing its dirty work underground. Hushed tears were even more bitter; conflicts sharper. A growing disorder had forced men to "reconvert," denying them any vocation, separating them from their friends and relatives to better dislocate them. They were ill from being uprooted and dulled by technology. They had bogged down young people in abstract studies for which they were unsuited, while extracting from failure, from unknown viruses, from thousands of abortions, divorces, unemployment, the drugs that distill death in the veins of heart-broken youth.

However, in spite of the reiterated attacks of the Iron Age, its traps, its treachery, some were still receptive to something other than intense conditioning and suspected the existence of a world other than the one where the hordes silently howled their despair.

Thus came the distracted who had forgotten their wallet at the cash register, the worried who had arrived two hours early and impatiently tapped their feet on the platform, the hypochondriacs who planned their funerals every day, the overly sensitive whose emotions were forbidden to them, the experienced intellectuals perched above themselves; they rushed to Job's pile of manure, the rich who had nothing and the well-off whose inner life was painfully poor; adolescents with pubertal pimples; the unstable, who fled each day by traveling, by attending meetings or parties, and can only put up with themselves by escaping; single women who cannot forgive themselves for never having children; forty-year old mothers who think they are good for nothing and become maids once the children are gone. They came, those who hoped to be heard by attempting suicide; the insincere who didn't keep promises and then accused others of the same things they themselves were guilty of; those who wanted to avoid the worst, if it wasn't too late, to try to strengthen themselves, to see themselves clearly, to put things in order before pretending to domineer over others; those who realized they had missed out on life, but who, before dying, wanted to hear that all had not been lost, or that they could still rectify their mistakes; those who lived in cowardice, but longed for the means to be courageous; those who, disgusted with memories of their poor behavior, launched mirages like snowballs and cried at seeing them melt; those who lucidly sought the causes of their problems, the meaning of their suffering, hoping to change their direction and who knows, even their nature; everyone who had the honesty, the courage to question their education, their family, their character, their opinions, their convictions; demolished by the Iron Age, desiring another metal. In short, everyone who still had the power to question.

They were surprised at being brutally trapped in this world where everyone celebrated their similarities, only to discover now that their only outcome was through an uncertain and provisional search of their inner self. At first, their attitude kept them expectant with regard to this "unknown god" that they were. Then, one day, they resolved to be crushed like the wheat kernels that become flour: they had to be ground to be transformed. (Curiously, the stairs leading to the chamber of dreams is a miller's ladder.)

Little by little, they discovered how wrong it was to incriminate others, their relatives, their neighbors or the circumstances; how vain it was to be interested in someone else's culpability for which nothing can be done, when one could change one's own. They admitted that the answer to the inevitable question: "Who am I, or what did I do to bring about such misfortune?" could only be found by an inner search. They admitted that this was neither a hobby nor intellectual entertainment, but rather the Affair par excellence of their entire life and they would have to invest completely and forever with faith, courage, and perseverance, renouncing any pretensions, consenting to completely abandoning the self; agreeing that self-understanding requires total commitment: a consecration.

Many times our couple may have at first appeared to them as one branded by the stigma of eccentricity. They could hardly believe us when we admitted that in spite of living in the country, under the same roof, we only saw each other at mealtime because we were both so absorbed by our work. They would often look at us as if we were extra-human curiosities, too mystic to be naïve, when we talked about our skepticism regarding technical progress, objective information, political promises, conventionalism, and trends, knowing only too well the suspicious character lying in ambush behind these words, or about our skepticism regarding large-scale humanitarian actions or loud demonstrations in favor of world peace that were orchestrated by men as if they were in a civil war.

How could we live so far removed from everything without a newspaper, without ever going out or having any visits, reading only books free of any official publicity, not finding it at all pleasant to look for wild mushrooms, attend social events, go on touristic cruises, play golf, belong to any groups or movement? And this without any arrogance, self-conceit, or any desire to stand out but simply because that's just the way it is.

They only understood us once they themselves had been sufficiently stripped of their hodge-podge of ideas, considering little by little the blandness of ordinary conversations that carefully avoid the essential subjects, measuring just how dull it can be to waste time playing solitaire; discovering that the most impenetrable country, the most unusual adventures are the ones seen and experienced from within, where beauty blossoms from the ordinary, where each moment can be richly unique, where splendor can be found where it's least expected, if only one knows how to recognize it. They finally realized that once they had reached the Stairs to the Inner Empire, everything else was barren poverty. In our refusal to participate in the decline, to trample millenniums of wisdom, to accept the reign of cynicism and the establishment of barbarianism, to be accomplices of ideologies, all of which spread one way or another with the idea of repressing consciousness, and converge on the excessive accumulation of possessions, they had at first suspected us, then joined us. They finally understood that this undertaking, in spite of its discretion, could arrest a collapse better than anything else. They, too, set about building their inner church, took to the maquis of God.

Lande-Helene showed them how to accept themselves just as they were, by ceasing to project their false unwarranted ideas on others, how to avoid definitively judging someone or something (the opposite of one's first affirmations is often revealed later on), how to accept the other as he is and not as we believe or would like him to be, allow him the same right to exist that we allow ourselves, that is to say, differently. She taught them how to remain calm and attentive, to accept reality, to welcome the good with the bad by continually alternating and to greet them with their darkness and their light. The ones who complained that those around them never changed, noticed that as soon as they started to change, the intolerant brother became understanding, their neighbor's music wasn't quite so loud, and their psoriasis cleared up. Their circle of friends was astonished to suddenly find that they were actually quite agreeable to be with.

She helped them to see what they already had rather than wanting what they didn't have and lusting after something without even knowing if it would bring them happiness. With tact, she uncovered the degree of infantilism that kept them prisoners of their past, of their parents, still expecting as they always had, admiration and immediate satisfaction. She made them see that the "elsewhere" they desperately sought elsewhere was right there inside, and that between the three poles that life rests on—the ideal, the possible and the real—it was wisest to hang onto what was real, all the while aspiring to achieve the possible and hoping for the ideal.

Before, they had watched their dreams like a show that didn't concern them; now they were discovering that they were one with their dreams and that even the most insignificant ones meant something to them. The problems that they considered tragically insurmountable when awake, blaming anyone who wasn't as interested as they were (without asking themselves why anyone should find their problems interesting), now paradoxically worked themselves out quite simply during sleep. If there wasn't any solution perhaps it was because there wasn't any problem!

For those who denied the existence of God because he didn't give them any answer, Lande-Helene explained that God didn't give the same importance to their torments as they did and that perhaps it was sufficient enough to put the horror into perspective; or perhaps, God's answer was not there when they asked the question but rather when they no longer needed to ask. Others still complained that they received no answer to their prayers; but they couldn't imagine that they themselves were the answer, because the same person who prays inspires the prayer. Those who called themselves atheists discovered that spirituality is something quite different from what they had thought; not something necessarily reserved for the superstitious or the obscurantist, but depending on an altitude and an unsuspected depth even in people who believe in God. The latter discovered, often for the first time, what they believed they knew or believed, and at the same time felt a lesser need for an outside ritual: a God showing himself through a liturgical apparatus was less imposing now that he was also inside them, seeking them just as they were seeking him; a God who needed limits, who himself is the Unlimited, who needs to take rest from his Infinity in their finitude. Because if God, by living within us, opens us up to the dimensions of the galaxies, we restrict him to the boundaries of the human being, this concentration of Creation.

And so it is that while huge organizations collectively strive for uniformity among millions of previously dulled individuals, Lande-Helene works alone at guiding certain individuals in their attempt at individuation. Every one of them, to one degree or another and each at their own pace changed their condition and points of view, discovered other aspects of their destiny, felt renewed inspiration, and by accepting the irrational and gaining access to their own personality, with letters, words, and tears, they were identical in their appreciation of the one who they felt had brought them back to life.

And so it is that over the years, the pioneer of awakening of one became the teacher of all.

The sad cancerous ones dying a slow death keep the memory of her hand on theirs for a long time.

*

*   *

Lande-Helene has sufficiently given up the idea of strengthening her ego, of imposing its will. She has created enough vacuity within herself so that from the mysterious center that is in communion with others, departs that invisible golden chain that unites her with others, and unites them all together.

Her love for others has nothing to do with a philanthropical ideal or religious rules. Perhaps she loves them because she loves love; she loves nothing more than loving them because it has always been her nature to do so.

She says: "Loving others means accepting them as they are without expecting anything in return."

She continues by saying: "My greatest wish is for everyone to be happy! I know now that the pain they inflict upon themselves is much greater than any pain they cause to others. I also know they hurt themselves much more unconsciously than consciously."

She adds: "In as much as possible, I try to resemble the idea that God had of me when he created me. God expects me to smile at their worries and help them recover."

However, I don't see her treat them with sentimentality and manipulation. She knows that true love is rigorous, that one must ask a lot of those who ask for everything: finding the meaning in words, reactions, and gestures; being able to say no; putting a stop to excesses and whims, refusing to be the perfect mother who gets up in the middle of the night to rock them back to sleep.

I don't see her idealizing humanity.

"Maybe because I was wrong to grow up too fast and was overwhelmed by the circumstances, I find that most adults are non-adults, chaotic beings who complain about their lot in life unaware of all the foolish acts they thoughtlessly accumulate, eternally adolescent and wilted."

And yet, in their deepest layers, she excavates for creativity, uncovering lodes they never suspected existed. Nothing is more passionate than helping them become what they are. It is hard not to imagine that if each one of the six or seven billion inhabitants on Earth accomplished the same exploration, then rather than being a small cohort of men and women with self-understanding, all of humanity would have access to its right to happiness by having finally found a meaning in life.

It would certainly be pleasant to see them lining up to have their souls scrutinized: Heads of State coming to reveal state secrets with the desire to better the people, confessing their dreams for improving themselves, revolutionaries in the streets preaching the revolution of consciousness, Christians who urge the (moral) slaying of each one of them so that Christ can succeed their ego. Businessmen would surprisingly escape from their ventures and run to exchange their assets in the stock market for eternal values, academic people would tear up their diplomas to board the ship *Argo*, oil men would drill for the black gold that springs from the kingdom of the Self. We would see converted research chemists extract several megatons of spiritual energy from atomic piles.

We're still a long way away. However, Heaven on Earth doesn't only reveal itself in our immediate surroundings: it emigrates. Words to regenerate and transform are now heard from those who have reconciled the lion and the lamb, the ambassadors whose credentials invite all the Chancellors of Ignorance to find peace within and among themselves. In turn they convey the message; and in this way, for others who we'll never know, life will no longer be poisoned by absurdity. The future of the world won't be changed by this, but their future will be and that may in turn change the world.

Is it due to her ego having renounced itself that people who don't even know her feel compelled to approach her, to spontaneously talk about themselves, to confide in her, while waiting for an hour in a station, in a waiting room, in a store, in any public area, hoping to remain in epistolary contact with her? Her smile captivates the most reserved child; they come forth, draw pictures, offer presents and fight over her, knowing that she'll teach them things no one else will. Parents sullenly watch the ploy. It's good for children to understand that one should part. Who knows if I'm not jealous of this confiscation, of her being simply more alert, having sweeter dreams and knowing how to interpret them better than me?

No one would be surprised to learn that when she passes by, even dead trees bloom again. Just as each human footstep raises clouds of atoms, each one of her words creates a tidal wave of feelings. It would be difficult to find less vanity. Slender, silent in her flowing black dress printed with colored flowers, she seems to be a princess from China going on ahead of herself toward a serenity that she had already won.

3. EVENINGS AT LA FRAGNIÈRE[*]

I

From 1951 to 1956 I spent several summers in Haute-Nendaz-sur-Sion, Switzerland. I was immediately seduced by the Valais, which is "set half-way between Heaven and Earth," wrote Rilke, who finished writing *Duino Elegies* in the Muzot tower.

I went on long hikes with Laurent and Fabrice Vust. Following the Vauchere trail or the Pré des Génissons, we passed vineyards, open orchards, and tiers of pastures, marked with chapels or tall crosses topped with pointed awnings. The hand-dug *bisses* crisscrossed the prairies like shiny ribbons beneath the wild flowers. With cupped hands we drank the herbal scented water, its wild strawberry taste even softer in our mouths than the sound of its cooing murmurs. We reached the spot where névés patiently grazed on solitary rocks; we came back down in the evening by the Navigenze ravine or another way near the Majorie where the Council of the bourg was held, passing Witches Tower with its pepper-box roof, near the Riedmatten de Crèvecoeur house.

The little chalet we were staying in had a lilting name: La Fragnière. With its bark roof, its straw colored pine walls and tiny windows, it looked like a dollhouse challenging the heights. Reigning throughout the *mayen*[1] were the scents of wild honey, resin, and Tibetan tea. The chalet was furnished with old hardback books, Genevan engravings, damask wing chairs, a silk spinning wheel, and a huge stone stove. We bathed in ice cold water, practiced shooting with bows and arrows, picked wild berries, dined on thick slices of country bread topped with butter and slices of Swiss cheese or Grisons dried beef, and drank rich fresh milk from nearby farms. Beeswax candles illuminated our conversations.

This is where I was to meet my friends' mother and hear her remarkable words of wisdom.

I had rarely had the occasion to meet a woman of more distinction than Thyra Vust. She had a serene face, deep blue eyes, and

---

[*] From *The Door to the Women's Apartment,* IV.
[1] Translator's Note: A Swiss word meaning "chalet."

hair like a frosty wheat field. Her way of speaking was measured, slightly accented with Swiss inflexions and very economical with words. Concerned with finding the exact translation of her thoughts, she seemed to eliminate ahead of time any useless term that might have misconstrued her idea. On top of this she probably took great care when speaking so as to avoid upsetting anyone.

Thyra didn't content herself with cheap aristocracy by addressing her husband in formal French or by appearing circumspect regarding women's right to vote and the manipulation of crowds; she was this way in that she was unable to live superficially out of fear of suffocation, although she never imposed her deeply rooted convictions on anyone else. Her respect and affection were an inspiration to others. She was inhabited by that sense of mystery so typical of people from the North who pay special attention to the importance of coincidences, creaking furniture, and tricksters' pranks. She said that after her mother's death, she heard her footsteps upstairs in the house, something that she never feigned to explain. We thought it was her relationship with the sacred that forbid her from mentioning it, not out of fear of shocking our immaturity, but in deference toward certain truths that cannot be adapted to an audience without distortion; at first, she merely told us that in comparison to the expression of an "emancipated human being" in India, the expression on the face of an ordinary man was scarcely any different from that of cattle. This passion for profoundness which intensified the indifference of most people around her kept Thyra in an isolation that I later discovered to be heroic, almost alarming.

Irritable, emotive, verbose, eaten away by feverishness, I observed with astonishment this image of serenity, these exemplary suggestions expressed with gestures and well-chosen words which gave her considerable influence over her sons and me. For all that, she was neither cold nor impassive: underneath this marble-like peacefulness spread a wide spectrum of emotions, which due to Calvinistic modesty, were only shown with great precaution. By her discretion and reserve Thyra lived in litotes; it wasn't surprising that one of her bedside books was *La Princesse de Clèves*.

She made it her duty to conscientiously set the table, to conscientiously move the teapot and remove its cover, to conscientiously open and close a door—I told her that *thyra* meant "door" in Greek—while at the same time learning to give herself leeway and see herself take action without actually taking any. It was as if by being the observer of her acts she detached herself from them, and with her deliberate attention hoped to turn them into a sort of prayer. Convinced that the world had gone mad, she tried to protect it, or at least those who were closest to her; watching the rest was a sight that filled her with disgust. This is what pushed her, in as much as possible, to live a simple life, follow a vegetarian diet, use natural medicine. She was quite often so lost in her books on Eastern philosophy that she had to forcibly tear herself away from her reading to chop wood, make butter, or spin wool (pin cushion, distaff lantern were her words). She longed for a return to country ways, and quoted this verse from Valéry which suited her so well:

> With her devastating grace
> Her brightness barely veiled,
> An angel set at my place,
> Tender bread, still, creamy milk....

Early on, an unusual friendship grew out of these small touches. But there was more to it than that. Thyra Vust was like the prolongation of Selma Lagerlof. The de Dardels, Protestants from Neuchâtel, sought refuge in Sweden during times of persecution. Thyra told stories handed down from her mother about Swedish farmers who got up in the middle of a stormy night, got dressed to leave, well aware of the danger and even prepared to face the Last Judgment, while men lost in the blizzard put their hats on backwards in hope of coming up with new ideas. Like Selma Lagerlof, Thyra believed that everything was animate, woven by invisible founding forces of the cosmic unit, where everyone loves, suffers, and rejoices imponderably over the fact that there is no absolute separation between life and death and that our ancestors play a part in this life. She contended that the universe sent us signs that were perceptible to us if we paid attention. She claimed that the images surrounding us had an imperceptible influence on us, and that the small Buddha that was always in her bedroom played a strong role in her discovery of Buddhism.

I had a vague feeling of skepticism, never for a minute realizing that Nature, with her silent language, was showing me my future. Every morning, when I opened the shutters to the dawn's bluing sky, I saw the rhododendron covered hills and beyond the Diablerets, the jagged outline of the Rochers de Naye. Little did I

27

suspect that ten years later Nay would become my home for the rest of my life. Once I had finally accepted that these omens were much more generously offered than it would seem, I better understood the expression "your eyes are for seeing."

II

My schooling was languorous. I remember the boredom I felt during never-ending classes: a boredom comparable to a feudal building with its heavy dormant blocks, oppressive vaults, and dungeons of despair. I tried to clear my mind in the school's gardens, but a teacher's voice always caught me like a fish hook, bluntly reeling me back into the heart of reality.

As my studies became more and more intellectual, I foresaw the risk of losing all my childlike wonder, and of seeing myself torn away once and for all from the state of enchantment where I had taken up residence.

The final blow fell during my senior year in high school. I conceded to my naïvete to the point of believing that "important people" knew how to solve the "important problems" that confronted young people who had the potential for thought. Why did the world exist? What is evil? What happens after death? Does God exist and what is he? Not only were no satisfactory answers ever given, but this kind of question was not even asked. We were told they were improper, incongruous; symptoms of shameful mental illnesses! It was much easier to encourage us not to believe in anything. After having quickly visited Plato's cavern, which denounced the unreality of phenomenal appearances, we spent the rest of the year studying phenomena! The age of adult thinking was born with Cartesianism. Everything that had preceded, a negligible amount, had been kept secret from us, as in China where millions of Chinese children are repeatedly told that the Chinese civilization didn't exist before the era of Mao Tse-tung.

The portrait of the father of modern thinking, by Franz Hals, let his gaze fall on our classroom buzz like some distant disdainful pout. Our teachers oscillated between skeptical humanism, incapable of choosing, always ready in the name of tolerance to tolerate anything and everything or to place bets on the worst, and atheism, activist for scientism, obsessed with the will to destroy the uniqueness of humans. Repatriated back home to the sky, metaphysics were sacrificed on the altar of understanding, in the name of history against mythology, structures against symbols, concepts against Ideas. What good was it, that being the case, that the world was simply the result of chance, metaphysical experiments, pathological cases, death, a total death? Between the "associationist empiricists," the "Kantian critics," and the "scientific nominalists," we really didn't know which to choose. Fortunately, we were distracted from the theoretical combinatorics that held us in a stifling mentality by the "little tummy" of Pavlov's dog or by the "dynamometer counter" that measured the pressure of joy and displeasure with its rubber syringe and zinc floater. Who could forget Theodule Ribot's imperishable sentence: "The pain of a corn or Michelangelo's pain because he was unable to attain his ideal are identical and of the same nature."

Was this what philosophy was all about? Was it all a formidable intellectual sham? Where was everyone with a "passion for Wisdom" hiding? What happened to this Wisdom? The refusal to refer to anything other than mankind—a mankind fallen and exhausted as the war was ending—seemed to be a tragic error, although we didn't know why. We were unable to pit ponderable arguments against the procedures used by adults with leather-clad diplomas who exalted reductionism. Our shy awkward attempts at disagreement lacked objective proof and quickly sounded ridiculous. Having asked our teachers for forgiveness, we swore allegiance to what they taught us. However, some of us still suspected they weren't telling us everything and that other points of view also had something to tell us.

As providential as Velleda, the German prophetess who emerged from the tempest at the last minute to save the warriors from being massacred, Thyra Vust was the one who would rescue us. What we were to learn in the little chalet during conversations continuing deep into the heart of the mountain night would prevail by far over any university knowledge, overwhelming for good our ways of being and thinking.

It all started the day that our teacher discovered the works of a completely unknown author, carefully removed from any fame, and who had just died in Cairo with the same discretion he had used in elaborating his works: René Guénon.

Nothing found favor with this author who appeared to be an absolute troublemaker, unable to compromise and obstinately undermining generally accepted ideas. That could only spark more interest! Although no one disapproved more of himself, what would happen to our world if Guénon were right? We didn't dare imagine the consequences of such an acknowledgment.

From the very first pages of *Crisis of the Modern World*, Thyra admitted feeling as if she were facing an "unfathomable mystery." Her vision of things had been radically changed; she began to find all other reading a bit pathetic, from *Narratives of the Merovingian Times* by Augustin Thierry to Gide's *Journal* which had fallen from her hands. She felt sorry for us when we had to study the philosophical speculations of Hume, Locke, and Malebranche, which seemed vastly sterile to her once she had discovered the symbolism of the Cross and the Holy Grail, the Zodiac and the "subtle organs of the human being," names like Thomas Aquinas, Ibn Arabi, Shankaracharya, Lao-tzu and other hallucinatory titles: *Bhagavad Gita, Tao te Ching, Futuhat al-Makkiyah.*

Amid a mass of ruins, while everyone continued to proclaim the advancement of humanity, it was in 1920 with an insolent conviction of argumentation that Guénon started questioning Darwinism, and through it, a society where progress, egalitarianism and other "secular dogmas" were simply imposed suggestions that were not discussed, where all hierarchy was reversed, where all ideals lived only in the "human animal" and "material comfort"; where, since man was no longer able to reach the highest levels, he brought everything down to its lowest; where the spiritually elite, who alone could still ward off barbarism, were decimated.

Unperturbed amidst ordinary worries, Guénon professed that time was not linear but cyclical. The general dissolution that contributes to the aggravation of all sorts of conflict, as well as the mixing and oblivion of vital truths, would accelerate decadence until the final cataclysm.—"Then, were we at the end of the world?"—"At the end of a world," Thyra rectified. This apocalyptic sentence corresponded to the *Kali Yuga* in Hindu cosmology—the Iron Age of ancient Greeks. *Kali Yuga*—the first time the sound of it echoed in my head I found it almost amusing even though so many terrifying realities lay beneath its four syllables. It seemed to hesitate between the affectionate name of a Basque grandmother, the name of Cretan candy, and the name of a Brazilian dance.

Lying on the floor, surrounded by her books, Thyra spoke in the dark; her voice rose as if in a cavern. We sat around her like children terrified by ghost stories yet asking for more, captivated by her, still not daring to believe what she was revealing to us. Yet, all in all, here was everything we had been feeling but didn't yet know how to put into words. The little bit that we knew about the world was enough for us to side with its denouncer. Guénon was familiar to us even before we had ever heard of him. Like him, we were unconventional, resisting; he would be our role model. Like him, we lived in Islam and we found nothing shocking about his conversion to Sufism. There was still a great deal of mystery about him and while he had already answered many of our questions he also raised many more.

To be honest, some of the progressive assertions held by the "servant to the One" still seemed outlandish, unacceptable. Even though the predicted curses have come to pass, today it is considered conformist to be proud of it. Over the years I would be able to verify the pertinence of the accusations, enduring like everyone certain inconveniences attributable to the *Kali Yuga* or even detecting several signs that Guénon either couldn't or didn't want to announce. He didn't go as far as routinely using iron which literally gave credit to the Age bearing the same name, although resorting to tools such as the wooden handled scythe still used in Valais attested to a time of weaker solidification.

"We were taught the benefits of industrial civilization; they told us that was the only one, born in the sixteenth century, after the long night of the Middle Ages."

"I'm extremely alarmed by that, my dears," Thyra responded. "There are numerous civilizations and even many that are more durable and more important than the West!"

Mathematics was not quantitative but qualitative; alchemy was not the ancestor of chemistry but rather the symbolic science of inner states. The history that we were taught was a falsification of facts; economical geography caricatured "sacred geography" by reproducing Heaven on Earth. Because reason was unable to attain the realm of metaphysics, it denied it. Beyond reason existed a subtle organ of understanding, the core of transcendent intuition that inspired the founders of religions, the great prophets, the "Awakened."

Concerning religions, we repeated what we had been told: synonym of "magism," superstitious obscurantism.

"Guénon has a very interesting idea," Thyra said. "Every religion has an outer envelope called the exoteric and a central core, the esoteric."

We learned that exotericism, which came from a literal interpretation of the Scriptures, was susceptible to variations, deviations, and intolerance as well, because each exotericism stems from feelings and claims to be the sole proprietor of the truth. Esotericism, on the other hand, was of a universal order originating from a superhuman authority; it held the keys to the symbolic interpretations transmitted in secret from the master to his disciple. Since mentalities were different, all the traditions differed from one another; but they all had a common core. The gradual distancing from the primordial Core brought about their decline and finally their disappearance. However, the original Tradition was periodically readjusted, revived by "divine Incarnations," the *Avatara*s.

All that sounded so different from everything we had learned by heart! Everything that we had meticulously distilled, having omitted anything inexact, crumbled into clouds of inanity within the lapse of several hours. We didn't notice our tea getting cold as the darkness in our heads thickened like the night's darkness in the chalet, plunging us into its eerie shadows. Outside the weather had suddenly changed. The rain gushed down on the barley fields; the gusts of wind were in the same league as our deepest reactions.

It was scarcely possible to avoid the theme of a posthumous future.

"If I have understood correctly," said Thyra, "the psychic elements of the deceased are usually promised to the 'Path of the Fathers' which leads to other conditioned states in the 'return to matter': Heaven and the Underworld for Judeo-Christianity, that is. The sage, totally purified, follows the 'Path of the Gods,' which leads to permanent liberation, to *Nirvana*."

For the first time we began to see the real reason for spirituality. It allowed you to take part in death, to obtain a happy destiny in the beyond. It was even the whole point of our time spent in this world. Whatever type of life existed after death and symbolized by a body was the direct result of everything our soul identified itself with during its earthly stay. Its "punishment" consisted of the discovery that the senses, instincts and passions had been poor choices. It was evident that the only thing left to do was to seek protection, as quickly as possible, in our soul. Not a minute was to be lost; maybe it was already too late.

Thyra explained the reading of *Bardo Thodol* had at first plunged her into a "dreadful state." For forty days that follow death, the deceased first had peaceful visions and then terrifying visions that were nothing more than projections of his subconscious. Identifying himself with these phantasms was the surest way of returning to illusory worlds. Sometimes she read excerpts from this book that transported us to the confines of the "Period in between": "In the intermediary state, beings with bad '*karma*' will see flesh-eating demons in horrifying commotion. The rain, sudden flurries of wind, humans being chased by wild beasts will also appear; deafening sounds like mountains crumbling, wildfires roaring...."

At this same moment the storm intensified, one of those terrible Valaisan electrical storms with the thunder rumbling over the roof. We were surrounded on all sides by mountain spirits and the souls of the dead. No one would have dared to look outside.

Vested with a providential mission, our hero, our god found his halo with these flashes of nature. Through him we detected the blatant lies of our time: a time that obviously prohibited the best, the most perceptive, from speaking out, the first ones, however, designated to help it out of its slump. That a brilliant mind such as Guénon could be the object of such an incredible silent conspiracy could only be explained by the scandalous contempt that these times held for anything threatening the pack of mediocrity in power.

It's difficult to imagine what such an upheaval provokes in the mind of adolescents already sufficiently conditioned to wander among "the signs of the times" like satisfied blind men, to imagine the collapse and the cracks that would create intense aftershocks of which we were the epicenter. Caught between two fundamentally antinomical views, we were quickly assured that the one that spoke the truth was not the one that we had been hearing for so many years. If our professors were our masters, we were no longer really their disciples. With an increasingly rebellious patience we tolerated the huge question marks furiously scratched in the margins of our dissertations each time we mentioned, perhaps with excessive juvenile awkwardness, "the sage who lived at the foot of the Pyramids."

III

Our visits to the village of Isérables always carried a certain amount of apprehension. The peculiar trait of its inhabitants was their slanted eyes; it is said that the Huns were their ancestors, having settled here in the fifth century. Due to this probable ancestry, even today they are still prudently kept in the background and bear the name *Bedouins*. Seeing the remarkable preservation of this Asian enclave in the heart of the Alpine Pennines gave us an even greater reason to maintain our Buddhist vision. Weren't the Mongolians related to the Tibetans according to Csoma de Koros? We liked to persuade ourselves that the people from Isérables descended from some horde that had escaped from the underground kingdom of Agarttha, where the King of the World lives.

Thyra often talked to us about the Buddhist lack of durability. From the stars to molecules, everything, from one instant to the next lives an accelerated history from beginning to end, everything being, in fact, infinitesimal sparks. The interval between each one was too tiny to be seen. Only the extreme speed of the glimmers let us believe there was any continuity.

"My dears, the only thing we see is what is left of our 'idols'; but 'idols' who are eternally alive because they are forever being resuscitated. And it is absolutely the same for everything we see."

"And for everything we hear?"

"Absolutely, yes!"

For the same reason, the ego was exempt of any real existence. There was only an infinite series of "egos," each one as fleeting, changing, and inconsistent as all the others. In fact, as soon as we wonder who we are, we're already no longer who we were at the time we asked.

That day, at the entrance to the village, the evening light (in these solitudes, night falls at 4 p.m.) was paling in the alleys, dripping from the rooftops, circumventing an abandoned cart. We were welcomed by a child's shout. We thought that if we had arrived just one minute earlier or later, the spot would not have been bathed in the same light, the cart wouldn't have been exactly the same cart, we wouldn't have heard exactly the same shout; as for ourselves, we, too, would have been slightly different.

We went into the little tavern. Shaggy-haired, primitive looking men spoke in a dialect that was never heard in the neighboring valleys, and sipped a kind of "pagan wine": lumbermen with red caps, cheese makers dressed in wool, who, it appeared to us, withdrew into silence while at the same time observing us curiously. Their wrinkled faces with small slit-eyes vaguely appeared through clouds of smoke; and with glasses on dingy oilcloths and a peaceful fire gently burning in the hearth, it was all we needed to believe we had halted in a makeshift inn on the way to Tachi-Lumpo in Gyangtse. Never before had there been, nor after, would there be these taciturn forms, the interrupted syllable upon our arrival, this heavy ambiance and such a kaleidoscope of flashing vibrations, millions of miniature beacons sending signals out in the galactic night.

"Well then," said Fabrice on the way home, "if from one instant to the next, Isérables died out and wasn't reborn from its ashes so it could die out again, Isérables didn't exist!"

"Nor did the lamas in Isérables," said someone.

"Nor the cart," I added, "nor the child's shout."

"Nor the child."

"Nor the tavern we went into," said Laurent.

"And if the tavern didn't exist, those rangers, that 'pagan wine' and that peaceful fire burning in the hearth didn't exist either!"

"And we didn't exist any more than anything else, not any more than the universe gravitating around the glasses on the stained oilcloth."

"And in the end, nothing existed except inexistance! And that, from one instant to the next, forever and ever," said Laurent.

"So, we don't exist any more now than we did before...!"

Thyra appreciated the bald language of Buddhism, its diamond purity. Tibet, one of the last authentically traditional lands before it became 471,700 square miles of nuclear arsenal, was revealed to her in tales by Alexandra David-Neel. She told us about sorcerers in robes made from bones, anchorites wearing flannel shirts in the Himalayan cold, and clever miracle-workers who could make it rain, move objects, and heal from a distance. Some of them went into seclusion, meditating and fasting for three years, and with an astonishing asceticism that allowed them to capture certain diabolical entities in order to force them into giving up evil. The *lung-gom-pa*, when in a trance with their eyes fixed on a star, could cross the high plateaux with amazing speed. Others, by mental concentration, could give a body to a phantom, animating it to the point where this *tulpa* shielded them from life.

Thyra knew that the energy diffused by every living thing and its inner energy were of the same quality. Thousands of irradiations condensed, dissolved and circulated everywhere, shaping the others in their sphere. They could either be tamed with the help of spiritual methods or left to their own anarchical profusion, triggering some of the worst catastrophes ever seen when rituals are neglected in periods of twilight.

"No matter, Fa,[2] do you want to prepare the tea...?"

Flickering candles cast their fantastic shadows. The scent of jasmine filled the chalet; fine scrolls of steam rose from our porcelain cups, creating an atmosphere in perfect harmony with the nature of our debate. Mystery was piling up behind each of our chairs.

If the least little vibration created such repercussions throughout the universe, even in the distant future, we could only imagine the responsibility that each one of our thoughts carried. This compelled us to think only positive thoughts, indeed, even forgiving thoughts regarding all beings, thoughts capable of improving, even sanctifying the atmosphere. "Ideas of force" always materialized: the more hate grew, the greater the risk of war breaking out.

With the generosity of our youth, we loathed suffering: obvious injustice and scandal proved the absence of God, his indifference! We had never considered that at the origin of all suffering was the quest for existence and the comparing of oneself to the illusions taken for reality, the appetite for pleasure, lust, and greed. The more man multiplied his needs, bustling about with a thousand wild dreams, the more he increased the number of causes and their effects. Joining one's *karma* with the group's only provoked one's own misfortunes and distress. The only solution was in the extinction of all desire, in the relinquishment of one's ego, in "joyous detachment."

Thyra's lifestyle, her frugality, her actions graced with simplicity showed that she had more than a basic book-like approach to Buddhism. It was much more difficult and undoubtedly contrary to nature to impose such a secret on our impatient vitality. However,

[2] Translator's Note: Fabrice's nickname.

36

something inside us adhered to this implicitly. Although we were far from living it, we sensed the greatness of her verity.

Thyra said that as we became aware of our own suffering we would start to see the pain of others all around us; we would share the pain of the sick, of everyone who cries over broken dreams, of abused children and animals, and even plants who suffer in silence. We would take a personal interest in the suffering of others. The more our own ego faded away, the more room we would have for the ego of others; the murmur of "the ocean of human tears" was even louder at the bottom of this "great compassionate heart" that needed to be awakened within.

What we barely understood then, we would come to understand the day that we, too, would need the compassion of others.

IV

When Selma Lagerlof revealed the world of creative writing to me, I didn't have a clue as to the torments that were in store for me. She didn't mention anything about the throes of writing, the silence of the public, the writer's desert. I ignored that this elegance of hers could also be a sort of curse that demanded lying about time and avoiding slave labor by force or by craftiness. I ignored that every author, even if relatively unknown, is held hostage by an unfair society, and that writing expects overwhelming ransoms. The ambiguous divinity it serves is also the one that devours it; heaping on the kindness and in return expecting its food for the giving.

By listening to Thyra, my friends and I were granted the opportunity to learn fundamental determining truths. But we had no idea that these revelations were to condemn us to taking a solitary road very much to the contrary of the world in which we were destined to live. We would soon be confronted with misunderstandings that could only result in endless skirmishes, hurtful disapproval, and suffering; the lucidity acquired when one has another value system, another outlook on prejudice and another inner state creates a vast difference with the surrounding environment and can be a source of suffering. For people like us, the times would be especially contrary: friendships would be more unlikely, even getting married could be compromised; the distance from the centers of interest where people in universal agreement congregate was growing. We would always be "somewhere else." In the midst of mass hysteria and unanimous false certainty, the only thing to do would be to keep quiet and live secretly.

Perhaps there was a certain self-satisfaction in knowing that we were isolated and in believing we were somehow better by acting like an "initiated person." This game would come to an end either as soon as circumstances brought us back to the reality of social contingencies and the tough demands of a job or when erratic transformations, born out of conflicts between our intimate convictions and the obligation to adapt as well as possible to a world where we felt excluded, would gain ground.

Thyra had told us, without a doubt, that every event in our lives had happened for a reason even if we didn't understand why at the time. We were responsible for our lives and for learning the lessons of experience. Hardships were given to us as signs at a specific moment in our life when we needed them and could benefit from them. But she also admitted that the hardships were always excessive and our means for overcoming them barely sufficient. Inner understanding required accepting this. As time went by, her words were confirmed, and far from holding it against our "awakener," we were, on the contrary, ever more grateful to her for having distilled our minds and having given us an acute awareness of earthly threats and intelligible knowledge. Several decades later, when Guénon's rigorous clear-sightedness would be acknowledged, we would be pleased to see an increase in the number of people who would gain the same understanding and allow themselves to think in the same language. A bittersweet victory.

Starting on this morning of awakening, everything began to shift. We now knew that "something else" existed; with a sort of indignant hindsight, Laurent, Fabrice and I began to think we had been betrayed. We'd been saddled with our own ignorance in order to take dead-end roads. Our future masters had also been abused before us. And we didn't know if we should be angrier with our own innocence of not knowing that what we'd been taught in the name of an indoctrination was both muffled and mandatory or with our professors who transmitted the ideas that they, too, had received with equal innocence. We began to suspect a diabolical will to destroy Knowledge, a worldwide project for the annihilation of anything that didn't come from a single source of mediocrity, narrow-mindedness, and simplification. Now we understood why so many intellectuals suffered from depression and why some of them even resorted to committing suicide.

Infinity cannot be put in parentheses: they would explode. Whether we wanted it or not, there wasn't just one kind of dead-end dialectics, one sort of mindless nihilism or one type of intellectual terrorism. This Knowledge subsisted, even if it was buried under masses of silence; it would resurface at the dawn of the New Times. With their accomplishments, some men had proven that Knowledge could be lived and integrated; men who had not in the least been made into legends but were extremely rare for our time. We would be instructed by them as long as we had the courage to start off with a clean slate. Not only were those who held the noblest truths scarce, but unlike the fake masters, they were never seen, and so one could easily conclude that they were absent. In reality, they continued to hold sessions in citadels of ether hidden from our view, supporting the invisible organization of things; but even if they had chosen to live in retreat, to stop voicing words that were foreign to our ears, they still existed; they were the watchmen of a nobler uniqueness, keeping the fire of secrets alive, awaiting the arrival of the "Great Disjunction" that would establish their return. They knew that all the fuss would upset their truths, degrading and disfiguring them if too widespread. Their excess of evidence would make them intolerable; far too removed from contemporary reasoning, they would be incomprehensible, even capable of backfiring on those who would spread them imprudently.

We were aware of the importance of these revelations and of how fortunate we were to have received so much before the age of twenty. We hadn't done anything to deserve it and yet millions of men who were older and more educated had never known any of this, even people who believed in God, ordinary clergymen had never heard of the tree of the *Sephiroth,* the symbolism behind the Three Kings, or the secret language of Faithful Love. This inexhaustible patrimony inherited from exceptional people led us to what was essential and in so doing we avoided roaming, trial and error, and the attempt to undertake too much all at once. We saved a considerable amount of time and our maturity took on the wings of *lung-gom-pa.* Consequently, we knew that our lives would follow this direction, and this one only, and that now and forever, the East would be our ultimate reference. There was almost something desperate in everyone who felt indifference or hostility toward such subjects, a sort of poverty among those who had never known this metaphysical nudge that transformed us completely. The most tragic part was that everyone who was convinced of serving and spreading the truth, quite recklessly accelerated the descent into the "Dark Age." As for us, we didn't have enough words of gratitude for Thyra and for everything she taught us. All we could do was repeat this sentence from the Gospel: "For whosoever hath, to him shall be given, and he shall have more abundance: but whosoever hath not, from him shall be taken away even that he hath...."

The last candle burned out in an immense silence giving even more shape to the words, and in the dimly lit shadows our cups seemed to stir by themselves. Frost glistened on the misted window-panes. It was almost two o'clock in the morning. Drunk with transcendence, we went out to breathe in the night which welcomed us with luminescent mystery. We could hear the Prince bellowing in the ravine. We would have never believed that we were in the middle of the *Kali Yuga*! From the huge wide valley that opened up like a grotto shaded in violet, the massive blocks of Valere and Tourbillon rose up under the stars.

As if struck by a thunderbolt, I had just fallen in love with God.

4. A Lifetime in a Flower[*]

I

"You'd certainly suffer much less," Tarini said one day, "if you put a little bit of order in yourself and if instead of thinking so much about everything you do, you put into practice everything you've learned."

Most assuredly, Tarini had always been good counsel for me and her comments on the East, which on several points were the same as Thyra's, were sufficiently eloquent for me to consider them with complete confidence.

"Do you know why I named my bookstore the *Lotus d'Or*? It's because the lotus is a complete program in itself; it's the perfect image of the inner transformation that man should accomplish during his lifetime."

She explained that, in effect, the lotus was born in the silt of a pond, grew up through the water, reached the surface with its swimming leaves, rose into the air with the help of its long peduncle, and blossomed in the blazing sun, thus passing through the four elements. She taught me that this corresponded to the four levels of a human being: the body, the soul, the mental state, and the spirit. Because in its weight and substance, our body is made out of earth, our psyche is murky and flowing like water, our thoughts in movement are as imperceptible as the air, and at the center of our being, the divine parcel is fiery. She also taught me that the four levels we were made of corresponded to the four stages of spiritual development, which consisted of successively purifying the physical, gaining of self-understanding, of not locking ourselves into intellectual mechanisms, and of joining our true being in the heart of ultimate Reality.

By encouraging me to experience this evolution, Tarini invited me to become a lotus worthy of its name.

First she showed me how important it was to get in touch with the closest reality, even the most manual, by teaching me the art of *ikebana*, which consists of "putting fresh flowers in water."

[*] From *The Door to the Women's Apartment*, V.

41

"With a simple bouquet," she said, "you can determine the level of consciousness of the person who arranged the flowers."

We must treat flowers with tenderness (they know that and will give us the same in return), be simple and delicate, respectful towards them, all the qualities we possess to one degree or another, or that we don't possess at all; we needed to create enough vacuity within us to exempt any selfish feelings or impolite arrogance, to open our hearts to the universal Heart, our inner vacuity becoming one with the Whole, with the intimate evolving of the essence of things; in short, become exactly the opposite of what I was. At the end of several years of learning and meditation, we would have some chance of revealing the suggestive richness of the mist surrounding an asparagus fern, a few maple leaves, a bramble branch, a single peppercorn placed in a shallow black lacquer coupe, or even correctly placing three stems of scabiosa or begonia grafts on an old moss covered stump, or some willow branches in a ceramic vase.

I have doubts as to having reached even the rank of a beginner; but I did have the first revelation of what could be called the Eastern way of life, especially, when after having taught me the art of arranging *ikebana*, Tarini explained the tea ceremony, whose purpose is to worship purity, and whose supreme refinement consists of slowly sipping, without any fuss, this precious beverage illuminating a simple bowl, and in sharing with one's guest.

I would have liked to know more about folding paper, how to arrange food on a platter and the assemblage of its colors, the ways of lighting incense. Not having read *The Art of Taking a Nap* by Li Li Weng, I took naps unskillfully, beneath the tulle. But I had already realized that these delightful marks of civilization were like the last flowering bushes in the field open to the invasions of savagery, and whose pollen now competed with the radioactive dust from a bomb that had exploded just seven years earlier.

I knew that we were living any old way by sitting in chairs, which twists the backbone, by eating and talking at the same time, which distracts us from both, and by not behaving in harmony with the seasons. I decided, therefore, to sit on the floor, keeping my shoulders and back erect and to walk barefoot on the pavement; I enjoyed paying attention to my nutrition, following the rhythm of the sun, reaping the benefits of going to bed before midnight, being surprised by unknown sounds heard when awakening at daybreak, smearing myself with dew, inhaling the garden's freshness before the rising heat. I knew that nothing was more barbaric than using a knife and a fork, and that by eating anything that moved horizontally I'd eventually end up thinking along the same lines. And so, I decided under my parents' questioning eyes, to return to the good old days when I ate with my fingers, and to convert to vegetarianism.

I became aware of my body by faithfully taking *hatha-yoga* classes organized by Tarini (I was the one who had never attended the mandatory gym classes). Yoga, like archery and *ikebana*, had not yet acquired a snobbish mercenary success. Once again, practicing the serious and disconcerting game of concentric acrobatics on a terrace meant arousing suspicion, exposing myself to ridicule. The best thing to do was to keep quiet; and for a long time, Tarini, Fernand Javel and myself could be proud of being the first "gymnosophists" on the entire African continent.

I was Fish, Gazelle, Frog, Locust; I was Plough, Tree. I did shoulder stands. I stood on one foot, on my head, put my arm around my left knee to grasp the toes on my left foot with the fingers of my right hand. I excelled at the "Sun Salutation," which Rigveda talked about three thousand years ago. I felt I was really breathing for the first time, found myself astonishingly svelte, easily passed all my exams. I couldn't think of any happier coalition than the natural joy of youth, the benefits of these exercises, small successes at university, and the delicious feminine fragrance of warm wisteria, which was inseparable from the memory of an entire adolescence.

By teaching me how to find vertical awareness, to comfortably control my breathing, to slip from one form into another, into one kingdom or another, Tarini had already helped me leave the animal state and come closer to the human ideal; because only man is able to change and grow.

II

Trying to emerge from the heaviness of my vase could only be a meager beginning. The lotus still had a long itinerary to follow before becoming a complete and dignified Nymphaeaceae.

Undertaking the crossing of the aquatic kingdom would require exploring and recognizing this uncertain and practically unknown psychic zone that official teaching excluded from its aims.

Some unusual dreams sparked an even greater interest than before. I was already intrigued by this allusion to the Russian pilgrim who, in a dream, had seen the ghost of his dead Father mark the page of the Bible with a piece of charcoal. When he awoke, he found the marked page as well as the charcoal set down next to the book.

I had barely started paying more attention to my dreams when they suddenly became more frequent and richer with meaning. I hurried to bring them, still moist, to the one whom I had chosen as their interpreter and who first taught me how to decipher their alphabet.

One night, I was passing over a swamp at high speed, scraping with my flight, a vast surface of foam, water lenses that I saw close-up, as if I were looking through a magnifying glass.

"You're afraid of getting mixed up with your deepest self," Tarini told me. "You're content to just stay on the surface of yourself. And you're speeding along because you're impatient. You won't achieve anything of value by hastening the process: you're staying in the ideal, refusing to live."

"But I can see this reality up close."

"That's because it is undoubtedly time to take the plunge."

Gifted with the rare talent of being able to evolve in space, I now leaped from the top of the Mangia Tower in Siena and landed softly—a magic paper glued to my chest served as a talisman—in the middle of the huge Plaza del Campo that is surrounded by old red brick houses. Quite a large group of people crowded around to see this new Icarus; every day I earned a considerable fortune. But fearing that my power came from an evil spirit and that God would eventually punish me with a mortal fall, I decided to donate half of my revenue from the spectacle to charities and keep the rest for myself.

Tarini indicated that this tower designated a state of confinement, an existence too separated from others. But this time I agreed to leave the heights, to descend into reality; this was notable progress. The allusion to earnings translated a concern for practicality, which didn't, however, refuse a place for sentiment: the lucky charm was placed at the level of my heart, or to sensations: the color red was evidence of this. The square symbolized the center of my being, its own center, "*la sienne*,"[1] that is to say, my deep and true nature. Undoubtedly, the public signified my need to be recognized, admired, but the fear of using a psychic power forced me to be generous: I shared my fortune.

Still another dream showed me descending without hesitation into frightening depths, and going down a long corridor where I opened doors that entered into gloomy kingdoms. The book that served as a guide was none other than *Bardo Thodol*. I was afraid that I was reading about my own death. Tarini reassured me: it was a part of myself that had died, the immature child, letting someone else who was much more like me in reality come to life. Furthermore, I showed my ability to handle difficult situations, perhaps even waiting to lead others.

That would come to me several days later. If my grandfather's death was not really too painful for me, the fact that there wasn't any religious ceremony to accompany him to his resting place greatly saddened me. That moved me to read in honor of him, over forty-nine evenings, the forty-nine chapters of the *The Tibetan Book of the Dead*. I was authorized by the fact that anyone, even a non-religious person could read it.

I stayed by his side while he contemplated the primordial White Light that follows the end of conscious life; stayed by his side at the start of the procession of kind and peaceful deities offering all sorts of mirages and charms, followed by irritated and fearsome deities creating all sorts of torments and dread.

"Acknowledge all of that as your mind's illusionary irradiations; don't follow it! Forge ahead!"

It was a matter of helping my grandfather avoid falling into the trap of fantastical projections born from work accomplished during his existence.

"Everything that you could wish for is coming to parade before you. Remember, oh noble son Louis, your relationship with the reader of this book! Chase away all attractions and all repulsion!"

---

[1] Translator's Note: In the original French text the author makes a play on words between the middle of the Plaza in Sienne, the city of Siena, and *la sienne*, the possessive form, in this case meaning his own center.

Calling my grandfather "son" seemed strange to me, but wasn't I his lama? At the time when he saw sounds, light, the numerous rays that fill up with helplessness, I was there multiplying my injunctions against them.

On the sixteenth day there was an especially dangerous passage.

"Now, darkness surrounds you like a mountain ravine; you hear cries, howling wind; hail is swirling all around you. Don't be distracted! Rest assured!"

And several days later: "Oh noble son, now you see your home, your family, and your body. The latter is the nature of vacuity: looking at yourself in the water, you won't see the least reflection of your face. It's the time where the Lord of Death looks into the mirror, where every act is reflected."

Next came the crossing of even more disconcerting regions watched over by the Guardians of the Threshold, strongholds of the goddess of the bells and the prophet of the animals; lands illuminated by the swirls of nectar and grains of light assembled in orbs similar to turquoise and coral bowls. And still, it was a matter of diverting the spirit of death from all of these illusions so that he could continue his march beyond all these "peripheral conditions," sources of new torments and unquenched thirst.

Thus, from October 12 until November 30, 1954, I guided my grandfather through the Beyond. I ignored that the dead saw different imageries according to the cultural settings that they had lived in. But, I carefully adapted my daily readings for easier understanding: the *Dakini* became Angels, Buddha, the All Compassionate, and Avalokiteshvara, God the Savior. And then, was all of that so important? If it's true that the dead still see the world of the living for a certain time, I still enjoy thinking that my grandfather felt an immense joy at seeing his grandson, seated in front of his photograph by way of effigy, tell him everything he had to do in order to reach one of those happy states that, for a short time at least, helps us forget the world's miseries.

III

To become a somewhat respectable lotus, I still had to conquer the aerial realm by starting with the disintoxication of integral rationalism. Learning on this occasion that in traditional Islam civil servants are selected according to pious criteria brought a smile to my face:

I would have gladly exchanged my leather-clad diplomas for a few hundred prostrations!

In the books recommended to me by Tarini on Eastern logic, I rediscovered certain ways of reasoning that had formerly been my own and that had been severely punished by my professors. Being introduced to Chinese numerology, where a black horse plus a white horse equals three horses, was like seeing a long lost friend that I had been forced to abandon. I began to wonder if I too, like anyone else, wouldn't have known how to bravely cross the ocean of numbers, if instead of having to solve the boring equations imposed on us by tough stiff regents, we would have been allowed to solve such figurative equations as those used by Monsieur Bhaskara when addressing the charming Lilavati:

"In the forest filled with the cries of parrots and cuckoos, the square root of half of a swarm of bees landed on a clump of jasmine near the swamps. Eight-ninths of the clump are also there. All alone, a queen bee stays and buzzes around a drone who is smelling a delicately scented flower. Tell me, oh ornament of calculators, how many bees are there?"

To manage my constantly recurring thoughts, Tarini had me reflect upon the teachings of Suzuki.

These amounted to saying that as long as we tried to find God with our mental state, we had no chance of finding him. Above and beyond all reasoning, we needed direct knowledge where subject and object coincided perfectly, or risk confusing the moon with the finger pointing to it. When all the oppositions and dualities blended together into a superior whole, Illumination, the radical and irreversible transformation of the entire being, would occur. To outwit the craftiness of thoughts and because the answers themselves brought about new questions, I was delighted to learn that the master didn't answer his disciple's questions, or he would give a silly answer, by cleverly side-stepping. As a child I was also criticized because my responses were "beside the point." Had I been a Zen monk and didn't know it? Was it during my childhood that I was the closest to the truth? I was close to believing it.

By training myself not to think, I easily persuaded myself that there "would be enough of a breeze from the fan to keep me cool." I freely admitted that the mental state was the devil and its present overdevelopment was a signature on the Iron Age; because it's a fact that the hypercerebral beings, the grinds we were turned into, generally had hardened hearts, were self-centered, insensitive to the pain of others. In Heaven, you didn't reflect on God, you reflected him, and the tragedy of contemporary thinking was that it forgot to keep on being a mirror. This suspension of thinking, which turned the spirit into a calm flat surface, was the best way of keeping some remnants of the Golden Age here below; the fidelity of the reflection, but also a certain courtesy of the heart, an amenity, a lightening of the surrounding opaqueness, is in short, what we call spirituality.

While strolling not far from our house, I sat down facing a hill where dry leaves were burning. The clouds hung low in silence over the countryside. There was only the smoke slowly unwinding from the fires, the crackling of reeds, the captivating odor of the undergrowth mixed with soil dampened by the first drops of a brief shower. And suddenly, the conjunction of all these elements triggered within me an indescribable state of rapture and serene exaltation that I have never really felt since with such native force; and yet, each time I revive this feeling, the intense flavor of its souvenir puts me back into the state that I had so thoroughly enjoyed.

Moreover, during these instants of absolute contemplation, I experienced a sort of dream buried in the very heart of wakefulness, a dream without any images, without any particular legends, without the slightest hint of restricted duration, in free moving action. I'm sure that what I felt was the real disappearance of the mental state: a unique state where even the hillside with its lazy curves, the scrolls of smoke, the nascent rain, the low clouds, the reeds fatigued by the flames, where everything is abolished, abruptly removed from its own presence. I had reached the edge of an inexpressible fullness. But what was most exquisite was that I didn't know it, wasn't aware of this extinction of everything because my ego had also extinguished itself. It was plenary and regained simplicity. Perhaps on this occasion and for the first time, I had forgotten to think; and contrary to the words of Descartes that had been drummed into us for so many years, I didn't think, I was!

What was I exactly? It was hard for me to answer precisely. In any case, no longer this *me*, eager to say "I"; nor another since I had rediscovered the beginning of an identity; but partly this smoke and the heaps of dried grass, partly some of the herbs scattered around, spreading over all the universe, and this very universe was stripped of its limits. I spilled over with a well-being that I couldn't attest: a sort of unconscious consciousness, as intense as it was impersonal.

IV

The hardest part was yet to come: reaching a spiritual level that would allow me to become an accomplished lotus, by learning to discriminate between the Real and the unreal, as the swan that separates the water from the milk that he wants to drink.

Taking advantage of my Valaisan vacation, I decided to spend time alone in a hermitage in the forest.

It wasn't too difficult for me to flush one out.

From up there I could see the enormous chain of mountain tops, inaccessible landscapes protected by the mirror-like armor of glaciers. In the distance, narrow towers rose like javelins from what must have been the towns in the nebulous depths of the diverging valleys. The only book I brought with me, which I had already read and reread, was *The Gospel of Ramakrishna*. In these words I found purity, tenderness, endless profoundness, the translation of the noblest metaphysical truths told in the language of familiar fables. It was only parables drawn from the water and the wind, filled with birds, frogs and monkeys flying from one branch to another, full of mangoes and betel nuts, and visited by a crowd of rajahs bedecked with rich brocades, humble craftsmen and sages; all of the parables were concerned with teaching the love of all beings because divinity resides in every being; all of them were an invitation to plunge into the core of the Absolute, to blend in, as a salt doll in the ocean.

Tarini had told me about the recluse who surrounded himself with a magic circle that protected him from attacks in the form of disturbing fantasies, like projections liberated from his unconscious. So, at sunrise, I started my day with this ceremony.

Standing up, hands clasped, turning in space to face each of the four directions, I tried to imagine the beings that could be found there and mentally spread over them the most intense force of love possible, wishing them a day filled with joy and peace.

Streaming behind my eyelids was the long procession of the suffering, the sick complaining from their beds of torment, the earth-colored starving, the blasphemous drunks, the human failures with their heartbreaking cries, the dying drenched in the sweat of agony. I could almost hear their clamoring and I unfurled the power of my tenderness towards them in successive waves. It was no longer only the weeping souls that I had surprised at the *Lotus d'Or* who came here, it was all of humanity who showed up, a dazed and woeful multitude; and the immense valley, a chalice overflowing with mist and rays, whispering Swiss mountain pines, babbling *bisses,* was a new *Lotus d'Or.* They were not assembled there for the Last Judgment, but for a banquet of love. Now that I better understood the uniqueness of each being, their hidden or open wounds, how much each one, in the end deserves more commiseration than blame, I better understood Tarini. Over the course of my visits, I discovered that her behavior, more than her words, had taught me how the bottomless pit of human suffering deserved compassion more than indifference. I understood why Tarini was equally patient with everyone, knowing that everything she heard—thoughts, opinions, projects, feelings—would inevitably be subject to change, that brutality concealed fear, just as aggressiveness covered up weakness, that for all of them, their inherent contradictions slipped out until finally surfacing to their consciousness. I understood that she had always known that, and that her maturity towered above ours. Her true colors appeared to me in this enlightenment. Measuring her being, I saw that she was named Profoundness.

From those heights, it was no longer possible to be angry with men for being nasty: their nastiness was the cause of their suffering. And it was on this level that Tarini stood, not in the back of a bookstore, since this was her vision of humanity.

Every creation was moaning and this moaning was a warning to me: bliss could not be allowed as long as one human being was suffering in this life.

Sitting in the lotus position under a larch tree, I tried to breathe slowly, calmly repeating the mantra that Tarini had confided to me: *OM Namoh Bhagavate Sri Ramakrishnaya!*

I only succeeded through trial and error: some parasitical thought always seemed to cross my mind at the worst moment, as biting horseflies streaking through the air. I had to surprise the transhumance of unexpected ideas, forgotten faces, and landscapes appearing out of old memories. But by way of consolation, I thought of what my master taught his disciples: "If you practice just one sixteenth of what I've told you, your salvation will be guaranteed"—although I had no sure idea of what this sixteenth could be. Perhaps, a simple dedication to his image of the snowy gentian, the purple striped crocus, the edelweiss gathered in the forest while remembering the *Gita*: "Whatever one offers Me with devotion: a leaf, a flower, some fruit, some water, this offering of love will please Me"; and to sing the hymn that had been taught to me in Sanskrit: "It is in you, you, friend of the humble, that I find my only refuge...."

I had given up wearing a watch. At exactly high noon, the sun passed behind a summit, the chalet momentarily darkened: it was night in the middle of the day. The hours grew listless in the silent idleness. Sparing any and all effort, gestures stood out in space with the same sharpness of the foliage against the sky. Another quality of time emerged from the absence of a schedule. With my breathing as slow as the passing of the hours, I slipped into the cosmos, repeating in miniature the phases of expansion and retention. From the massif of silence I soon loomed over the futility of words. A subtle modification of the consciousness was taking place, the first signs of which appeared in my handwriting—I was keeping a hermit's diary—which suddenly became miniscule. Without any resistance I gave into myself as the angles of my personality rounded out. No longer regarding me as an intruder, the animals quickly understood that I was not a threat to them: a dormouse settled under the roof, never hesitating to appear; and while I was yielding completely to meditating, a family of marmots dutifully whistled at me.

At the end of an intense week, I began to savor that special quality of things that signals the emergence of another reality, of a transparency, the gustation of serenity where each dot in space widens endlessly. I had the confirmation that an entire range of different levels of consciousness existed, like a stack of fabrics with the thickest sheet on the bottom—our vegetative, coarse, raw consciousness—to end up, after having passed through a succession of hemp, cretonne, twill—our animal nature,—percales, satins, velvets—our intellectual nature,—at the most subtle laces, where silk victoriously rivals with the light. And since these days gone by, in hazy hours where the foghorn of discouragement could have bellowed, I have always found comfort and renewed faith in the thought of the boundless inner wealth of each human being.

It occurred to me, however, that it might become dangerous to continue the experiment. My imagination made its first attempts, risked suggestions. At first I thought that someone had entered the chalet, was prowling about. Sometimes, when the mountains creaked, I feared that an avalanche would come hurtling down these slopes. I had strings of insomnia. Snacking on the last of my cookies, I started to wonder how I would fare, isolated in the mountains, if ever I should have a medical emergency.

I remembered *L'Auberge*, a short story by Maupassant that takes place north of Loeche. (I was just twenty kilometers as the eagle flies from this village located on the other side of the Rhone.) The old guide, Gaspard Hari, had gotten lost in the Wildstrubel massif, which is crowned with fir trees and glaciers. Ulrich Kunsi went out looking for him, but in vain. He was obsessed by a shout that he had heard; maybe from Gaspard who had fallen into a crevasse. Ulrich ended up shut away in an auberge for the entire winter, stuck in the middle of sudden gusts of wind and snow storms worthy of those in *Bardo Thodol*. The torment intensified the howling of Sam, the dog, unless it was the footsteps of a ghost. In the spring, they would find Ulrich overcome with madness.

This story seemed like a caricature of a spiritual quest; the incandescent altitudes of the Absolute were replaced by the abysses of ice, the rapture of bliss, by nocturnal terrors, mystic madness, and mental illness. Strangely, the name of Sam, started like *Samadhi*;[2] the name Kunsi evoked Kunti, Arjuna's mother, like the name Hari evoked the God Hari, who was asked by the sage Dakshinesvar to sing praises.

The fragrance of flowers can't float against the wind. In learning solitude, I remained in isolation. To become fulfilled, man needs men; it's only later that he can withdraw, has the right to do so and the vocation. Ramakrishna taught that "Nothing will come to pass until the right moment comes." This solitary foolhardiness proved to be premature, exposing me to an upside-down life, and for a long time afterward I no longer ventured there. I would repeatedly follow the cycle of the lotus flower: it wasn't just a matter of a few years of precocious blossoming, from flowers that reopened, then wilted, to new flowerings, but the whole of an entire existence, as the water lily that fades before the next flower completes the four stages of its development. However, the difference between a man and a flower is that one starts over again from the same stem and repeats the same cycle, whereas the other, each time, departs from a rich under-

[2] "Supreme ecstasy" in Sanskrit.

standing of past experience and notices that each new path is marked with progress made on the paths that came before.

Before sacrificing my ego, I had to acquire one, to construct it. I was at the age that wanted its commencement; and this commencement entailed shaping the man, maturing. Before dying myself, I would first have to live: return to the cities, survey the land of people; blend in and confront myself. And maybe I would also have to suffer and love.

II

The Modern World

5. STRATAGEMS AND GREAT MANEUVERS[*]

Demagogic by vocation and by necessity, Subversion finds choice ground in political and social arenas. It knows its chances of success are greater here than in areas coming under human control, too human, and that established order offers more shortcomings than qualities: no temporal regime has ever made everybody happy. Thus, from a certain point of view, the Roman church's outrageous prerogatives at the end of the Middle Ages, or the slow technological growth that affected Russia under the rule of the tsars, or the Middle Empire in China at the beginning of the twentieth century were able to justify radical reforms; these were even more destined for success since the structures they attacked bore the marks of wear and dilapidation. But just as a current power tends to take a tougher stand on its rights, to neglect its duties, and gives in to hegemonic temptations, Subversion, likewise, becomes more questionable from the moment when, intoxicated with its conquests, it reveals its true nature and starts adopting what it scorned in the system it is replacing.

Subversion always resorts to double talk. After having encouraged disorder for as long as necessary, it devotes itself to passing on its order as the only one that is real and fair; that is to say, in the case of passive and unconscious resistance, by insinuating itself into minds by gradual conditioning adapted to the circumstances, or in the case of active resistance, by imposing itself on them with force and terror. It goes into its plan by discrediting in advance everything that risks opposing it. For example, to challenge the idea of hierarchy, it will proclaim absolute equality among men, but in order to do this will create inverted and parallel hierarchies, and when the former are finally destroyed, will impose its own hierarchies as the only legitimate ones. While contesting the principles of the opposing side, it will borrow them when it finds them effective. Thus, it will denounce chastity for the religious as being unnatural, but will be capable of requiring it of its activists, not as a method of spiritualization, but as training for moral strictness and the concen-

---

[*] From *Return to the Essential*, I, "Aspects of Subversion," 1.

tration of energy to serve the cause of the revolutionary ideal.[1] This will not prevent it from spoiling at the same time the milieu whose soul it *wants* with pornographic suggestions and debauchery. Not acting openly itself, Subversion will push its pawns onto all the scenes of society. It will erode society from the inside. It will take over and use the goodwill of those who ignore how they are being used as instruments; especially, many an idealist and nebulous intellectual—"the last of the imbeciles" said Bernanos—driven by the sole dictations of theoretical thinking and naïve sentimentality, always ready to rush to the rescue of falsified causes. Those who are really responsible are obviously behind, keeping their guard up to avoid getting caught. In troubled times like these, it is difficult not to unknowingly side with the forces that one disregards or even pretends to combat, even more difficult to know what they are.[2]

It is easy to observe the process that, in accordance with cyclical laws, allowed the establishment of social classes substituting themselves for castes by increasing and reinforcing the lowest values and by gradually eliminating those that prevented or held up the degeneration. Like the weakening of individuals, weakening societies see creative forces slow down and the references to the transcendent source, dispenser of energy, disappear. Habit and routine replace initiatives, hamper inventions; the world loses the freshness of early morning, its native spontaneity. The destruction of the natural authorities and the massacre or suicide of the elite leave a clear field for the unfurling of obscurantism. A sterile coating settles over the best; discouragement does the rest. The only recognized "great men" are recruited among the incompetent. Subversion will entrust them with its greatest responsibilities, consulting them as infallible oracles. The death of a transitory and insignificant star will plunge an entire nation into despair; that of a sage who holds answers won't even be mentioned in the organs of information. Those who would

---

[1] In Hindu mythology, the demons (*asuras*) try to vie with the gods (*devas*) in piety and in asceticism to overpower and deregulate the social balance in their favor. Moreover, we are acquainted with the symbolism of the "Angel of Light" and the hidden side of "angelism" in general.

[2] In this order of ideas, even the East, reservoir of possible solutions, can be diverted from its real role and contribute to the aggravation of the Western "crisis" rather than easing it. Here as well, the "prudence of the snake" and the qualification of mediators are essential.

still be capable of having certain responses will be prudently left aside as enlighteners and troublesome; and the denouncers of Subversion will pass for subversive! They themselves won't undertake anything themselves in order to be heard, except a minority who will have escaped from the quelling, knowing that in such degrees of blindness, their message would be untimely, unheard or confiscated, and that any reckless use of energy would be as vain as a voice shouting in the desert.

When things get to this point, the cracks of the Great Wall widen to become royal doors that the hordes of Subversion sweep through. The latter then has no trouble satisfying what is the lowest in a human being: vulgarity, mediocrity, petty bureaucratic subservience, jealousy, all the passionate elements that are just waiting to be aroused. It also has no trouble making the last chances of salvation detestable, scattering confusion onto confusion by destroying the mind's insightfulness, its sense of proportions, and replacing them with capital myths that can only have a hold over uneducated minds. And thanks to advanced techniques, it no longer requires any effort to exploit rumors and hysteria, denials and diversions, in order to establish a climate of permanent uncertainty and instability, and to divert the real problems, which are and remain those of interiority. In a trembling silence, in muffled hypocrisy, the individual no longer thinks or speaks; he will be thought and spoken. A thousand subtle influences will squeeze him, shape him, while at the same time establishing him as the one who is responsible and the decision maker.[3]

Subversion is very good at arranging life in such a way that business as well as pleasure (known as "organized activities") contribute to lowering the mental level of the greatest number possible. It secretes incommunicability between people: man, a stranger unto himself, "alienated," can only be a stranger to others; it sets up unhealthy social relationships, signed with indifference or reciprocal surveillance, spitefulness, brutality: the men of the *Age de Fer* (the Iron Age) are themselves *en fer* (made of iron)—which puts them in *Enfer* (Hell). A Hell that they impose on others because for

---

[3] Instead of using the words of Saint Paul: "It is no longer I who live, it is Christ who lives in me," modern man, still lucid, would be able to say: "It is no longer I who think (or speak or act), it is the newspaper that I read every day (or television or the union or the political party) who thinks (speaks, acts) in me...."

others to be exempt is intolerable for them: Hell, too, is contagious. It compels individuals to have bloodless activities, devoid of any real interest, taking as much time as possible from them—time that becomes even more precious as it runs out—so that they are confronted as little as possible with themselves, with the memory of the "only necessities of life (*solum necessarium*)." Everything is good for it provided that the "only necessities of life" are not served, provided that no one thinks about them, that what they signify or whatever interest they hold have been forgotten, and that they pass for the only things that are useless and unnecessary. To divert man, Subversion will multiply worries about well-being, conflicts in human relations, family dissension, social drudgery, meanness and pettiness, the incredible ennui of bureaucratic dullness, mandatory meetings, never-ending discussions, harassment, disguised persecutions and even rewards....

A colossal enterprise for demolition, it starts discreetly with engineered rumors altering energetic tendencies, incessant provoking or denouncements, and finishes with the vast manipulation of ideological intimidation, brainwashing, correctional camps, summary executions. When Subversion has reached its goals, when it has taken possession of the state machinery, the police force, information agencies, publishing houses, social and cultural departments, judicial, military, university and ecclesiastical hierarchies, when everything already belongs, even though nothing seems to belong to it yet, then it can be considered that society is nothing more than a mere shadow of its former self. Like the decomposition of a cadaver whose bones emerge after the flesh has already vanished, the social structures remain, but the driving and creative conscience has been disbanded and annihilated.

Subversion excels in blending truth and error. Regularly transmitted to new generations, these clever or laborious, officially enthroned falsifications are looked on as anti-traditional traditions.

Nowhere is this more clearly seen than in the field of university information. The choice of authors and texts, the images that illustrate them, the omission of embarrassing passages, the underlining of certain others contribute to the alteration or deviation of objective reality. History offers a privileged area for this kind of manipulation in accordance with the ideological options of those who narrate it. History has mastered the art of isolating events from their context, interpreting magical behavior through modern mentality, condemning itself in this way to not understanding the events, evading what would risk going against the prejudices of progressive messianism. It has been forgotten, for example, that the mistakes made by the emperors of China were punished by the people's rebellion; concerning the Nordic kings, they were taken to trial as a result of social calamities, which concluded their disqualification; or even concerning the condition of women: they had the right to vote in medieval mayor's offices. Every effort is made to belittle anything that does not meet the demands of established dogmas by abusively identifying what is represented and its representative. Just as medicine would be condemned under the pretext that there are quacks, all religion will be condemned as a whole because of some bad monks. Certain embarrassing corrections will be kept silent.[4] One imagines how easy it is to influence young minds, which by definition are receptive and malleable, still deprived of a critical sense, sensitive to the supposed objective neutrality, but lacking any contrary argumentation.

Much more instructive than official History would be the possible investigations in "metapolitics," whose role at the level of the occult war cannot be neglected. Disraeli's words are well known: "The world is governed by very different personages from what is imagined by those who are not behind the scenes." Rapidly appearing as filigree work in History would be the existence of *plots* by rival allegiances, plans designed and followed step by step by clandestine promoters. Disinformation—strangely camouflaged by information overload—disorganization, the destruction of the last values in view of the planning of humanity at the lowest level, are certainly not the effects of hazard alone, but the application of an implacable will and concerted programs, in which the demoralization of those whose loss is desired is also included. No doubt, the real situation of the world requires lucid consideration; and it would be misleading to ignore the most threatening aspects. However, such an acknowledgement, if its only goal was to bring about despair, could only

---

[4] For example, the call of the anarchist, Proudhon, will be popularized: "Property is theft" (*What is Property?*, 1840), but one will forget to cite what he later wrote about it: "Property is the natural counterbalance, necessary to political power"; "it is the triumph of liberty" and "the greatest revolutionary strength capable of opposing power" (*Théorie de la propriété*, 1865).

serve Subversion. It must aim to inform people's consciousness and make them aware, not for preventing the collapse of the Empire, but to watch out for the signs of what must follow it.

$$*$$
$$* \quad *$$

If we now take a look at the world of art, we will see that the modern world presents the image of a "civilization without culture" or at best, a "culture without knowledge."

If there are still some isolated serious works of art, the gulf separating current works from the mystical poetry of Sufism or Elizabethan theater, Gothic cathedrals or Hindu temples, and the metaphysical corpus from both the East and the West is overwhelming. Even admiration for scientific achievement quickly loses its keenness; "technical miracles" no longer generate enthusiasm among crowds that are already bored or always hungry for something else. Talent is thwarted. Detectable behind the waste of vocation is the visible signature of Subversion that knows full well that "with the destruction of intelligence (*buddhi*) man perishes."[5]

And it begins with the destruction of language. The intense consumption of words weakens them, dries up their savor. Using them without distinction or limit depletes their magical effect, their intensity and density. The systematic recourse to crude language when there is no reason for it is supposed to replace overused terms while waiting their turn to be eventually overused themselves. The creation of sometimes unpronounceable acronyms is multiplied with abstract expressions reduced to initials. Words are diverted from their original meaning to the point of meaning the contrary; several languages are mixed without any guiding principle; the harshest terms are used for the most insignificant subjects; spiritual meanings are used at the most profane level. An even more subtle technique consists of surreptitiously removing a certain number of words from dictionaries with the pretext that they are no longer in current use or are incomprehensible for most. *Hazard* wants these words to carry philosophical or spiritual notions; the concepts they

---

[5] *Bhagavad Gita*, II, 63. Simply reading administrative instructions contributes to confusing the mind by the totally "alexithymic" nature of their style.

englobe disappear with them.[6] What is practiced at the same level of words is practiced with people's names. With the conspiracy of silence, true parody of the "law of secrets" practiced in initiatory brotherhoods, the systems and doctrines that make the mistake of not following the "course of History" will be suppressed. Consequently, certain major questions are carefully omitted from debates; the works of eminent minds, precursors condemned to solitude, withdraw into the past and disappear from memory; the widespread downfall of thinking happens periodically, without the public being informed.

No field is spared by Subversion: everything is its business. In advertising, spelling is defaced and altered; one talks about getting rid of it under the pretext that it contributes to maintaining oppression! The approximative nature of style and syntax, combined with that of vocabulary, leads to the poverty and diminishing of an uncertain, perturbed thinking that reflects a defeated psyche. The last enclave of a sacred language is poetry, but the public's loss of interest in it is well known, unless it chooses to lock itself into an unreadable obscurity or the spread of cancerous words. Here, many of the symptoms of the end of a language are present. Yet, it so happens that the end of a language is the end of those who speak it insofar as it is inherent to their attitude, psychology and unique sensitivity.

"New music" that only manages to establish itself by cultural terrorism has been at a dead-end since the first half of the twentieth century—the era when Schoenberg invented the "serial technique." It renounced the system of intervals, the hierarchical relationship between the notes. Their distinction between the fundamental, keynote, leading note and dominant expressed the relationships that the polytonal and atonal systems entangled without destroying; but their disappearance ruins any possibility of "communication." Contemporary musical art abounds in sonorous collages, in random and repetitive pieces (the parody of incantations); it multiplies the dissonances, breaks rhythms, reproduces in its own way the fragmented violence of the Western psyche. By integrating the sonorous

---

[6] The process of the "vaporization" of words, with the idea of an agnostic conditioning of attitudes, was described by George Orwell in his novel, *1984*, concerning the "newspeak." In comparison, all the languages of early civilizations—Greek, Sanskrit, Chinese—display, to the contrary, an abundant semantic richness.

elements of electric origin, which are submitted to algebraic treatments, fiddled with in laboratories and programmed on computers, it removes any kind of emotion or imagination, any therapeutic value susceptible of having an effect on the psychic core of human beings, as does traditional music. If the latter is the "sound of Heaven's door opening and closing," as heard in the expression of the dervishes of Mevlevi (and that certain works of Messiaen would still like to imitate), the recording of the cries of the damned, the spasmodic gasping of humanity knocked around by the shock wave of an atomic explosion is made possible by electronic music. Music's role is assuredly something else: to change the level of consciousness, to temporarily spare earthly weight and turbulences, to suggest pre-ecstatic states, to reconcile man and creation, to help him forgive himself.

As for sculpture, it aims toward an abstraction and densification of volumes in perfect harmony with the mass attitude. Rather than lightening the matter, it makes it opaque, prohibiting the final incursion of the Spirit to show even the slightest transparence, flexibility. Caesar's scrap heap eloquently provides evidence in favor of the Iron Age. With the exception of several artists likening Plato—Klee, Matthieu, Bordet, Wulfing—painting has also stripped itself of tremors and divino-human reflections, affective and subjective vibrations that are its *raison d'être*. The reign of anguish that immediately arose after Impressionism, the refusal of nature, the dislocation of shapes, the division of the world starting with cubism and futurism (to the point of being unable to recognize the subject of a painting by Picasso), contributed to this wrong-way evolution where man, contemporary of the winter of the world, discovers that he is cold, is no longer *linked*; a world where nothingness is the only thing left to paint. Whether it is through larvae that have risen up from psychic decay, or from geometry that is similar to dismantled metal superstructures, or else through the degrading of the faces and bodies of humans, pictorial art displays a complete spiritual void where one is persuaded that flashes of genius, snobbish outrageousness and mercantile advantages are reconciled.

In all of this, nothing is susceptible of holding one's attention for very long. Instead of making man worthy and preparing his assumption, Modern art has chosen the easiest path: to follow cyclical degeneracy. The prophetic spirit has stopped inspiring, perhaps because there is no future. If, according to the *hadith*, "God is beautiful and loves all beauty," it cannot be seen how he could recognize himself in these grimaces and fragmentations. None of the three criteria for perfect art—nobility of the contents, exactness of symbolism or harmony of composition, and purity of style—has any significance for artists who have allowed themselves to be surrounded by Luciferian elements whose accelerated exhaustion accelerates the end of art.

Art refused the "keys" which permitted boundless possibilities for creating; it exhausted the possible harmonization and combination of elements and ranges that had given birth to different artistic tendencies and schools; it opened itself unilaterally either to the untempered *yang*, bringing the stiffness and hardening of forms, or to the *yin* in the pure state, bringing their liquefaction. Undoubtedly, one of its rare options would be to turn to the East, to return to its roots, to renew itself there by drawing on certain forgotten eternal principles and by adapting them to an appropriate language. Music, for example, would rediscover its own role: not the expression of equations, but of "qualities" and "states," of discovering new rhythms, tones and instruments.

In conclusion, we will just mention a word about one of the most recent discoveries whose worrisome development solely for economic necessity has reached the point of supplanting man in his last realms of liberty and of implementing a transfer of creativity in its favor: we would like to talk about the computer. Its inexorable invasion guarantees us a sort of frozen universe, with no possibility of errors or lies, one of complete boreal purity, quasi-divine. But this universe is divinity gone amiss, diabolically innocent. Because computers, regardless of how perfect or perfectible they may be and despite their *absolute knowledge*, will always lack what some might call a soul, in any case, a *je ne sais quoi*. These top-quality metal angels, capable of breathtaking calculations at incalculable speeds (which only serve to accelerate the cyclical movement), and next to which men trudge at the pace of oxen, appearing by far inferior to the machines that are however their creatures, presenting only one flaw—total and implacable—that of being nearly infallible compared to all the weaknesses of human intelligence. Barring a Spirit from the spheres of Up Above, their providential Emissary, here below it seems dangerous to know everything and never make a mistake.

In the same way that an Arabian tapestry always has a flaw (albeit done on purpose by the craftsman), a missing stitch is evidence that all work done by man falls short of the perfection that belongs solely to one Creator; in the same way that absolutely pure oxygen quickly becomes unbreathable because anything living needs germs and impurities, it can be considered that the whole of advanced technology seems too impeccable to correspond to human standards. It is tempting to praise error as a vital necessity, the errors of the unfulfilled as the signature of a normal world. The world of computers resembles perfection too closely to remain unsuspected—a sterilized perfection with something automatic and insensitive, a *straightforward* perfection—it comes too close to God to not be suspected of being the Devil. *Errare humanum est, non errare diabolicum.*

6. DEBACLE OF A THOUGHT[*]

Much more than other disciplines, general philosophy becomes the agent of Subversion by allowing even more room for systems that reduce man to technology, sociology and biology, and by ignoring the whole of non-European wisdom, which could only cause its collapse. Everything that, for the time being, would risk expanding the spiritual horizon has been relegated to small study groups that have no influence over the course of events and are tolerated because they are inoffensive—which maintains the illusion of respect for free thinking.

The history of ideas in the West has appeared for centuries—with the temporary stabilization of the Christian episode—as a series of shifts, slow drifts, imperceptible betrayals whose sum has led to the philosophical dead-end that we are aware of. We do not have enough space here to show that all throughout this history there was rivalry between the different existentialist trends, from *humanitas* in the sixteenth century, its "culture" and "scale" to Husserlian phenomenology, in passing by Kierkegaard, Jaspers, Heidegger and Sartre. It is all too well known that the main origin of the contemporary slump lies in what has become of dualistic Cartesianism, which, from divisions to successive exclusions, has managed to deny the most important half of Reality—which corresponds to nine tenths of the Whole!—and to provoke an offensive and systematic skepticism. After the resulting scission, life was proclaimed absurd, the world, deprived of meaning. Consequently, not only does "existence precede essence," but only existence exists, before sinking into inexistence in turn. The refusal to confront the metaphysical *quid?* is not a solution, rather it plunges man into the ravines of desperation. In effect, he no longer has the possibility of averting the crises of the phenomenal world by finding the resources in the Self, by settling there in an unshakable manner. Man sees himself condemned to "anguish," "melancholy" and "nausea," the many stages of panic in the face of what he ignores and cannot explain. The remedy of the scourge, which is not given to him, is in the *knowledge*

---

[*] From *Return to the Essential*, I, "Aspects of Subversion," 2.

that allows the vision of all things in the supreme Principle, in the Center of gravity of the visible and invisible universes, of knowing that all apparent contradictions are the elements of total order. There is no doubt that this anguish and hopelessness, which demoralize the West, weaken and undermine it, also enter into the programmed destruction to which we alluded in the preceding chapter.

As for structuralism, we see it substitute the visions that preceded it, which are as much realist as idealist, with an option according to which the sole reality is a simple interrelationship between the "ego" that perceives and the things perceived. In this way it destroys the edifice of all human thought and imprisons man in stiff and artificial corsets. Levi-Strauss proclaims that "the mind is also a thing" and that "the ultimate aim of human sciences is not to constitute man but to dissolve him" (into the sole physico-chemical state). It seems difficult to reduce to even less something that had already been condemned to being only a "reasonable animal" or "an accident of the universe."

These recent interpretations of man all concur in denying him any intellection. And yet, not only can intellection be lived and proven experimentally—fulfilled individuals are living proof—but human understanding alone is incapable of reaching any intuitive proof concerning the Absolute; it can only collide with its prison walls and the implacable antinomies of a partial and immanent experience. That would be a lesser evil. But since it lacks the means of reaching the Absolute, rationalism and its derivatives have preferred to deny its existence, to "absolutize" man instead, whose strength of will no longer knows any limits.

The ultimate result of the evolution is the nihilism predicted by Nietzsche and which embraces both "the death of God" and of man; first, the death of God, because now references are only made to what is human. And yet, as Dostoevsky points out: "If God didn't exist, everything would be possible." By following this idea to the letter, Sartre was able to establish the absolute freedom of man, and Camus to justify his revolt against an empty and silent heaven. Afterwards comes the death of man, if it is true that he is "in the image and likeness of Elohim," therefore solidary with his own mortal destiny; or, if the human being is stripped of all value, as Feuerbach and Bakunin affirmed before. A product of pure chance, lost in the "unfeeling immensity" of the universe, of which

Monod speaks, he no longer has, in effect, any significance or special vocation; he himself is an eternal question that has no answer. A double death certificate whose consequences spread over nearly all the works of the twentieth century, and that can only trigger cynical and destructive behavior. How can it be otherwise, when there are no longer any references for the slightest ethical attitude, and to fill the nothingness, for lack of Totality, there is only its caricature, totalitarianism? Such a vision leads to totalitarian fanaticism, bringing with it young people who cannot know anything other than what they are told and are not objective enough or sufficiently informed to judge otherwise. As a matter of fact, such teaching, underneath its kind neutral exterior, constitutes a stronghold of intolerance. Kept in the ignorance of essentialism, one has the right to wonder, along with Jean Servier in *L'Homme et l'Invisible*, if young people who at the moment "are fighting against a destiny they don't want" will manage to "shatter the material world that is closing up their minds," or if their thinking will "be forever crippled."

It would be easy and interesting to make comparative lists for many Western philosophers who, starting from sound premises, always ended up skidding on a turn somewhere along the way. It could even be the subject of a conclusive book for the history of ideas: to follow the different deviations of Western thinking from its Greek origins through the main philosophers, and showing how, from step to step, this thinking multiplied dead ends to result in an "intellectual night" where the "black suns" of Subversion shine. We can only give some outlines here.

Aristotle also deals with metaphysics and Platonic "Ideas." He adheres to the existence of a God who is the motor of the universe, entirely "substance" in actuality, thorough and perfect; *but* he formulates a theory of the concept that is no longer metaphysical but logical. His "realism" is that of sensory objects, refusing to separate the essence from the thing itself. He brings metaphysics back to ontology; and the entire history of Western metaphysics will be marked, preventing it henceforth—barring exceptions—from belonging to *philosophia perennis*. This *reduction* brought about an abstract and theoretical conception of knowledge, resulting in modern intellectualism, unknown to any "experience." God becomes a Principle separated from the world (before completely disappearing from the human horizon and human concerns). Thomas Aquinas will study this same separation that Descartes will definitively confirm. Rational understanding will replace metaphysical Intuition. Not only will the Super-Being be completely set aside, forgotten, but the study of the Supreme Being will gradually be reduced to that of the "categories" of the physical world; the world of Illusion will be promoted to the point of becoming the only reality. God, conceived as the supreme Individual, paves the way to the personal God of the theologian, of the exoteric who will be unable to get past this personal aspect of Divinity: first limitation, although still of a principial order. Everything is already in place for inspiring conceptions of the Absolute that are increasingly limited, "systems" that are natural or rational, purely theoretical, exclusive, dogmatic, dialectic; everything is ready for transcendence and universality to be removed from view.

Spinoza, a familiar figure in Hebrew theology, clearly integrates traditional elements into his philosophy; his doctrine of salvation is linked to knowing God, possible in that human understanding is formally identical to that of God; *but*, as a Jew uprooted from his spiritual tradition—as Freud, Marx and Einstein would be later—he is opposed to theological dogmatism in the name of his own rational dogmatism: his monism obliterates freedom of choice or of the "person," unlike non-dualism—such as Vedanta—which integrates them into the universality of its perspective. Kant adopts a similar attitude: he assumes the existence of "noumena," those "things-in-themselves" independent of any relationship with our rational mind, beyond the "phenomena" of apparent reality; *but* unlike skepticism, which can only logically affirm itself by also having doubts about itself, all of Kant's reasoning for proving that one cannot use reason to be acquainted with "noumena" shows all the faith he still has in this reason. Hegel refers undoubtedly to Christian theology and seems profoundly linked to a spiritual dimension; he puts Incarnation at the center of his system; *but* he confuses the pure Supreme Being and nothingness. For him, the necessity of Incarnation means that it adds something to the Supreme Being of the Father: God would have needed to be incarnated to become real. Yet, such a necessity no longer corresponds to divine freedom, but rather to a lack: it is simply a matter of profaned Incarnation, of a new rationalization of metaphysics in favor of theology.

The same ones who, referring to the East, could be worthy of more confidence, display similar deviations. Leibniz discovers a binary notation based on the exclusive use of one and zero; *but* while admiring what the Jesuits of Beijing tell him about the *I Ching*, he gets lost in the interpretation of the *yin-yang* and the trigrams of Fo-hi. Schopenhauer recommends the renunciation of the will to live and of life, which he considers with Buddhism as pure illusion and nothingness; *but* it is for passing into a *Nirvana* that is itself just another nothingness, and not the death of the ego, death of the mental, nor the state of absence from pain and ignorance. Bergson rehabilitates the notions of intuition and life force; *but* it is for immediately adding to it the virtues of mechanism, progressive evolutionism, the efficiency of "human action" placed above contemplation. Steiner encourages returning to a "spiritual science" whose panorama he describes, indicating the modes of access; *but* this "science," under the weight of pseudo-visionary rambling, darkening and alienating psychic influence, quickly becomes the opposite of a science.

In this case and in all the others, the tactic is always the same: circumvent the greatest geniuses so that they serve the purpose of Subversion, make them sow in the fields of Truth, without their knowledge, and without looking back—that is to say without suspecting the consequences of their words—at the teeth of the antique dragon, that then rise as warriors and transform themselves, behind their backs, into battalions of error.

*
* *

Because the psychic sphere is particularly indistinct, ambiguous, and operating behind its erratic dunes is easy, Subversion long ago understood the benefits of using psychology. It uses psychological "functions" to its advantage, corrupting life from within, and confusing unrelated ideas. From the moment it occupies this ground, it is free to do nearly anything it pleases with human beings.

Is it a question of men with a special gift for *intuition?*— Subversion will devote itself to perverting it or getting rid of it. Intuition will see its right to existence kept; but its premonitions will not occur, will be inexact or grow scarce by a system of training that will dry out its sources, insist on the abstract, on fastidious calculations, and on the automation of the mind. By increasing the shocks, the traumatisms, by forcing the most fragile souls to an unsteady lifestyle, by undermining the keenest aptitudes, Subversion attains its goal: impaired, the psyche no longer responds.

Is it a question of beings whose *mental activity* is predominant?—Subversion will use intellectual weapons, will refine the resources of specious dialectics where any argument can, without any inconvenience, be turned around to the contrary, and convince that one will never be right, even if one should always be wrong! It is a question of trapping man in a sort of inexhaustible sophistry, until he realizes that no answer will ever get out of the groundless conceptual game and that all exits are closed to him. His torment can become acute enough to push him to the thresholds of madness and death.

Is it a question of beings whose *sentiments* prevail?—Any occasion is good for touching the right chord, for trifling with elementary emotionalism, exploiting indignation at a level of opposites that are as simplistic as black and white, for using pathetic eloquence: in admirable improvisations, Subversion becomes the *passionnaria* of the collective psyche to establish and impose its own conception of the common good. It will know how to move a moving versatile crowd and make the "heartless" who try to resist it feel perpetually guilty.

Is it a question of beings dominated by *sensation?*—Subversion will continuously unfold the panoply of visceral impressions and multi-colored seductions, praise the body's laziness and the sluggishness of subtle perceptions. It will know how to orchestrate the dance of primitive sensations, restrict life to a forever unappeased epicureanism, use unexpected suggestions to return to instinct engineering, which will then be impossible to get rid of. Subversion is no stranger to the fact that nearly anything can be gotten from men when they are held by the pleasures of good food and the blandishments of the flesh.

Much more than being in communion with people, the group is the juxtaposition of individuals. Getting several people together to form a personality only dilutes the personal possibilities of each one, maintains infantilism and a gregarious mentality, reduces the chances of taking initiatives and of inventing. The bigger the group, the more it conceals the particular components, proceeds with perfunctory examination. It forces the highest level of participants to conform to the lowest level, that of the majority. It molds attitudes in such a way that they consider the lifestyles, ways of thinking, work methods, and human relations at the sole level of the masses, the level of this demon who is himself called "legion," to be normal and legitimate. Anyone not sticking with the herd will be considered antisocial, "marginal," and this even sometimes more quickly than he would be at the pathological level. These demands direct the group as well to side with the subversive forces since it is in the best interest of the latter to block the development of the personality, the only thing capable of really opposing them. Finally, aware of its force in numbers, the group reinforces in its members the certainty of being right, and leads to an intolerance toward those who are on the outside. As such, it is the group that goes against the love of his fellow man. The barricades surrounding it are not so impenetrable that an exterior element cannot get through: emissaries of Subversion, responsible for penetrating the group, and after having created disorder, division and scandal, give their report on the state of affairs.

It can never be repeated enough that the only possibility of having a strong bond with another is if one is really linked to oneself, reconciled with oneself, not as the ego but as the supreme "Self." Without the prior self-understanding that is accomplished in the secrets of the heart, without passing through the "desert" and the confrontation with oneself, without individual and coherent discussions where no stone is left unturned, without regular meditation in rapport with one's individual character, relations with others can only be one more pious illusion, random harmony, a worthless brotherhood.[1]

At the very level of psychological analysis that "groups" claim to adhere to in varying degrees, there is another process that consists of bringing the analysand down to a level beneath ordinary individuality, of pushing him to regress toward obscure and chaotic forces, and basic embryonic elements; this works in the same manner as spiritism and all the techniques that work on the residue of psychological decomposition, without, however, helping him later rise up again from animality; or else, by keeping him there in the

---

[1] Jung noted in *Mysterium Coniunctionis*, 1, 2, that "the current tendency is reflected by the replacing of man's interior coherency by the exterior community, as if someone who was not coherent with himself was capable of any exterior community. This deplorable tendency lays the groundwork for civilization en masse." And, we can also add, for mandatory collective living, dictatorship, and war.

same way that the head of a man one wants to drown is held under water; even more, by pretending that the lower levels of the "sub-conscious" are the levels of the "supraconscious." Abused by the "confusion of the psyche and of the spiritual," some will read in such superficial dreams real archetypical "thoughts" that, when interpreted and applied literally, lead to the worst disasters. In reality, these dreams only emanate from the lower zones of the unconscious where "impressions," "impregnations," latent "tendencies" stay,—the *vasana*s and *samskara*s of Indian psychology. Undoubtedly, with other deeper dreams, dreamers can gather information of which they are deprived by the usual censorship, about their neuroses, frustrations, repressions, about the origins of their conflicts and anxieties. Enlarged or mythologized in the sense of Jungian "amplifications," their interpretation can help change outlooks and initiate the first process of transformation. But, putting it into the realm of a total experience would be to endow it with a dimension it does not have. It is nevertheless interesting to note that Subversion, which is capable of dissolving the psyche by throwing it into the swamp of Freudian sexualism, is also capable of exalting it toward mystic altitudes which are in reality the sphere of *pneuma*;[2] and that, in spite of itself and without its knowledge.

Contrary to this maneuver that allows for the inferior to be thought of as the superior with the sole aim of absorbing and swallowing the latter, there is another one that reduces the transcendent notions to the most immanent level, by only seeing religion as a work of the human hand and as a simple therapeutic additive. Or else, the myths included in the Scriptures, stripped of all symbolic meaning, will be simply connected to geological or atmospheric phenomena, to historical events that would have been passed down to us through naïve spicy legends from archaic beliefs, even though they refer to the eternal relationships between the ten *Sephiroth*! Or yet, humanity's greatest wise men will be assimilated with eccentric dreamers, victims of hallucinatory wild imagining, barely worthy of our commiseration, and will eventually end up in insane asylums. Those who are the least apt to judge these things are likely to get carelessly involved, without any fear of sinking into the ridicule con-

---

[2] The *Talmud* says (Berachot 57b), "the dream itself is a sixtieth of prophecy"; it contributes to spiritual awakening by revealing a truth.

ferred by ignorance. And yet, here again, certain authors such as Henri Corbin, went to the effort of specifying the distinctions that are mandatory at the outset of such investigations. It would be useful, for example, to inquire somewhat about the demarcation established by the Shi'ism between the physical and the material world—*alam hissi,*—the intelligible world—*alam aqli,*—and the "imaginal" intermediary world, which only the "Perfect" reach. From this "land of theophanic visions," prophetic knowledge, inspired words, the secret meaning of the Scriptures, ritual symbols and modes of prayer are returned to humanity; as many sparkling fragments from the landscapes of the "eighth Climate," captured by an independent spiritual power from the psychic organism, associated with the subtle body, and whose function is not the construction of the unreal—that is the role of the "imaginary"—but the uncovering of the Real that is hidden behind appearances. In relation to this "agent of Imagination," the "imaginary" is a matter of simple mental activity, a producer of overlapping fantastical images connected to noticeable perceptions. As such it is degradation, obscuration, and for this very reason, serves the aims of Subversion.[3]

* * *

But out of all the objectives that Subversion intends to attain, the spiritual world is the most highly targeted because it represents what is the most contrary to it. To conquer it, Subversion employs all sorts of procedures that would take too long to properly analyze. For the moment, we will only take a look at these two: the support of sects to compete against established churches, and an erroneous use of the Eastern doctrines with the sole intent of spiritually weakening the West.

To be accepted, sects convey a certain number of truths, and even some of the truths that churches tended to neglect; but these truths are inextricably mixed with errors that, for the most part,

---

[3] This is a job that Surrealism carried out by shamelessly confusing the "supreme Point," reconciler of all the contraries, with the lowest point, condenser of all the obscurities, and thus making the superessential Non-Being the totally blanked out non-being.

come from a literal reading or a defective interpretation of the texts. To attract individuals who have been disappointed by churches,—it would be better to say by unfortunate personal experience or by a deficient clergy—sects persuade them to leave the multitude of faithful to join the small number of those who hold the "truth,"— who are, as it happens, nothing more than the insignificant or tragic imitation of the elite initiates, and who never transmit anything other than a "contra-initiation." They flatter these same individuals in their strength of will by promising them the acquisition of "powers" that will convince them of a high degree of spirituality, when these "powers" are known to be obstacles to inner development. They continue to flatter them by investing them with a greater mission, that of converting at any price, by spreading a presumptuous proselytism that quickly becomes intolerable and can only further indispose with regard to "religion." From here, the belief that one is "chosen" when one hasn't even been called, there is only a quick small step, from one illusion to another.

The origin of sects is questionable, even if the founder carries the insignia of sincerity: one can be sincere when mistaken. But there is always a flaw, an imperceptible signature that betrays the heterodoxy somewhere; sufficiently trained, a discerning mind will notice it. If the great spiritual revelations that punctuate the future of humanity—the famous "sects that succeeded,"—directly reflect the light of superior levels (this light is only the shadow of the "brighter than bright Darkness"), the teachings of sects emanate more from the gloom of below. They adopt pernicious influence, morbid or abhorrent doctrines, mongrels of Gnosticism. One often finds in sects an even greater passion than in parishes, a veritable zeal for God, without knowing, however, if this fervor is the expression of a visitation by the Spirit or a collection of cleverly crafted suggestions. Sects sometimes reveal a lethal will, going as far as ritual murders and collective suicides. They show their true colors: nightmarish prisons where drugs are a beverage for immortality, orgies, liturgical festivities, and where the master of initiations will be the ambassador of the Lord of Evil. Recruited from its bosom are the manipulators of psychic powers, fake masters keeping disciples at their mercy, all these patented imposters, or the ones who have been so abused that they are sincere in their imposture. As for the disciples, they are generally fragile and easily influenced beings, with no formal intellectual training, in frail mental health, thus even more likely to accept as real the unbelievable that lacks proof or that has evidence proving the contrary. These are the kind of individuals that greatly contributed to starting the rationalist reaction; this reaction, to a certain degree, could have been useful for cleansing the atmosphere of the miasmas of occultism.[4]

The traditional East has not been taken over by the forces we are denouncing. In as much as the numerous Asian contributions can help the West regain its normative references or practical support, other contributions from the same origins, which cannot be assimilated for various reasons or are deformed by incompetent transmitters, can only add to the psychological and mental disorder of Europeans. The vulgarization of certain techniques that are only worthwhile for a handful of qualified individuals is regrettable. The "democratization" of Zen has plunged more than one into disastrous illusions, who, devoid of any sort of academic culture, thought they had already reached *satori*, when they hadn't even started out: books should certainly be burned, but only after they have been read and assimilated! Likewise, certain reinterpreted Tantric methods are such that the poison taken as a remedy acts as poison. Sexual obsession, characteristic of every crepuscular era, wanted to justify itself here, confusing the liberation of the senses (which is another constraint), with the final Deliverance. Trivialized love uncorks disgust; the wasting of nature's greatest magic energy, camouflaged by the practices of the "left-hand Path," gives wasted generations a pale imitation of telluric ecstasies. The latter have nothing to do with the hyperphysical union of the followers of Tantrism, who, in the image of Shiva and of his *Shakti*, reach an initiatory death and a state of non-duality.

Poorly interpreted, poorly transmitted, the East encourages an arbitrary syncretism. At the level of principles, this is nothing more than an artificial juxtaposition of fragments, a mosaic of miscellaneous loans from any provenance, without any profound connection between them and perhaps even from opposing

---

[4] The refusal to believe without proof is not due to Descartes; Buddhism advocated it long before. In the *Anguttara nikaya*, Buddha recommends not believing anything based on the sole authority of masters or preachers: "What you will have experienced yourselves, recognized as real..., believe it and behave accordingly." The error of rationalism is in systematizing skepticism, of having tossed out the baby with the bath water, that is to say having refused at the same time certainties and conjectures, authentic masters and charlatans, religions and sects.

categories—the complete opposite of a synthesis that connects elements coming from the same metaphysical order and that which directly ensues. At the practical level, nothing is more dangerous than the mixture of paths: even if all of them resort to analogous methods, these are not necessarily identical; they even come from distinct spiritual climates. From one religion to another, rituals transport different influences, the confusion of which is the source of cruel misadventures. It is certainly advisable to stick to the path that circumstances have determined to be *the* path, and to concentrate on it, thoroughly exhaust the contents, something for which one human life is insufficient.

This is the type of illicit and improvised connecting that prevailed at the birth of religious internationalism, which is the exact opposite of the Unity of spiritual traditions: a race of false recapitulation and reconciliation that, far from restoring this Unity, works at meticulously destroying each religion. Whereas the universal Unity of the Spirit was revealed in the beginning to a unified humanity, internationalist syncretism is the inversed version, contemporary of the times of the end, for the benefit of a humanity deprived of all discrimination.

Since Subversion acts on all fronts simultaneously, the forces that are seen edifying syncretism are the same ones that work at erasing the last remnants of Unity, creating opposition between religions by insisting solely on the exterior differences and dissimulating what they have in common. In their will to divide and conquer, these forces use anything available to them, from political interests, ethnic susceptibilities, to metaphysical doctrines insofar as they have been sufficiently deformed to agree with error. For example, monotheism will be conscientiously opposed to polytheism without seeing the different divine principles that constitute the former, or that the fundamental One prevails over the second one. In their vast majority, these religions' believers do not go beyond the level of exoteric divergences, and encouraged to continue by a clergy worried about keeping their credibility and their followers, will serve Subversion by pretending to defend their faith; and without noticing that by opposing each other instead of joining forces, they are at the mercy of what they think they are fighting against.

Not content to oppose the believers, Subversion, which knows how to be hateful when the tactics at hand demand it, also knows, on other occasions, how to seduce. Nowhere more than in the dialogue between believers and non-believers, do the "voracious wolves" easily invade the sheepfold. On the occasion of such meetings, the atheists, or those who pretend to be,—but there would be a lot more to be said about this—are almost always guaranteed in advance to get the better of their partners, not because they are right or hold the truth, but simply because they are better trained dialectically. Deprived of the keys to esotericism, reduced to the notions of morality, to sentimental subjectivism, to "good will," the believers are obliged to remain on the defensive. The idea, which is as seductive as it is fallacious, that consists of "forgetting what divides us (or separates us) to share what brings us together (or unites us)," is one of the most equivocal; because what can eventually be brought together comes from fields that are infinitely more relative, alien, bordering on the religious domain, than those that exclude any possible compromise coming from the Law, faith, theology, and gnosis. Alone, the naïve believers, unaware of the doctrine of The One who arrived on the earth with the sword of discernment to dissociate good from evil, truth from error, alone, the "half-hearted" loathed by Heaven can accept this game of fools. They perfectly exemplify the saying according to which "God blinds those he wants to lose."

The success of these diverse undertakings, which seem opposed to each other, disorganized and contradictory, has an even better chance of being complete in that, on the one hand, religions dating back several thousand years show a certain fatigue, offer their flank more easily to an attack and have a lesser capacity to retaliate; on the other hand, in a climate of general mediocrity, conceivably the vast majority of men will be inclined to spontaneously choose easiness and what avoids any extra effort; therefore, opting in the end for the indifferentism where Pilate washes his hands.

7. THE PROFANED SANCTUARY*

Subversive action at the spiritual level offers an especially interesting example to study. This action is easily discernable in what is acknowledged as the "crisis of the Church"; furthermore, it is sufficiently related to our subject for us to dwell on it somewhat. We do not intend to examine either the origins, which are long prior to Vatican II, or the effects, which are multiple. In any case, it is certain that the shaking of the pinnacle affects the entire edifice, and what is seen to occur at present at the ecclesiastical level is nothing other than the repercussion of what is happening in all of Western society.[1] The slight decrease in vocations, the lack of interest in questions that do not concern human immediacy, the absence of religion's direct hold over the mass of the baptized has already planted the "decoration" of this spiritual desert promised to Christ in the Second Advent.

Evil comes both from the outside and the inside. Outwardly, it is the result of the tireless offensive of militant atheism's forces against the rock of the Church; inwardly, it is the result of doctrinal weakening that, with the best intentions, has too many Christians working themselves unknowingly at destroying Christianity, or doing nothing to help it.

In the West, the ideological battle is fought against an established Church, but for whom the comfort of the *establishment* and past errors have dulled the fighting ardor, led to a certain caution. This battle took arguments from these same errors: the schism of Rome and Byzantium, the courts of the Inquisition—even if the number of victims was knowingly exaggerated—the fratricidal wars of a fraternal religion; and, behind all that, the heritage of the Judeo-

---

* From *Return to the Essential*, I, "Aspects of Subversion," 3.

[1] The ancient texts of India had already mentioned the ruin of religion as major evidence of the *Kali Yuga*. The *Vishnu-purana*, VI, 1, alludes to the *aggiornamento*: "A simple ablution will be regarded as sufficient purification." And then: "Men of all the castes will presumptuously imagine that they are the equals of the brahmans. They'll say: 'Who gives authority to the Veda...?'" A theme taken up again by the *Bhagavata-purana*, XII, 24, following: "In the *Kali* Age, men are short-sighted (meaning: limited metaphysical intelligence), the *Vedas* are corrupted by the heretics.... He (Ashyuta, the master of the three worlds) is no longer honored by anyone...."

Christian attitude encouraging even more, with the initiative of the soldier, the jurist, and the administrator, the missionary conquest, the suppression of minority particularisms, the solidification of bureaucratic structures, and the intellectualization of the doctrine to the detriment of its interiorization. When Subversion decided to bring down the Christian institution, it was obviously these facts it evoked; it forgot to mention the efforts of the first monks' work toward civilization, the figures of Saint Francis, Saint Bernard or Saint Benoit, the Rules and Orders of which they are the founders and their influence for centuries in the face of the spreading of barbarity.

If nothing can be done against saintliness, there is more to be done against the intellectual notion of the Revelation and the dogmas that will soon be replaced by the social, political and economical "good news" spread by the multitude of new "apostles." The latter organize everywhere, and in the name of the goddesses of Liberty and Reason, institutionalize "secular and mandatory education." Following religious fanaticism, from which the past was not exempt, would then be free thinking, which, by appearing to give more respect to personal opinions, would influence and condition minds in such a way that they could only opt for agnosticism. Soon religion would only be tolerated as long as it communicated in a conventional and insipid language deprived of the invigorating breath of its origins; or, it would adopt the most relativistic interpretations of the Gospel, therefore, the most compatible with modernist opportunism. Anything not understood would be accused of being prelogical, superstitious, obscurantist thinking, indeed Machiavellian inventions of a clergy whose only interest was in exploiting an ignorant people. Science would quickly be called to the rescue—however, it is itself subject to so many variations—to contest or demolish what would, in any case, continue to escape it so long as the esoteric and symbolic levels remained unconnected to the literal level.

A situation that is more radically tragic for the Eastern Church, that refuses unprincipled compromises, is passionate about faithfulness to origins, and also maintains, perhaps, a certain taste for martyrs. Here, the hard method replaces insinuations.

It can be said that Subversion's persecutions apply to the letter the phrase from the Book of Revelation: "He who would not worship the statue of the Beast should be killed." Without even mentioning the material destruction of thousands of churches—who still remembers that by dynamiting the temple, man dynamites himself, since the temple and man are analogically built according to the same plan?—the physical suppression of tens of millions of Orthodox seems to have saved, at least in the Christian East, this "honor of God" too often scorned in the West. The twentieth century will have broken all the records as far as properly-attested-to persecutions, and for which only a certain Western spinelessness pretends to reduce or ignore the polymorphous horror.[2] One of Subversion's titles of glory will have been to add to the classic methods of torture that act exclusively on the body, the entire range of psychic torture, capable of depersonalizing the individual and turning him into the antithetical shadow of himself. The chemicals which alter or destroy the conscious managed to prove *a contrario* that the believers in God were abnormal, since the State, expression of normality, did not believe; thus, it was an act of humanity and public health to cure them by making them deny their faith! As for the psychiatric cohabitation of the believers and the mentally ill, its only aim was that of confusing folly and faith in a diabolical caricature of the "folly of the cross": once the believers have in turn gone mad by contamination, it is easy to show that the believers are crazy. In the face of such refinement in sadism, one has every right to wonder who the real madmen are, the victims or their torturers.[3]

And in truth, the easiest way to kill a people is by killing its faith. By eliminating this, hope is eliminated, and when men are deprived of hope, the means to the end are even easier: they die from within, become everything one wants, even embrace those false hopes of enchanted tomorrows. However, if the witnesses of the Spirit can be killed, the Spirit that they bear within cannot. It is well known

[2] Among the many testimonies, we will cite the one from Alexander Solzhenitsyn, consecrated to *The Gulag Archipelago*. The history of underground Churches could be inscribed with this verse from Ovid (*Metamorphoses*, VI, 202): *Quodque licet tacito venerantur murmure numen* ("All they can do is whisper in low voices their prayers to the divinity").

[3] One cannot help thinking of this apothegm that is astonishingly relevant to our time: "A time will come when all men are mad, and when they meet someone who isn't, they will say: 'You've lost your senses!' And it is only because he will not resemble them" (Abba Antony, *Apophthegms of the Fathers of the Desert*). This is echoed, under different heavens, by Ramana Maharshi: "Since the world is mad, it thinks you are mad."

that the blood of martyrs always incites more, that resistance is organized, that any spiritual doctrine finds renewed vigor in the caves of torture, in the catacombs of silence. This was true of the first Christians who, under Nero, Decius and Diocletian, were handed over to the beasts and the torches, and it was still true until recently for the Christians of an East where the sun rose secretly. But it was also true for the *Hassidim* who were dragged to crematoriums, for the Tibetans massacred in Lhasa, and in general, for all peoples who, when fleeing from under the screaming wind of terror of the "Dark Age," still embrace the word of salvation, the syllable of eternity. All hits strike the knowing, none strike Knowledge. If the fierceness and duration of torment is astonishing, it is because Knowledge, even disfigured, always forgives ignorance, and that is what ignorance cannot forgive it for.

*
* *

The destruction of Christianity from the outside would still be relatively slight if it were not coupled with an inward destruction, to which consciously or not, both clerics and laymen contribute. Minimalism, torpor, disregard of the sacred aura, alteration of the Scriptures under the pretext of adaptation to the current way of thinking create adequate conditions for this kind of demolition.[4] Cleverly maintained ambiguities and uncertainties trouble the souls of the faithful only as much as is needed. Sometimes, a supposed animal origin of humanity will come to "scientifically" contradict the story of Genesis; sometimes the calculated existence of other men in other areas of the universe will relativize Incarnation. Doubt is cast successively on the sacerdotal minister, the value of the sacraments, the dogmas of the Trinity and Christology, and the real presence in the Eucharist. Religion becomes the most discreet of the possible humanisms, shows gratitude towards the temporal authorities that are hospitable to it, makes a pact with them, fights for their

---

[4] As an example of the disregard of the sacred aura, notice the use of applause (resurgence of the pagan amphitheater), which turns sanctuaries into community arts centers or political assemblies. As an example of an error in translation, the replacement in the Apostle's Creed of "consubstantial with the Father" by "of the same nature of the Father," is a formula that reintroduces the heresy of Arius.

points of view. Vague considerations of a moral, social and senti-mental nature nourish the ordinary content of the sermons, suc-ceeding only at further distancing from the Church those whose demands and aspirations are of another order. Even the attitude becomes perverted: certainty is presented as a suspicious need for security; doubt is hailed as criteria for sincerity. Behind the attempts at ecumenism that all too often would like to reconcile the irrecon-cilable, the house continues to split. The conservatives maintain an obsessional stubbornness at keeping values that no longer neces-sarily coincide with the needs of the era, a tense blockage to any adaptation and validity of other religions that are obstinately ignored, and the conviction that anything that is not fundamental-ism is sulfurous heathenism; for the progressive, who love conces-sions, the severing of the very principles that religion is based on are sacrificed by pretending to renew it or restore it to the asceti-cism of its beginnings (in reality, to the destitution that reigns once the Spirit has departed), because the intention of impoverishment is not a vow of poverty.

Once the sources of its esotericism had been lost or denied, it gradually became impossible for the Church to give complete and satisfactory responses to the essential questions: after having for-gotten "knowledge," religion could only refer the faithful to "faith." This had a twofold consequence: those who refused the mystical attitude of "faith"—*pistis*—without, however, being in a position to attain "knowledge"—*gnosis*—organized the fight against a faulty spirituality that was charlatan-like in their view, demanding to *believe without proof*; as for the believers, deprived of decisive arguments, they were won over by the limitations of open-examination and dis-cursive reason, were entrenched in the dogmas, satisfied with spheres that had less and less to do with religion, and that were, indeed, even unfamiliar with its competence. Yet, to situate the deep meaning of a religion in the external is to situate oneself on the outside of this religion; being married only to one's times is to divorce from eternity. What's more, beyond trial and error, one must not exclude the active and occult influence of certain pressure groups whose interest is in the eradication of Christianity, if not to say the *spiritual thing* itself.

While Christianity insists on the notion of the "human person," at a time when psychology confirms the uniqueness of each indi-vidual and the therapeutic necessity to recount everything in minute detail, confession becomes hurried and voluntarily collective. The Last Supper appears to be a "fraternal meal" at a "common gathering," even though it is a ritual and sacred meal: the Eucharist is an "act of giving thanks" making Christians participants with the three Persons of the Trinity; it is "hierogamy," the Sacrament of the union of Christ and his followers, reunited in the mystic Body. The loss of the meaning of a transcendent mystery reduces Mass to a simple friendly meeting where the music, vague imitator of primitive trances, becomes more chthonic than celestial, excites passions instead of calming them in a humbling silence; where the word replaces the chant, when in fact it should be actualized, vitalized by ritual or psalmodic recitation, and become manducation of the divine Word—the whole in an abstract decor (especially the stained glass windows): veritable nonsense in the religion where the "abstract" becomes precisely "concrete" by Incarnation.[5] Even more serious is the liturgical celebration before the people, during which, in every Church traditionally turned toward Jerusalem, the priest henceforth turns his back on the East.

Much could be said about contemporary Christianity's *socialist* attempt. Undoubtedly, the economic situation of certain milieux and numerous underdeveloped countries justifies an intervention of the Church in the name of justice and charity. As Thomas Aquinas, who cannot be accused of progressivism, had already written, "the use of a minimum amount of possessions is required for exercising virtue."[6] Moreover, there is something "social" about Christianity: one clearly insists on helping one's neighbor, the sick and the unfortunate, on the notion of "sharing," even more than on the notion of "giving." One is reminded of the word of the founder: "For he that is the least among you all, the same shall be great." Poverty is a prerequisite for passing through the "eye of the needle" (that is to say the doors of Heaven). It is often recalled that the sole owner of richness is God, man being simply the manager of grounds that do not belong to him.

[5] As much as abstract art has its place in Islam where God cannot be depicted, except by the geometric iridescence of a multiplicity near to the Principle, it has no place in the religion where God, coming out of his impersonality, makes himself out as a body and a face.

[6] The words of Ramakrishna echo back: "Religion is not for empty stomachs."

However, such "socialism," if there is "socialism," owes nothing to Proudhon, Marx or Engels. Possibly having Buddhist origins, it greatly inspired Christianity from the beginning, through Asia Minor. What's more, reducing the message of Christ to a simple "socialism" tinted with devotion is impossible, just as is reversing the order of the precepts of love; the love of one's neighbor does not come before the love of God. *Tackling social issues* does not require being Christian: it is enough to be a socialist. In fact, it does not seem that a politico-social interpretation of the Gospel is defendable if it is admitted that the latter is supposed to be essentially a guide for inner life. The absence of any political directive in the Gospel is even a sort of implicit warning against the divisions created by political passion. Wanting to mix politics and religion is once again, as India would say, to work for the confusion of the *dharma*s. We cannot love only men and forget the divine priority without frustrating men, God and ourselves at the same time. But the ultimate blindness consists of taking the message from the ideal City (and, as it happens, ideological), for the message from the Heavenly City of Jerusalem, of which it is the opposite; because the Prince of this world is capable of "seducing the chosen themselves," Christians believe that technology and socialization are the irrefutable signs of a new effusion of the Spirit.[7] Must one be reminded that Christ refuses to serve two masters at the same time and that his Kingdom is not of this world; that the "kingdom of God is within you," and that the builder of the real Jerusalem is not man at all, but God?

It must still be added, from the Christian point of view, that the "meaning of History" is not the assumption of the economy, politics and power of the state; it lives in the Coming of the "Kingdom of God." To say that History has a meaning is the same as saying that it has an end; and the end of History—the accomplishment of which Christ died for—is the union of man with God. This end of History is transcendent to History; it would not know how to come within the sole temporal level, it demands a separation from the natural world and a transfiguration of a human life into a divine life. In this

---

[7] The Spirit, undoubtedly, will return to the world, and such is the meaning of the heavenly Jerusalem; but the new cycle will start off on completely different facts from those that are fashionable today, the best of which can improve man's practical condition, but remain remarkably incapable of transforming the "inner man"— the citizen par excellence of the new Jerusalem—because that is not of its "order."

sense, no Church has to adapt to the world; the duty of the Church is to adapt the world to God. Christ did not say to have a revolution, and evangelization will follow, but to seek first the kingdom of God and these things shall be added unto you.

*
*   *

All of this not only brings about the collapse of religion (which is sometimes blocked by the miraculously favorable initiatives and the invisible influence of anonymous supplicants in the last deserts or the house next door, in the heart of the city), but the establishment of a counter religion, the one of Man. Already, at the doctrinal level, it is surprising to see certain omissions in the "mandatory basics" of new catechisms. The result of such toning down is the outrageous humanization of the Divine and the evacuation of Transcendence. The disappearance of the supernatural removes all vertical dimension from existence, does nothing to legitimize the preservation of *religion,* whose aim is precisely to connect heaven and earth.[8] This situation only reflects the general tendencies of the theology of the "Functional Age," which, according to Robertson, succeeds the "Mythical Age" and the "Ontological Age." (Are we really that far removed from the three Ages of Auguste Comte?) Whereas Bultmann undertakes to "demythologize" the Gospel, and Bonhoeffer recommends a "Christianity without religion," one sees the "Son of God" hand it over little by little to the "Son of Man," theology becomes anthropology. More and more, Christ tends to be just "Jesus," not only stripped of his tunic but of all transcendence: a sort of great man, a benefactor of humanity, having a great love of democratic equality and justice, but lacking any divine power that could in some way make him resemble something superior. Whereas a great man can be admired, he is not adored in spirit and in truth, he is not worshiped. This is how liturgy is increasingly put

[8] Translator's Note: The word *religion* comes from Latin *relegere* meaning "to take in," or from *religare,* to "link" or "connect." The author has used the French *relier,* which has the similar origin *re + ligare,* meaning to "bind." It is interesting to note that "rely" in English, which implies placing faith or confidence in someone or something, also comes from *re + ligare.*

into perspective, until it no longer finds any other justification; the divinity of Christ being ever more eluded, one manages to ineluctably proclaim his death, then that of God in his Son on the cross, and in all logic, the final death of Christianity. The "new theology" gives the deathblow to this religion.

The "death of God" no longer has here the death of man for correlative, but his "divinization," which is just the counterfeit of his "deification" in the Holy Spirit. It really is a question of a substitution of humanity for divinity, a humanity that takes itself for the object of its own worship, and where Man, to repeat the words of Protagoras, has become the "measure of all things." As a second Creator, he rethinks and redoes the world; intoxicated with his power, he applies the words of Christ to himself: "Behold, I make all things new." The rational animal deifies himself and makes himself absolute in a *logos* that is no longer the Word but the only reason; his flight to the Moon is taken for the Ascension of Humanity. The "Holy Matter" denies God as the "motionless Mover" that sheds the universe; the "Holy Evolution" has God finding Himself being swept up into the rising "cyclone" of Matter: he is a "cosmogenesis" God, captive of the Existence and the Future he created.[9] In times where inversion rules, only a counter religion can pass for religion. It can apparently continue to celebrate God: Man is exalted by it; it can evoke sacredness; this sacredness is the profane that passes for its opposite; it can announce the coming of the messianic times: these times in reality are not the dawn of tomorrow but the crepuscule of today. What is said of the "other Beast" applies to it: "He had two horns like a lamb, and he spake as a dragon."

In this respect, it can be said that Subversion has its most complete victory; because not only is it the ruler over an entire territory, but in the mind it is perceived as the most unbiased and most ordinary thing. Its grip is such that it embodies normality and legitimacy. Its accusers are the ones who are considered, from then on, as undesirable; and in effect, the same accusers who warn Christians today against certain plots are seen accused by their co-religionists

---

[9] The "conical cyclone" of the "mass of consciousness" dear to Teilhard de Chardin, a mass rising toward Omega that becomes increasingly complex over the centuries, is only the caricature of the continuity, which in traditional cosmology, descends the Spirit through the states of the Being.

of militating against the Church. With the speed of change, the last keepers of Christianity will be considered as suspect members of a sect on the road to ruin. And while Subversion advances in hierarchy to the point of dictating its decisions—and the recording of a suffering pope—those who die at its hand will imagine they have died for Truth!

The entire question amounts to this: how can the Spirit be protected? Basically, it is a good idea to remember that *there is no worse enemy than reductionism*, and that the refusal of the vertical inevitably condemns it to the horizontal—the position of cadavers and those who are asleep. The recollection of certain facts is undoubtedly unpleasant for many who have no desire to question themselves, who confuse adaptation with pure and simple elimination, and who still believe that anything new mandatorily constitutes progress toward an anterior state. But we have never chosen, as far as we are concerned, the side of demagogy, and it is the responsibility of the love toward one's brothers to know how to accept saying certain truths that are unpleasant to hear.[10]

Our intention is not to discourage or drive anyone to despair—men whose faith is questionable do that all the time. But before closing this chapter, we would like to recall two important words of Christ that should accompany his disciples in all circumstances, and today more than ever, even if they should one day dim to the point where it seems that all that remains of the edifice is rock upon rock and that "abomination and desolation" reign everywhere. The first of these words are: "The gates of Hell shall not prevail against my church"; the second: "I am with you always unto the end of the world."

Yet, acting as the instrument of destruction of the cycle, Subversion also works at the abolition of its own reign, since the latter is par excellence the very expression of this cycle. All those, who, in the name of Subversion, exalt that which they cannot avoid, all those who claim to be the forerunners of a new Age, are in reality the rem-

---

[10] Saint Paul recalls in 2 Cor. 7:8-10, that certain words may sadden, but "sadness according to God" is salutary, stimulating, and leads to revision, the reversal (*metanoia*) of false certainties.

nants of an Age that is ending. Tragic victims of a power for which, out of self-interest or ignorance, they became the propagators, they will collapse with it into the chasms it will have made them dig. On the other hand, if it enslaves the weak, Subversion strengthens the strong, those who, no matter what, never despair because they know it must be this way momentarily, that order is born from chaos, light from darkness. And assuredly, the veritable forerunners of the coming new dawns have completely different faces from the ones exposed to view today.

8. About an Intellectual Reform[*]

One of the main traits of these times is the *disoccultation of esoteric teachings* and their popularization among a growing and interested public. In fact, in today's Western world, access to the different traditions, which in the middle of the twentieth century were still only known to a restricted number of specialists, is available to everyone. The appearance of an increasing quantity of translations, commentaries and documents suddenly revealed in the face of official reductionism, some doctrines, methods and approaches susceptible to completely casting a new light on a unilateral and belittling vision of the world. The disclosure of initiatory teachings brings around another way of questioning, destroys the numerous apriorisms, answers the metaphysical interrogations on which religious exotericisms as well as profane philosophies remained silent for centuries. It supplies the lost keys concerning both qualified time and the doctrine of cycles, the subtle make-up of the human being and his posthumous destiny, the multiple states of being, the tripartition of the worlds, the notions of "eternal *Avatara*" and "supreme Identity," the fundamental unity of the traditions and the significance of universal symbols. Within the darkness of the *Kali Yuga*, we probably don't realize how lucky we are, and how envied we would be by previous eras, for having such easy access to these teachings. We need to read the sign of the times in the fact that the Spirit allows itself to be so profaned, that the law of silence has been broken, that the seals of Knowledge have been removed everywhere. It's up to us to make the most of our good fortune. This crop of texts that were unknown or inaccessible up until now must seem to be the necessary compensation for the monstrosities of the times, a veritable blessing over the field of the ruins of intelligence. Didn't the Bible announce that "at the time of the end, knowledge shall increase"? This knowledge might correspond to the "human sciences," whose development is intensifying, but it also concerns the rediscovery of the "sacred sciences." Another sign of the times is when the oldest past must resurface at the end of the cycle in order to guarantee the recapitulation and to serve as the starting point for the elaboration

---

[*] From *Passports for New Times*, II, 2.

of the next cycle. Only esoteric teachings carry enough weight to counterbalance the destructive theories, to the fore but condemned to discredit, just like the rigid and dying scholastic of the sixteenth century was gradually replaced by a humanism vitalized by antiquity. It could be said that our era is going through a similar Renaissance from Eastern sources this time, but a Renaissance that, more than at the basic intellectual level, is located at the psychic and spiritual level, and that instead of exalting the mental and moral man to the detriment of the rest, returns man to his proper place, in his deepest relationships with himself, with the world and with God. Only such teachings restore intelligence with its cardinal function, which is the discernment between the Real and the illusory, the Permanent and ephemeral, the Essential and the accidents, and its possibility of making use of the means that allow for the realization of the "one thing necessary." As soon as this new direction is taken, hope for rediscovering the spiritual ways returns. The fearful, ignorant or irresponsible minds, teaching everywhere that the eternal is outdated, can from then on be considered outdated.

Certainly, this multiplication of information in fields that had been reserved up until then, entails the risk of mixing impurities, of inciting tendencies, of altering truth, and of adding to the confusion of ideas instead of making them clearer. And this will occur each time that intelligence does not discriminate enough. No doubt as well, it can be recovered by the insatiable European mental state, finding here a new pretext for dissipation without giving any thought to the least experimental verification; unless certain poorly or unguided attempts at putting it into practice lead to the worst failures and destroy rather than build the being with their improvisations. It is nonetheless true that the pearls have been spread and that as the vice of materialism tightens, the sources of adamantine truth spring forth more intensely.

In this rediscovery of esoteric doctrines, there is little need to recall the importance of the East, without however forgetting that Western thinking also carries Eastern aspects that, as neglected as they may be at times, are still part of our patrimony or come from the East themselves.[1]

---

[1] Among these Eastern aspects, reference can be made first to the pre-Socratics and

*

* *

We would like to mention at least three of the most likely contributions to the mental restructuring that we are dealing with: the notion of "points of view"—the *darshanas* in Hinduism—, the critical elements of certain philosophical clichés, the priority of the practical over the speculative.

While for Western logic it is impossible to accept as true two contrary propositions, these will only have a subjective and pragmatic value for Eastern logic. They are not necessarily true in every case and other ways of looking at the same question exist that are just as justifiable and in no way inferior. For the West, A cannot be both identical to and different from B; for the East, A can be identical to B, different from B, identical to and different from B, neither identical to nor different from B. Counter to an analytical, separating, unilateral, incomplete thinking, sensitive to dualities and dichotomies, and as such, the source of conflicts and never ending oppositions, the East brings a synthesized, encompassing, unitive thinking, reconciling and going beyond pairs of contrasts. For it, the different "points of view" are relatively true. They are more complementary than contradictory.[2] To renounce a firm hold on an acquired stance that is inevitably rigid, stubborn and transitory, to fade with one's own thinking in perpetual renewal, "to value no opinion," according to the Zen precept, to be with Lao-tzu in the middle of the ring of contradictions without answering them, and by staying linked to the sole reality that is hidden behind arbitrary delimitations is what the Eastern attitude advises. It knows all too well the relativity of good and evil, of true and false, of free-will and

---

the Greek Tragedy, the stories of the Round Table, Shakespearian theater, initiatory works such as *The Romance of the Rose, The Divine Comedy, Don Quixote, Faust*. Diverse Eastern elements circulate through Rabelais, Nerval, Whitman, Eliot, Blake, Rilke, Novalis, Hesse. The hermetist movement must also be included: Paracelsus, Eckartshausen, Boëhme, Lull, and the "Christian Kabbalists," Martinez de Pasqually, Fabre d'Olivet, as well as the mystic movement (in the best sense of the word): Meister Eckhart, Ruysbroeck, Nicolas of Cusa, the Greek Fathers: Gregory of Nyssa, Gregory Palamas, Denys the Areopagite, and Maximus the Confessor.

[2] When asked who was right, those who pretended that God exists or those who pretended that He didn't, Ramana Maharshi replied: "Look for what the two propositions have in common."

necessity, of action and contemplation, of the consistency and inconsistency in the world, of life and death. With each loss of a point of view, progress is made towards a higher truth; man does not progress from error to truth, but passes from the truth of a certain level to the one of a superior level, until that time when the most diverging points of view are harmonized in a transcendent synthesis.[3] Such an attitude of the mind especially explains the Easterner's tolerance in philosophical and religious matters; each system describes more specially this or that facet of the Divine, which neither excludes nor invalidates the others.[4]

One guesses that this way of looking at so many "problems" could be useful and salutary for the West at the level of intellectual relations. Only admitting one's own truth by putting it in the wide range of truths, only admitting it by simultaneously admitting the possibility of its contrary would greatly contribute to the rehabilitation of the mental climate and human relations.[5] It would put an end to or slow down the endless debates that lead to nothing, exasperate passions, widen gaps, accentuate differences, stir up apocalyptic incandescence; it would help politicians, sociologists, economists, teachers, theologians to understand that, each intelligence being finite, it can only apprehend a minute part of the whole truth, that there are several ways to consider a question and to resolve it, that there is an art of "thinking without thinking," just as there is one of "taking action by taking none," where the "middle road" has no middle.[6] By revealing the existence of the "points of view," esotericism brings us back to the distinctions between simple

---

[3] Something from this reasoning can be found episodically in Western thinking. Thus, the dispute between physicists over the composition of light (wave trains for some, photons for the others), was partially resolved by Louis de Broglie's wave mechanics, which reconciles the emission theory of light with the wave theory. Likewise, modern science has stopped opposing Matter and Mind by distinguishing in the first one a plurality of planes in permanent interaction, a density scale going from the most compact to the most subtle, just as it has stopped opposing time and space, which it has replaced with the space-time continuum.

[4] Who hasn't heard the parable about the elephant told by Jalal ad-Din Rumi (*Mathnawi*, III, 1259 and following)? The men who touch the elephant in the dark each give a different description of it: a water pipe, a fan, a pillar, a throne.

[5] The West is not systematically unfamiliar with this mentality, but is, one might say, Eastern in flashes. Pascal, who deplored that a river separated error from truth, was careful to remark in his *Pensées*: "Error comes from forgetting the opposite truth."

[6] According to one *hadith*, it is true that the theological divergences are a "sign of

individual and discursive reason, source of subject-object dualism, combat area of hypotheses and contradictory axioms, and meta-physical intuition, the transcendent intellect, of an informal order, capable of reaching the supreme Principle where opposites are abolished.[7] The *intellectus* is this "organ" of the spirit that moves in the order of a unity and a supra-individual and supra-rational con-tinuity, and corresponds to the inner certitude of the causes pre-ceding all experience. Its own metaphysical perspective escapes the relativity of reason, implies a certain inexpressible certainty with regards to which opinions are simply gossiping and cacophony; it is the special spot where "one is what one knows." Only the atrophy of the superior faculties of the being, correlative to the development of the inferior elements, leads to the dispersion and exclusiveness of unassimilated "points of view," that is to say the inability of reach-ing the Truth, and consequently, to the frantic desire to deny it.

*
*　*

The revelation of esotericism will be sure to take a closer look at many of the undiscussed points of the few philosophies taught to millions of young people today who only adhere to them out of ignorance of arguments to the contrary, which are either carica-tured or silently passed over. Subjecting these philosophies to eso-teric screening would fill an entire book, at the end of which, only the straw of the very limited *darshana* they represent would remain. As an example, we will just isolate here some of the axioms for which the refutation in the light of esoteric teachings can only lead to ruin, and afterwards, that of the philosophies based on them.

The *cogito, ergo sum* of Descartes.—The Eastern doctrines will first reveal that the thinking organ is only one of the vibratory centers existing among other forms of the conscious, and that subject to

Divine Compassion," but precisely inasmuch as the destiny of the antinomies is to be exceeded. The best way to avoid the antithetical sectarianisms of uniformity is to harmonize the different aspects of Unity.

[7] Note that the reasoning reason, or the faculty of thinking, corresponds to the *manas* in Hinduism, the transcendent intellect to the *buddhi*. Also corresponding to it are the "Eye of the Heart,"—*Ayn al-qalb*—from Muslim esotericism, and the *aliquid increatum et increabile* from Eckhart, leading to direct and illuminating certi-tude.

continuous variations, it cannot be confused with the unaltered independent conscious of the *Purusa* that lies behind it, and which Descartes did not sense. Next, they will show us that the "I" is only an ever-changing, elusive, evanescent and unreal aggregate composed of habits, faculties, dispositions and tendencies without fixedness. Finally they will show that thinking is only an attribute of the being, and that the *conscious* of being cannot be subordinate to the *experience* of thinking. By reversing the order of its terms, the all too famous "I think, therefore I am," may be able to express a truth much closer to the Truth.

"Religion is the opium of the masses," according to Marx.—For the author of *Das Kapital*, religion perpetuates the relationship of the dominant and the dominated, by promising the people an illusory happiness in the beyond, and by beguiling them, keeping them unaware of their miserable condition. Recall first of all that as far as religions go, Marx only knew Western Christianity, too often subservient, it must be said, to established powers. But he ignored that in Hinduism, for example, the men belonging to the highest castes were equally those who were subject to the greatest duty and most devotedly served the vow of poverty.[8] Concerning an illusory happiness promised to people in the beyond, Marx ignored likewise that the beyond is not necessarily contemplated in religious conduct,—as such, for certain forms of Buddhism,—and that Hell and Heaven are first found within us, during our terrestrial sojourn. Finally, far from wanting to desensitize, religion offers an awakening to a higher degree of consciousness. Due to simple spiritual inability for the most part or by falling into routine, the goal is rarely attained; religion should not be incriminated for all that.

The "Oedipus complex" of Freud.—For the founder of psychoanalysis, the belief in an all-powerful God would only be the revelation, at the age of the adult, of a child's perception of his parents. In this way, the adult would be rebuilt with a protective Father by a sublimatory mode; religion would be an infantile fixation, neurosis, illusion. In supposing that Freud's explanations can be applied to monotheistic religions of a patriarchal type, the only ones he knew,

[8] It must be noted that poverty had not always been considered in the same way in the hierarchy of values, and the voluntary and ascetic quest for the limitation of consumer goods had nothing to do with the pauperism stemming from the industrial civilization of the nineteenth century.

how could they pertain to the case of spiritualities whose principle is the Divine Mother, or better yet, a neutral entity above and beyond all sexual specification, such as the supreme Brahman or Tao? How, in the case of polytheisms where gods designate all the possible archetypes, all the human and cosmic energies? Even if these gods are illusory, Hinduism recognizes the psychological reality and therapeutic value of illusion; all illusion has a truth as its original basis. Likewise, if God is an idea invented by man, one may wonder where this idea came from. If the idea of God, and therefore God himself did not exist before man, how could he have pieced together God's existence?

"Man is condemned to be free" according to Sartre.—The Sartrian man is not free to accept or refuse being free. He cannot withdraw himself from his freedom. The East denounces the inanity of this attitude: a perfectly free being would be God. Yet, the human being, limited by the movement of forms and the condition of his existence, cannot enjoy total freedom: he is neither born nor dies when he wishes; he is subject to heredity, a slave to conditioning, who could only be emancipated by the techniques of spiritual awakening refused by Sartre. Man is only free to remain or not in his slavery, to choose or refuse God.[9] The Sartrian existence is freed overall of any transcendental principle or value. The East teaches us that "existence" is nothing if it does not serve "being," reaching for something that is more than life, by activating within ourselves all the possibilities of transfiguration. The slow exploration of within shows that Hell is not "the others," but ourselves and the others in us; the awakening to the sentiment of love (which guarantees the only authentic freedom because it leaves us free to choose or refuse God), reveals that our Hell is the suffering of others until the end of the world. Undoubtedly, Sartre detected the "fundamental suffering" (the Buddhist *dukkha*), but by revolting against it instead of sharing it, he made himself a slave to his revolt. The traditional sage, on the contrary, will look for the cause of this suffering; he will find it in the "ego" and will scientifically envisage the inner means of overcoming it. As for the nihilism that Sartre comes to, it can only be, in these conditions, the reversed reflection of the superessential "Non-Being."

[9] Recall the patristic adage: "God has all the powers, except that of forcing man to love Him."

With their irresistible temptation for the seediest kind of thinking, their way of proclaiming the human being without referring to anything else, before denying him by their refusal and their inability to provide any means of inner liberation, with their success at totalitarian forms of teaching, society and political regimes, these philosophies despair without consoling, destroy without replacing, accelerate the fall into chaos, diffuse the gospel for twilight terrors. They are very much those of the lowest castes, which are those of the final hand of cards; they are very much the cornerstone and drive of the great breakdown. The far reaches of their extreme limits sign the end of Western metaphysics. Only replacing them with their contraries would constitute the element susceptible to help escape from the *Kali Yuga*, or insure the safe crossing of it, or yet, its take over. For that matter, it's possible that this limit prepares the pendulum's return to the other pole at the same time; that this auto-destruction carries the seeds of a reviviscence, as long as the mental conversion we're talking about occurs, and as a result of a complete reversal of the situation, "existentialism" gives way to "essentialism." The doctrines of the "death of God" and the "death of man" may well lead to the transpersonal "Non-Being." For that, it is enough that "nothingness" is integrated into the Universal and reversed in the perspective of metaphysical Non-Dualism, due to the inspiration of "eternal Philosophy."

*

* *

Another Eastern contribution susceptible to contributing to this conversion: the priority given to the practice and experimentation on theoretical speculation. The hypertrophy of the Western brain corresponds to an imbalance that is accepted today. All of thought's arabesques, no matter how imperious and remarkable they may be, translate or dissimulate a worried or anguished state that is trying to exorcise itself with the help of discursive reasoning. It is even easier at this level to deny the possibilities of the human being's metaphysical realization as they are denied to him, since putting this into practice is excluded and replaced by the sole exercise of conceptual oppositions. The obligation to think, not correctly, but as much as possible, indicates an all-quantitative conception of "culture," full of voluntarily abstract jargon and academic scholarship. Endless discussion of the exact date of birth of Christ or the apocryphal nature of any verse will never force the doors of Beatitude. Any answer to a question is simply one answer among others, momentarily acceptable, but destined to revision or rejection; any answer is already a potential question that will in turn require an answer. The solution does not resolve the problem, it dims it, deadens it, foments new ones. Taking interest in spiritual ideas does not result in any change of consciousness. Even spiritual questions are all arborescent and parasitic creations of the mental state. All the traditions teach that intellectual reflection, like ignorance, is part of the "stains" and is useless for "salvation" or "deliverance." Metaphysical discussions only lead to further torment.[10] One might even maintain that a huge part of spiritual literature only serves to disperse and divert the mental attitude: the experiments are passionate, as long as someone else is performing them!

All true knowledge is primarily lived and integrated rather than being thought. The processing comes later, with the risk of hindering, complicating, deforming the initial enunciations, whose ineffable character never gains by a translation into a cerebral language. The East is here to remind us that the only way of knowing Truth is by becoming it. The only proof we have of the Absolute, although decisive and definitive, is by experience, which risked sinking into madness or death. Experience is essentially the detachment from and the surpassing of the limitations of the mental state, its volitions, its continual encroachments; it is the supreme illustration that we become what we know, and that we only know authentically what we are.[11] At this level of realization, all dialectic or search for "proof" evaporates: we ourselves are the proof we're looking for, we demonstrate it to ourselves. Even if in the *Kali Yuga*, this passage from the *discursive* to the *operative* is a complete success for only a few individuals,[12] this should not be a pretext for not attempting

[10] This justifies Buddha's attitude of refusing to broach them. As he explains to Malunkyaputta, the questions concerning Deliverance and *Nirvana*, irrelevant to the renouncement of and the destruction of passions, are useless for obtaining Deliverance and *Nirvana*. Yet, reaching it is the point. The lack of explanations that Christ gives for the same type of questions tends to prove a similar attitude.

[11] When the *Maitri Upanishad*, VI, 34, declares "one becomes what one thinks," we must understand: not what we think with the *manas*, but with the *buddhi*.

[12] *Bhagavad Gita*, VII, 3: "Among those who strive for perfection and attain it, only one here and there knows Me in all the principles of My existence." This comes close to Matt. 7:14: "Few there be that find the way which leadeth unto life."

the venture: doesn't Islam recall that giving a dog one drink will do for joining the cohort of "those brought nigh"? This small number of men testifies that a priori, any man can make a leap into the Infinite, that for any man, so long as he is prepared to pay the price and truly wants it—which can mean wanting nothing—this intuitive Seizure where the manifestation coincides with its principle is possible, that for any man, the immediate and instantaneous Evidence, pulverizing the opaqueness that separates us from a Divine that is closer to us than we are to ourselves, is possible.[13]

Thus, to the aforementioned reforms,—rectification of errors and prejudices, broadening of thought by the rediscovery of other fields of knowledge, acquisition of complementary rather than opposing "points of view," giving priority to practice over theory,— a final one will be added: *the suspension of intellectual activity.* Therefore, in the face of reputedly difficult or insolvable "problems," one will no longer be satisfied by simply wondering if the questions were poorly or correctly asked, if the separated elements were really separate, even if the different aspects had been examined and integrated; one discovers that the so called "problems" were only secreted by a mental state in upheaval and that they only existed there.[14]

Two preliminary attitudes will efficiently help the suspension of thought: avoid pointless discussions, work on mental silence.

We can quickly assess the uselessness of discussing spiritual questions with those who are deliberately hostile to them. Such discussions steal a great deal of energy and time without persuading the opponents who know that any intellectual argument can be confronted with another. Besides that, they force truths to be lowered from a superior level to the grasp of minds that are not mature enough to receive them or who have even decided not to receive them. This *prostitution* harms at the same time these truths, to the extent that we are forced to distort or betray them to make them

---

[13] "God is closer to man than his jugular vein" (Koran, 50:15).

[14] Some Westerners rediscover this way of "overcoming the question," especially at the psychological level. Wittgenstein notes in *Tractatus logico-philosophicus*, VI: "The solution to the problem of life is in the disappearance of the problem." Jung writes in his *Commentary on the Secret of the Golden Flower*: "The most serious and important vital problems are all, in the end, insoluble, and they should be, because they express the necessary polarity that is immanent in any system of self-regulation. They can never be resolved, but only overcome."

acceptable; these unprepared minds, uselessly troubled and some-times pushed to an excess of blasphemous words they would not have expressed without our intervention; and lastly ourselves, when, in the heat of the debate, we get carried away with passion, the desire to convince, and arrogance. We also won't forget that we are rarely as noble as the doctrines we are pretending to expound: to what degree have we really assimilated what we would like to teach others? Not only do such discussions lead nowhere, but they trigger and exasperate hostile vibrations that only add to those already present in the fabric of the era, and succeed at leaving deep inci-sions in the unconscious: the achieved goal is the opposite of the desired goal. In all truth, the viewing (*darshan*) of one sage is more effective on souls than all the unfurling and artifice of eloquence hoping to be persuasive.

The second attitude consists of the daily practicing of mental silence, of attempting to establish a state of peace with oneself and by that, with others, by remembering that "the remedy to all illness is to calm the mental state."[15] On this point we can only refer to the instructions given by the supporters of *dhyana* or *zazen*, concerning in particular the most favorable moments and places for medita-tion, the postures and exercises that should be regular and disin-terested, the means of controlling thoughts and breathing. The Westerner should not try to achieve supreme ecstasy—*nirvikalpa samadhi*; he should stop if he feels troubling symptoms. "Meditation about the Without-Form" will be less recommended to him than "meditation with attributes." The most important point is that once his appropriate path has been found, he should stay on it without losing sight of his goal: first slow down, then cure the hypermental-ization which does him so much harm.

Such a practice will make clear the future necessity of "burning books": as necessary, in fact, as they are at the beginning of the course to inform and stimulate, they prove to be an obstacle when one holds onto them without surpassing the uniquely theoretical

---

[15] Ma Ananda Moyi, *Enseignement*, I "Therefore, all will be physically and psycho-logically in harmony." This will be related to Confucius speaking about a state of happiness where "the ten thousand beings evolve without harming each other, where the contrary doctrines are practiced without clashing" (*Chong-Yong*, XXX, 2). Thus, the soul is in the "happy medium." This will also be related to "the pover-ty of the spirit" of Meister Eckhart, introducing the notion of Emptiness, already evoked.

plane they represent.[16] Finally, what counts is nothing other than the reversal of our being with the recovery and exercise of this "princess faculty," the most fundamental and innate in us, that which mental activity has buried to the point of forgetting its existence, and that allows us to rebecome what we never ceased being.

The Hindu tradition presents six brahman students entering the hermitage of the sage Pippalada. He bids them to meditate and be silent with him for one year; only afterwards, each one of them may ask him one question. This is to say how much the modern Westerner must, even more so, learn to unlearn, stop thinking-for-the-sake-of-thinking, open up to the inner emptiness, receptacle of all fulfillment; how much he must convince himself that no science is of value if its purpose is not for liberating man, "otherwise," the *Upanishads* repeat, "nothing is worth knowing." But first, he will have to discover that this "nescience" is not written in any book, is not found in any program. It spurts forth at the most unexpected times in life—those that nakedly expose our true nature, the extreme and incomprehensible situations, on the edge of which reason and its pretensions stagger, flashing wounds in the face of which logic flees. It rips the thick clouds blocking our horizon, dissipates with the swipe of a sword the opaqueness of the mental state and the self, illuminates solitude, like a burst of laughter over a cup of tea.

---

[16] In its History, China is shown to be an expert at this type of periodical "purification." So, in 213 B.C.E., Li Si, Prime Minister of Qin Shi Huang, had all the commentaries that were considered subjective and useless, all of the basic works, destroyed. One will take care not to confuse this type of destruction with the one resulting from wars or barbaric outbursts, as was the case for the fire at Alexandria's library that contained 700,000 volumes, or at the time of the Maoist Cultural Revolution with much more prejudicial damage.

III

Traditional Societies

9. THE THEOLOGY OF THE ICON[*]

The icon not only has its aesthetic; it also has its theology. The icon includes an *alchemic* aspect concerning the spiritualization of matter: its transfiguring function; a *symbolic* aspect concerning the transposition of the archetypes into visible images: its purifying function; and finally a *liturgical* aspect concerning the "descent from heaven to earth," which is its cultural function.

Plotinus had already glorified a vision of Nature that, aimed at the "inner eye," neglected the appearance of forms in order to reveal their essence. Orthodox Christianity adopted this philosophy while at the same time adapting it. Origen would outline the study of the five spiritual senses and the organ used for contemplating incorporeal objects, in other words the "eye of the heart." This is not analytical and discursive learning, it is an immediate intuitive knowledge offered by the spiritual core, from *logos* to the heart of sensitive things. The job of the artist will be to successively peel away the bark that covers them to let the being emerge. This explains the disappearance of all perspective, shortcuts, external lighting, and earthly horizons in the icon; this also explains the translucent aspect of the characters and objects, which is comparable to petals arranged around and throughout a luminous source. These coats, these tunics whose folds retain the memory of gowns, drape the souls more than the bodies.

The icon foreshadows, here and now, the glorification of mankind of the Eighth Day—not only mankind but all of Creation. The small wooden board, the egg yolk base paint,—symbol of the triple world—holy water diluting colored paste are the humble beginnings of the substantial Redemption that should operate during the Apocatastasis. For by becoming flesh, Christ made the metamorphosis and the deification of the physical world itself possible. If the Fall was not only Adam's, but the occultation covering the entire universe, the paradisiac modality, likewise, the final Salvation concerns not only humanity but all the atoms of the cosmos. A precious idea in Orthodoxy: by descending into Jordan, Christ sanctified the waters in advance; stretched on the cross, he sanctified the wood (this wood which also designates the cosmic substance);

---

[*] From *Athos, the Transfigured Mountain*, V, 2.

buried, he sanctified the earth; by breathing our air, he sanctified the air; and by manifesting himself in Hades, the fire. This is what the first aspect of the icon eloquently teaches.

Its second aspect recalls that the icon is a mirror in which Eternity, Paradise, the future Century are reflected; a window onto the Absolute, by which Essence, the supraterrestrial Beauty descends. The gold of the background suggests the deifying Grace penetrating everything. Its light arouses things more than it illuminates them since things illuminate themselves; it is the vehicle of archetypical presence. The icon procures the "sensation of divine things" by revealing them; it purifies the place where it mysteriously shines and attesting to the presence of the Transcendent there, it is as such, *theophany*. It is the point of convergence of a precipitate and a concentration of energy, the expression that Ramakrishna consecrated to the divine image: "a condensation of conscious" could be attributed to it without syncretism. On the one hand, it is above all the place where God puts on a face, that of a man, where the human face of God appears unveiled; on the other hand, the place where man can contemplate at the same time—reminiscence—the original image of the Face that was his before the cosmic catastrophe, and—anticipation—that of the Face that will be his in Celestial Jerusalem: one and the same Face in the glory of Pleroma.

There is no greater miracle than seeing the Invisible become visible; no better confirmation than discovering that the Face of God is also that of humanity. But the wonder of wonders is that this Face has a gaze, a tear through which Heaven surges, unfurls to meet our eyes.

The third and last aspect concerns the liturgical and sacramental role of the icon. The liturgy of the here below only reproduces the one that, uninterrupted, takes place in the other world. The icon is perhaps the visual echo of this Liturgy. Placed on the iconostasis that simultaneously separates the nave from the altar, the profane from the sacred, and regards the profane as sacred for presenting them to the Kingdom, the Holy Images are located at the confluence of the terrestrial and the celestial; and as the divine truths are reflected in the human mind by images, they reflect likewise Heaven on Earth.

The icon sanctifies the gaze of the one who looks at it, transforming the former into a "sense of vision." Free from any sensualism, it inaugurates the "fasting of the eyes," pacifies, illuminates. It is also a support for meditation, canalizing the mental and psychic currents. It facilitates the repetition of the Divine Name pronounced before it by helping concentration—an exercise that recalls that of the Hindu *manasapuja*. Moreover, the contemplation of the icon is this gaze of the silence that awakens within us the appearance of the archetypes and the desire to bring them together. Little by little, the divine-human Face becomes part of the firmest tissue of the human being; it gives him order, purifies him, prepares him for the vision of God. Has it not been said that "he who has not seen God in this life will not see him in a future life either?" And because "man becomes what he contemplates," said Plotinus, he who has contemplated Love will obviously become Love, first by reflection, then by imitation, and lastly by identification. Likewise, the one who has contemplated ugliness, vulgarity, violence and hatred will become ugly, vulgar, violent and hateful, and the seed of criminality will germinate in him. In the rampant "image oriented civilization" that marks the times, it is unfortunate that the actuality of the icon, mirror of holiness, is so poorly understood by our contemporaries.

This *impregnation* works toward inner transformation and is the preparation for the Face-to-face meeting at the moment of the great passage. The icon is a tool for the acceptance of death. It immerses, empowers the deep layers of the unconscious. Its memory is kept above the immediate and superficial memory of the brain; and the face it represents and buries in the depths of the human being lets him recognize the Face located on the *other side,* and to feel, in the beyond, that he is in the land of knowledge.

The supporters of the goddess of Reason, with her authorization, denounce the worship of Images. In the eighth century, the Iconoclasts were already criticizing Christians for wanting to represent God, and in the way of the pantheists, of deifying matter. Constantine V *Copronymus* (surnamed Dung) would have them tortured and dragged through the streets, sewn into sacks then thrown into the sea. One can admit the possible existence of superstitious deviations, of an idolatry. But let the debate be raised to the level of the Fathers.

The latter reply, on the one hand, that if God cannot be represented, the Word became flesh, and it is possible from that moment on to "represent the likeness of The One who showed himself"; on the other hand, the substance is not adored, but through it, the Principle is. In a definitive formula, Saint John Damascene explains,

"I do not worship matter but the Creator of matter who, because of me, became matter, and with that matter saved me." A strange irony of sorts: the one nicknamed *Chrysorroas*—"Gold flowing" (because of the eloquence of his words), had to defend the icon in the Muslim state, not against the Muslims, but against iconoclastic Christians: he was lain to rest in a mosque. According to the Council of Nicaea in 787, "Anyone who worships an icon worships the person it represents." The holy Fathers have said it more than enough that "honor given to the image passes to the being embellished by imagery," and that "by looking at an icon, the spirit ascends to its prototype." By becoming flesh, God did not divinize matter, he deified it; he made it the Spirit's receptacle.

By turning to abstract art, Western religious art proves today its complete lack of understanding of the meaning of Incarnation, and that by doctrinal weakness or out of concern for demagogic adaptation it has lost intellectuality to intellectualism. Insofar as abstract art can be appreciated in Islam, the religion of divine Impersonality, it is unjustifiable in the religion where, par excellence, God gives concrete expression to the Face. As for profane art, faced with the world of icons, it only translates a fragmented world of decomposed shapes that favor the appearance of imprisoned structures instead of the essence; a world where matter, unfamiliar with assumption, disintegrates under the aspect of haunting monsters or mechanical grins, where the psyche, uprooted from all references, agonizes in the dregs of the human misadventure ... Nightmarish depiction of a glacial Hell into which Christ did not deign to descend. Exaltation of the Triad of inversed hypostases: titanic *Arrogance*, facing the discretion, obliteration and absence of all rhetoric from the Word; hateful *Folly*, with respect to God's "passion" for mankind; *Nothingness*, like the parodic reply to the divine kenosis, made from spareness, renunciation, and sacrifice until death.

Contrary to the dryness that is characteristic of naturalism, cubism and tachism, the art of the "saints and precious icons" soothes the eyes and rejuvenates the soul; it arouses a dream that is truer than reality, presents the plenary Truth. After having discovered the splendor and diverse levels of meanings, one can only turn once again toward this sea that brings us everything to see if other icons won't sail toward us; this sea that, from ages to ages, has brought to the shores of Mount Athos, these floating images, slowly pushed by the wind, collected by a monk, and that the traditions loaded with miracles, and piety, with flowers.

10. THE PARADOXICAL COUNTRY[*]

Should the reconciliation of contraries to which I just alluded be attributed to the Hellenic geography where earth and sea blend in more than confronting each other? With the exception of northern Thessaly, the sea is never more than one hundred kilometers away from the innermost regions. Imagine how the capes and bays, the inlets and promontories, the strings of islands sublimely run into each other to the point of no longer being able to distinguish the mist of sea spray from the swells of ploughed fields, in continuous penetration, reciprocal and complementary, where each of the two need each other, like the effect and its cause, illusion and reality, a letter and a symbol.

In truth, the Greek spirit seemed predestined for this. Five centuries before the vulgar era, Heraclitus had already assured: "opposites agree.... God is day and night, winter and summer, war and peace.... The beginning and end are the same in a circle...." We shouldn't be surprised that the wildfire that burned at the contact of water is a Greek invention, or that in architecture, the passage from a square plan to a circular one was easy with the simple addition of a pendentive at each angle, allowing for the thrust of the dome, or that the Tetramorph of Vatopedi, instead of being an incredible teratology, accomplished the synthesis of the impossible by enveloping a young man, an eagle, a lion and an ox in ocellated wings. Grammar itself, in the agreement of different genders,—*he Theotokos,* "the Mother of God"—gives the example of feminine words declining to the masculine or—*to Pneuma,* "the Spirit"—the example of neutral words transcending the masculine and feminine.

At the beginning of the reconciliation of the contraries reigns paradox. Yet, the true nature of Christianity is foreseen when one realizes what constitutes it and brings it to life is specifically the paradox. One also suddenly realizes that the paradox is exactly at the antipodes of logical, rational, separative thinking, which we have become accustomed to since our childhood by an education based on dualism. Because for dualism, things are obvious a bit too quick-

* From *Athos, the Transfigured Mountain,* VII, 1. 2.

ly; they are either this or that, left or right, good or bad. Dualism makes scission its kingdom. Consequently, nothing bothers it more than expressions like "sweet and sour," "clear obscurity," "gentle violence," which threaten the satisfied primarism that is its own. However, such is Western thinking, whose Latin alphabet, with its straight and angular lines, targets clearness and efficiency. One would look in vain for the flexible, complex, gentle ornateness offered by the *dzeta, xi, phi, psi, omega* in the Greek alphabet, or the Cyrillic in the *ji.*

Nicephore Gregoras harshly criticizes the Aristotelian scholastic, sees a "mode of reasoning for mediocre intelligence" in syllogism. Eustrat of Nicaea hears himself reproached for resorting to it. Pope Saint Leo I (the Great) had already revealed a Manichean influence in the fact that believers in the blood of Christ did not receive communion, thus separating clerics and laics. From the same origin comes the celibacy of preachers, assimilated with the monks starting in the twelfth century; celibacy going against the orders instituted by the Apostles and by the Gospel: "What therefore God hath joined together, let not man put asunder" (Matt. 19:6). And we will not say anything about the serious consequences for the future of our civilization of dualist philosophies born of the gnosticism mended by Cartesianism.

The loss of, or oversight of the latter, of *tertium datum*, prohibited the West from surpassing the opposites, even aggravated it; the West has mastered less and less the separations and differences; its discursive reasoning has specialized in analysis, maintaining without knowing it and in spite of itself, an atmosphere of pre-conflicts. The Christian East has managed to maintain the plan of syntheses, of systemic vision, under the light of intellective intuition, of that "supramental" (*hypernoetos*) that Gregory Palamas spoke of before Aurobindo; faithful to the Divine himself, who includes in the himself the manifested as much as the unmanifested. Such a thought is located well beyond the separative mental state, triumphant everywhere today. The conciliation of the contraries mandatorily guarantees a metalogic and keeps it there.

It is quite certain that reaching such a degree of perspicacity of things is the undisputable proof of an exceptional series of coincidences, of an ancient civilization. Not all religious understanding, throughout time and places, has always been capable of stopping the rudimentary opposition between God and man or of conceiving a Three that transcends the One. We owe this to Greece and its "great lights," the Fathers of the Church.

To Greece, let's say, and primarily to Constantinople, haunted by the synthesis of Spirit and Matter. The Palace, the chamber and the imperial staff were described as "sacred"; the Emperor was "equal to the Apostles," "representative of Good and Beautiful," wrote Theodosius II Lascaris. In his *Book of Ceremonies*, Constantine VII Porphyrogenete concludes the preface in this way: "May the imperial power, exercising with order and moderation, reproduce the harmonious movement that the Creator gives to all this universe." In this work, the eighteen administrative dignities come forward on two levels; below, the real, effective functions attributed by decree to the state employees; above, their "principles," the *ideal* offices, purely honorary, constituting a veritable parallel hierarchy, invisible but indispensable, legitimizing the lower functions, enabling them to exist and to express themselves, giving force and effectiveness to all of the Constantinopolitan administration.

In an atmosphere that is so greatly inhabited by spirituality, it is not surprising that the same temporal head had been under the influence of attraction. Even though crimson is a beautiful shroud, according to Augusta and Friend of Christ, Theodora, several Emperors voluntarily descended from their thrones to embrace the monastic state: in the eleventh century alone, Michael IV of Paphlagonien, Isaac the Ist Comnene, Michael VII of Parapinace, and Nicephore III Botaniate. Others will build monasteries, supplying them with goods. In the sixteenth century, Constantinople will have one hundred of them; they will be spread in colonies to Mount Athos, Egypt, Sinai and Palestine all the way to Mesopotamia. The supernatural impregnation of the era is such that, in the Church of Blachernae, every Friday, the Mother of God faithfully performs a miracle.

*
* *

Hama, "together," "at the same time," "both": that's one of the most precious adverbs frequently found at the tip of the Fathers' calamus. This word could be inscribed as an epigraph to all of Eastern patristic thinking and could float on all the banners of Byzantine theology.[1]

It is not at all surprising, that being the case, that Christianity's emblem par excellence is the cross. That a horizontal line starting at any point in space meets a vertical line starting from any other point is a possibility of telescoping that had one chance in a billion to occur in the sidereal immensity. Yet, this is what occurred one day; while man was looking on, the figure of the cross suddenly appeared: the simplest, the most elementary there is, and however, the heaviest and most revealing of paradoxical *gnosis*. The wedding of earth and heaven, the miracle of miracles happened: a horizontal marries a vertical and with that, the first successful reconciliation of opposites, veritable challenge for the unilaterality of dualistic rationalism. At the moment of accomplishment, the cross, instrument of torture, shameful object reserved for slaves, appeared, as both, and at the same time, a throne for the King of kings, a sign of liberation, the key to heaven. And what may be said of this veritable geometric scandal can also be said of all the theological paradoxes that abound in the Christian tradition.

Let's glance at some texts for examples.

God himself is *both* Essence and Superessence; his Darkness is "more than luminous": it is light more than light, dark by its excessive brilliance; it is the blackest obscurity, because it is beyond all light. Moreover, it is "the brighter than bright Darkness of Silence": admirable metaphysical synaesthesia that marries sight and hearing! In his *Ambigua*—an already revealing term—Maximus the Confessor writes about God, "movement and rest," and "beyond one and the other," that "He hides by revealing himself and reveals himself by hiding." He inhabits the visible forms of the cosmos and the readable words of the Scripture: in each created thing *Logos* speaks and remains silent. The same one also writes: "In the diverse is hidden The One who is one, in that which is composed, The One who is perfectly simple, in that which began one day, The One who

---

[1] *Hama* in Greek corresponds to *simul* in Latin, *samu* in Slavonic, and *samah* in Sanskrit. These terms of Indo-European origin express the ideas of gathering, identity and totality. They evoke the inclusive movement of the embrace, the one of love. The language of birds connects it with the imperative *Ama*, "love," that Augustine requires as the condition that should rule over everything one does (*Ama, et fac quod vis*). *Samadhi* in Sanskrit translates the same idea of completion, of absolute union; the *sannyasin* is the man of total renunciation.

has no beginning, in the visible, The One who is invisible, in the tangible, The One who is intangible." In his *Mystagogy*, Saint Maximus adds that the spiritual always manifests itself totally in the totality of the perceptible world: "In this one is that one by the essences; in that one, this one by the symbols; the work of both is one." While in *The Divine Names*, the Aeropagite writes that "the love of God envelopes the spiritual in the perceptible, the superessential in the essence, gives shape to the shapeless, and through a diversity of symbols multiplies and represents simplicity without a face."

God is Father and Mother *at the same time*, and this is why, in the Book of Genesis, man, created in his image, was created "male and female." God is equally One, and he is the Trine. The equation $3 = 1$ is heresy for philosophers, who, trapped in their exclusivist reasoning—it's either one or it's three—do not discern here the Christian *koan* par excellence, the pure expression of a "meta-mathematical" number, according to Basil of Caesarea, which, always identical to the One, from time to time marks the excess of opposition in fullness, the "immobile movement of Love" between the Trinitarian Persons. This cantor of qualitative accounting, who had already served for the Pythagoreans and Taoists, knows that in the transcendent perspective, this Three is located on the outside of both the isolation of One and of the division of Two that leads to dualism—which in turn leads to the fragmentary, the multiple, the splintered. This Three gathers together in the most complete fullness, the One, the Two and their countless descendants.

The fact that there is no absolute opposition between Matter and the Spirit, that a certain intelligibility resides in the substance and a certain substantiality in the Spirit—only the absolute Principle staying in the beyond—authorizes the existence of a human being who is *at the same time* bearer of God. Mary, born of a sterile mother, becomes Mother herself without losing her virginity. Like her very distant Egyptian ancestor, the goddess Neith, she is *both* virgin and mother. "Her lips touched The One whose embers make the angels of fire retreat. She nourished The One who gives life to all the worlds with her milk." So sings the Syrian, Jacob of Saroug. The Acathist Hymn, which extols "the Bride and Maiden" (*nymphe anympheutos*), the one who "gave birth in intemporal time," does not hesitate to see in her "the one who reunites the contraries" (*tanantia*).

117

What can be said about Christ, paradoxical figure par excellence, who in the same Person groups together divine and human nature? Christ is fully God and *at the same time* fully man. "Strange and paradoxical mystery," proclaims the Troparion of the Nativity. "The cave is heaven..., the manger, the place wherein lay Christ God, Whom naught can contain." The one who is all light is born in the heart of the night. At the time of the Crucifixion, darkness falls at high noon. The tomb will be the "wedding chamber" where God and humanity marry each other. With his death, Christ vanquishes death. The Nameless is incarnated to the point where he can be named. The One who is absolute becomes *kenosis*: he empties himself, denudes himself, humiliates himself to the point of being only a scorned captive. By becoming Flesh, the Word becomes the reverse of the Word; and however, it remains Spirit. At his incarnation, God "descends without moving"; because being infinite, he is here as well as elsewhere, on earth and in the heights; being omnipresent, he descends less than he appears at any point in space, and, it should be mentioned, at the junction of the East and the West. Christ is the "synthesis of the limit and the unlimited, of moderation and excess, of bounds and the boundless, of the Creator and the creature," said Saint Maximus. Christ himself declared to the disciples: "For he that is the least among you all, the same shall be great" (Luke 9:48). In the Book of Revelation, the sacrificial Lamb reveals itself as a swordtail.

The teaching of Christ does not escape this perspective. What is taken for contradictions by superficial minds is nothing more than seeing things from a different angle. This teaching is offered to everyone because every man should find his salvation, and *at the same time* it is reserved for a few because the ones who ascend to deification are rare. "I spoke openly," said Christ, "to the world; I always taught in the synagogue and in the temple where Jews always resort; and in secret I have said nothing" (John 18:20); but simultaneously, after the experience at Tabor, he asked the witnesses not to say anything about the prodigy that they had just listened to and only explained in private the meaning of his parables. The doctrine of deification is only disclosed by allusions, but it is also proclaimed "from the rooftops."

The stages of spiritual accomplishment are sealed by the same nature. During the Divine Liturgy, the spirit, which expresses the holy word, the meaning, purified and sublimated by incense, the icons and chants are conciliated. The preparatory fast and the eucharistic banquet conciliate hunger and the satisfying of it. The prostrations reunite what has been dissociated; top and bottom, thought and dust, thus imitating the descent of the Spirit into the cosmic substance where it takes shape. The psalmody is *both* a spoken and chanted word. The "Prayer of Jesus" conciliates speech and silence: the oral repetition of the divine Name is gradually interiorized, settles in the heart, symbol of the center, from which radiate the four directions of corporal space. By resting during the day and staying awake at night, the supplicants not only reverse moments and invert the ordinary temporal succession; in a way, they pour night into day and vice versa, thus contributing not only to the rupture of a physiological reflex, but to a better balance in the order of things, to reducing their unilaterality, and therefore dualism. "Incredible and paradoxical union and mix of contraries," exclaims Gregory of Nyssa about this: "I sleep, but my heart waketh." When all physical and mental activity is asleep, the soul, in the sobriety and nudity of the spirit, receives the Beloved's visit: sleep becomes awakening. Likewise, shattering the temporal categories, the Kingdom that will come, has already come. The Eucharist, reconciliation of solid (bread) and liquid (wine), of earth and fiery water, of flesh and blood, in its conciliation of the man and the god, reconciles them.

The very foundation of Christianity is in the fact, which is constantly repeated and recaptured in a thousand different ways, that for love of man, God becomes man, and that for love of God, man deifies himself. By descending to him, God raises man in spirit toward knowledge; man manifests by his virtues the God who is invisible by nature. The orthodox non-opposition between Nature and Grace further facilitates, clarifies the understanding of things. Maximus the Theophorous writes on the subject of the deifying process that the mystic remains entirely man, body and soul, according to Nature, and becomes entirely God, body and soul, by Grace. "United with God according to Nature, he knows The One who knows him, and he is known by The One he knows."

Divine Energies are to metaphysics what the intermediary bodies are to a governmental system. They constitute precisely the *tertium datum* that establishes a relationship between what seemingly could have never been linked, considering the disproportion between the Absolute and the very relative; they link the two poles that were the most infinitely separated from one another, at the origin of all incommunicability. With them, God ceases to be absent, he is no longer the God of philosophers: an entity, an abstraction that is so blurry and inconsistent that it ends up no longer existing—deism is very much the antechamber for atheism.

God becomes the Living.

This real knowledge is itself "unknowledge." The closer we get to God, knowing him by his energies, making our participation in him possible, the more God escapes from us into his Essence, where our participation is impossible. The more God is known, the more he reveals himself as unknown. Gregory of Nyssa writes: "Both can be said: 'the pure in heart see God' and 'none has ever seen God.'" In a vibrant formula of restrained lyricism, he magnificently assures from mysticism that he goes "from beginnings to beginnings through beginnings that never end."

Throughout the ascension, the Word-God is able to *both* enflame and refresh its servant's soul, to appear to him as devouring flames and salutary dew, as the upholder of rigor and merciful clemency. This alternation expresses the *one* double face of asceticism and its modalities more than it opposes two successive influences that neutralize each other. Likewise, "life in Christ" will be "a mix," writes Nicolas Cabasilas, a fusion of the created and the Uncreated, but fusion without confusion.

In short, who is the deified being? The one who, in himself, has realized the Kingdom. And what is the Kingdom, if not the perfect harmonization of the different parts of the human being, their reunification—and their surpassing, the actual realization of the psalm: "The wolf also shall dwell with the lamb and the leopard shall lie down with the kid" (Isaiah 11:6), which is nothing other than the restoration of the paradisiac state? It should be mentioned that this reintegration of dualities is the only serious display of the disintegration of the multiple, of the anarchic proliferation for which the nuclear bomb is the illustration in nature as is cancer in man.

The *conciliatio oppositorum* is inseparable from the "reversing of the poles": it responds to automation by creativity, to discord by concord, to non-fulfillment by fulfillment, to the incomprehensible by astonishment. Concerned with unity, it neither excludes nor condemns the human being's negative tendencies: it turns them around positively. Even though it seems to oppose, it unifies.

Undoubtedly, when Christ says: "I have not come to bring peace, but division" (Luke 12:51), it would be tempting to carelessly link him to this other master "divider" (*diabolos*), the devil. But, to borrow the modern terminology of one Stephane Lupasco, the saving separation with which it is concerned comes from the *contradictional* realm, whose harmonics require being found in the light of a peace that is not of this world, while diabolical separation comes from the *contradictorial* realm, where opposites are so by nature and essence, remaining definitively incompatible with each other. If the "Virgin Mother" is just an expression of contradiction, thus soluble, "God-Satan" would be one that is intrinsically contradictory. Christ is certainly a "sign of contradiction" (Luke 2:34), a cause of dissention between members of a family where some will believe in him and others won't, while the devil is the sign of the contradictory in that all the members of the same family will agree not to believe in him. Christ separates to reunite; the devil separates to destroy by separating.

Whoever has understood the fundamental role of paradox in Christianity has understood Christianity. The paradox is the source, the essence and the meaning. This is why it is not surprising to find it in this country of the paradoxical: Orthodoxy. A paradox, this mingling of an outer appearance of robustness among numerous monks and their inner state of tenderness; a paradox, this marriage of the immanent and the transcendent through a savage and inhospitable nature and these oases of culture that monasteries are; a paradox of thunder, sign of elementary violence, in a smooth blue sky, sojourn of serenity.

11. DEIFICATION*

From the beginning of this life, man creates on Earth the *atmosphere* that will be the content of his posthumous existence. This point must always be kept in mind when questioning the why of religions. Salvation is not a "reward" of a moral or legal order, but a very natural consequence, if not to say normal, of the work man accomplishes on himself, of his inner dispositions, of his lifelong voluntary orientation toward acquiring the Spirit. "God being present everywhere," Father Cyril told us, "divine Love fills everything, including Hell. But whereas Love is the flame of joy and life for those who love God in mind and truth, it appears as the flame of torment for those who do not love Him...." To become Love from the beginning of this life is to remain Love after it.

This immediate concern is coupled with the even greater dimension of deification—*theosis*—as the final end of the human being. The Fathers make this their basis, Christianity's *raison d'être*, proclaiming: "God becomes man so that man becomes God," with countless variations of the same theme. With his "philanthropy," God becomes man so that, with Grace, man becomes God by reuniting in his hypostasis the divine and the human. By his very birth, man is a being that tends to surpass himself, who aspires to *everything else* but himself; for he is consubstantial to the humanity of Christ, as the latter is to the divinity of the Father; patristic adage: "God only talks to the gods." Gregory of Nyssa goes further: "He who is not moved by the Holy Spirit is not even a human being."

The devil's greatest trick isn't in making one believe he doesn't exist: it consists in creating confusion between *deification* and *divinization*.

Yet the latter is only a twisted caricature of the former. *Deification* consists in losing one's ego to be overcome by God; it is the complete reversal of the human being, the *kenosis* where man empties himself to become Spirit in response to the *kenosis* of the Spirit. On the contrary, *divinization* consists in man considering himself and passing himself off as God, extolling his own worship on God's cadaver, edifying the religion that renews the world instead of its

* From *Athos, the Transfigured Mountain*, XX, 2.

Creator and restores idols, the substitutes for divinity: Money, State, Work, Progress, Techniques. The first lets man recover his paradisi-ac nature, woven with beauty, lightness, ontological transparence; it secretes these men who, as Saint Isaac the Syrian says, "If they sur-rendered ten times a day to the flames out of love of humankind, they would find that it wasn't enough...." The second is the inverted Muse who inspired the fallen man with the evilest inventions, the most terrifying regimes, the most attractive lies, capable of seducing even the chosen themselves, and who, after having proclaimed the death of the Father to him, now makes him commit the murder of the Mother, great Nature.[1]

If deification concerns each Christian, is his essential vocation as a member of the "royal people," and all the more reason for each monk and each anchorite, it is another aspect of eremitism, which concerns all of humanity.

Self-sacrifice for God means self-sacrifice for all others. All per-sonal salvation serves the salvation of the human community. Far from being evasion, eremitism appears here as open-mindedness towards others; the combat of a few scouts for the communion of men and the realization of their unit—"Find inner peace and ten thousand around you shall be saved," said Seraphim of Sarov. As such, eremitism is not only cleansing work, it is the special tool of counter-divinization. By beaming mysteriously, the hermit's invisi-ble presence tempers the dissolution process, attracts the graces from above. It shows men how they are linked to the Absolute, and that they are capable, it they so desire, to restore and achieve Heaven on Earth, to live Eternity from here below.

The hermit keeps a window open onto the sky, without which the world would perish from suffocation, ugliness and boredom. He is

[1] In a previous version of this book, a footnote made clear: "At the time of writing (1980), the oil spill in the Gulf of Mexico that has been spreading three thousand tons of oil a day for several weeks, is submerging *Corpus Christi*. The 'coincidence' is obvious ... by recalling that the men of the Middle Ages called oil *aqua infernalis*." Today it is possible to prolong this footnote with the help of another equally elo-quent example: "At the time of writing of this revision, the oil spill in the Siberian tundra has reached the Polar Circle." The symbolic value of the combat between black and white speaks for itself. To be added here, that for Indo-Europeans, the extreme North, now devastated by the *aqua infernalis*, has always meant the Hyperborean Land, dwelling place of the original Tradition.

the only one, along with the poet, who still speaks the language of the beyond, who makes existence sacred, who gives life this verticality without which humanity is buffeted about beneath itself. He is a rampart against the assaults of mediocrity, nastiness, hatred that is intolerant of its opposite. He is this force, made out of weakness, that warms the atmosphere, melts the winter of the world. For men turned toward secondary things, his presence recalls the existence of the essential things: the order of the world, knowledge, the priority of salvation and the adoration of the Supreme, by imitating the sunflower whose heliotropism has much to teach us, who never turns away from the trisolar brightness. Model and prototype, the hermit represents, in a chaotic and dehumanized world, a final landmark, an ultimate axis for reference. He allows man to remain standing by recalling the Absolute; when deprived of the Totality, man becomes totalitarian by compensation. At precisely the time when this world would most need this counterbalance, we see it, in a characterized suicidal tendency, refuse him all existence: absurd, the world for whom the hermit is absurd.

A living reminder of the transcendence, the hermit teaches this world that he is of other values, those of truths other than the world's. Seeming to live the opposite of a *normal* life, he is, in fact, emancipated from physical and psychological mechanicalness. Immobile in a consecrated place, he exorcises space and turns it into infinity. With his prayer that removes him from quantified time, he is situated in an intemporal instant. Situated at the center of himself, he has every chance of being in God. Being himself in God, humanity has a chance of arranging itself, of becoming harmonious all around. Reversing the disorder, the arbitrary, the accidental, in the crucible that separates Paradise from Pleroma, he inaugurates that which was; he remembers that which will be.

Undoubtedly, like the Deserts of Egypt, Palestine, Syria and Athos, that of the modern world echoes the same worrisome sabbats. The West is very much the land of demons in liberty. But the Deserts were or are equally haunted by pneumatophore and theocentric saints, victors of centrifugal and diabolical forces, whereas no one sees our own: the West kept the night, and it lost the watchmen.

The Earth is indebted, however, to the greatest mystics for not being worse off than it is. A world where no one works anymore at integrating the obscure elements is promised to obscurity; a world without vision is condemned to losing its outlook. Hermits and anchorites are the salt of the earth who keep the earth from completely rotting. They are the ones who, in spite of their small number and anonymity—or thanks to it—can still to a certain degree, weaken or neutralize the poisons fabricated by society in its politico-social activities (even those that have a humanitarian mask) and by all of humanity in its psycho-mental activities. Today, these men are the last and the only ones able to stop the generalized dissolution process, to avoid the definitive crumbling of everything.

There's more. These *involutes* are the true revolutionaries, the true heralds of the future. The revolutionaries below, stealing the expression from Saint Paul and thinking they can do better than him, pretend to create a "new man" without first killing the old one, and by physically destroying whoever opposes them; this is the error that condemns them to constant reiterated failure or to an artificial victory, imposed by force and temporary. The true revolutionaries are the ones from above: the ones who, by *first* killing the old man within themselves, work at acquiring new trans-subjective, transhistoric, transhuman knowledge, and in this way, foreshadow the man of tomorrow, citizen of the veritable perfect City that is the eternal Present, and inhabited ahead of time by daring pioneers, the ones that Tradition calls the "crystal torches."

12.   A FLOWER-LIKE GESTURE[*]

When it isn't a slap on the back or a thump on the belly, a hand-shake[1] is our greeting: optimistic, a bit vulgar, extremely egalitarian. A miniature hug. The engaging, vigorous contact seals a military-like pact that can quickly become a chain. The handshake is the greeting used by meat-eaters.

The *anjali* is that of the others.

This gesture has shone through tons of centuries without the slightest alteration. This simple movement of vertically bringing the hands together, this gesture performed by Arjuna before the Supreme Lord is still performed by elegant hostesses in modern airports. The spontaneous gesture of childlike wonder, the controlled gesture of prayer and adoration, with its gracious profile resembling a magnolia bud, is the one used in India billions of times a day for opening or closing any dialogue, and does not show any signs of tedium or of being worn out. Because of it, India is the country of perpetual Grand Flower Shows; it appears among men as the arche-typal and auspicious sign par excellence. Hands are held this way when starting the breast-stroke; and if man could fly, this is how he would soar from the top of towers. These hands wrinkled by servile work, these hands capable of cursing and of strangling are liberat-ed and transfigured by the *anjali*.

Not touching the other is not scornful. It is for keeping one's finest energies inside, according to the Hindu concern of squan-dering nothing but of strengthening oneself instead; for preserving the quality at the confluent of other currents perhaps loaded with impurities. Thus, the risen Jesus cannot tolerate being touched by Mary Magdalene: that which is soiled is separated from the sacred. On the human level is the added precaution of reciprocally avoid-ing any tactile impression that may tickle a subconscious desire with its feather. For a people that is all sensuality, where nervous radi-ance turns the body into an eolian harp, where the lightest graze has the value of an invitation, touching is already considered to be one familiarity too many, the antechamber of intimacy. Trying to

[*] From *The Pathways of Passion*, 4.
[1] Translator's Note: Handshake appears in English in the original French text.

find a Hindu couple holding hands in public is a search in vain; and I recall having seen here in my own country, male and female Basque dancers gaily performing a folk dance, counting on a scarf to join them together. Lastly, in the Eastern spirit where everything is in iridescent nuances, an exchange of looks is sufficient; empty space becomes the support for subtle efflorescence. Treated this way, the margin is a hanging garden, reserved for the accomplishment of an instantaneous mystery; either it forms a word of welcome, as *"Namaste!"* ("Greetings to you!" where the intimate way of addressing even a stranger is a reminder that you have always known each other, that you are in the Primordial Age and that you have just met each other again), or it swells into a pure space of reverential silence.

The *anjali* represents both a supplication and an offering; it makes you the offering of a supplication. Hands softly joined together with their fingers floating up like seaweed in anarchic directions are now wiser, reconciled, humbly edifying the mute request for nourishment and affection that the immemorial Beggar solicits from you. Anyone greeting you this way considers himself inferior, confesses to being indebted to you, whispers a testimony of admiration and anticipated acknowledgment.

The hands are also a recapitulative offering composed of five elements, the one that the devout person places at the feet of his divinity. With the very substance that constitutes them, hands offer the earth; with the slight sweat that moistens them, they offer water; with their enlacement, fire; with the emptiness of upturned palms, air; the whole giving birth to a trembling flower, to which ether ritually corresponds; a fleshy brown flower, delicately veined, whose four half-closed petals and pistils are nothing other than the lateral and median fingers and whose nails are the shimmering dewdrops. Thus, a veritable miniaturized form of worship is given to you at each salutation.

Indicating the double symbolism here will not dull the chalice.

First of all, it is axial symbolism. Raised to the height of the forehead, the hands represent the flame shooting out from the "third Eye," the flame of Brahman, the "Being-Consciousness-Beatitude," as perceived by the yogi between his eyebrows. Near the mouth, they designate the flame of words, the Word that contains the creative formulas, the *mantras* of *salutary* blessings; they are also the wings of the most modest kiss born on the discretest lips. Near the chest, they give concrete expression to the flame of the heart and become its messenger; they reveal the salutation that is not really addressed to your person, but to the essence that lies within you (this lamp shining straight onto the lotus of your heart whose configuration is like the coupling of the hands), a tribute to the internal god for whom you are the tabernacle.

Horizontal symbolism is a reminder of the intrinsic unity of the two halves of a human being. We know that the right side corresponds to action, the masculine and conscious aspect, while the left corresponds to dreams, femininity and the unconscious. In Western handshaking, two right hands clasp each other: the conscious of one superimposes itself over the conscious of the other, although all by itself, the quickness of the exchange leaves no time for the left hands to feel foolish out of frustration. In *anjali*, in each one of the two greeters, the conscious and the unconscious are married without being confused together. Thus, at each *anjali*, we are shown exactly what we should do with our hands: reunify our two natures, become once and again a total harmonious being, in short, recover the original androgynous function.

But the *anjali* will not tell you all this: it is too aristocratic for displaying its virtues. It is up to you to discover them; and to help you do this, I have only unveiled a miniscule part of its secrets.

As for myself, even though I arrived in this world deprived of all luck, I would not have regretted anything had I only known that by slightly bowing the upper part of my body and so joining my hands together, I would have had the privilege of dedicating, every morning and evening, from the summit of my mountain, as the Himalayan anchorites still do, my salutation to the four directions of space and to all the creatures that populate them. From up there, in a succession of waves tumbling down the steps of clouds and escaping into the valleys, my vibrations of love would have descended on earth to unclench fists.

This aerial diagram possesses so much restrained respect, natural distinction, and contemplation, so much gratitude and deference, and lightens and ennobles so naturally the one who draws it on the horizon of friendship, that he feels an inner desire to make *anjali* his only function, to practice it as an art or a kind of yoga. This simple, even mechanical, gesture, appeases him, strikes an even balance, assembles him in his core and makes him sacred. The *anjali* is the most beautiful gesture invented by men for undertaking the most marvelous of adventures: communication. Or rather, that they inherited from the gods who use it when beginning the oldest poems.

I salute you with the salutation they taught me.

13. SANDALWOOD[*]

Delicately take out a stick of sandalwood. Light it with your right hand. Rather than blowing on it, gently shake the stick to put out the flame. Then, place it in its holder, sit back and be silent. The stick is there, trembling, almost always ready to snap; its slenderness is ample with all the miracles it will unfold before you. It quivers at the threshold of the offering.

Weightless, bluish smoke starts to rise into the air. It forms slow volutes that embrace each other then detach themselves, whimsical arabesques, corteges of changing profiles, knots that untie themselves.

The stick of sandalwood uses space for its page. Even if its quill of light never moves, the sentence it traces is never the same. You will see affected arborescences that seem to entwine invisible columns of air, or like delicate carnelian foliage, wind their way up the snowy Taj Mahal. You will follow the changes of this flexible unfurling, of this subtle ballet of symbols. And you will wonder about the debris of an incoherent mystery whose evasive identity escapes you.

With slightly heavier breathing, the architecture becomes alarmed, rebels, running to reconstruct itself elsewhere. You will see the dream wander.

You will soon discover that this elusive and constantly renewed dance is a perfume. You will guess that all these forms reproduce the letters of the Sanskrit alphabet, and undoubtedly many others— with keen alertness they can be decrypted in flight—the human body's countless attitudes during love, the choreographic game, sacred gymnastics, all the species of leaves, all the corolla of the great forest, all sorts of animals, and all the ornaments on the canopies of temples.

If you observe just a little more, you will tell yourself that all these graceful smoky accidents mimic and dance the thoughts and reveries of the spirit, that the fragrant stem resembles a tranquil stylet carving the empty space spread out before it, precisely depicting the shivering of outlined shores, the meandering of the imaginary; but it also describes the sublime metamorphoses of the human

[*] From *The Pathways of Passion*, 14.

future, and while lingering in nostalgia, passing through periods of exhilaration and despondency, it is telling you the story of your life.

But such is also the image of the universal future. Because while it is slowly being consumed, you will see the stick inscribe the cycles of eternity that develop, become harmonious, crumble at the angles of destiny, tirelessly reinvent themselves under the immobile squall of the Spirit, and are reborn of their own evanescence.

Until that moment when obscurity finally arrives, the only thing left shining before you is a drop of imperceptible light, like the glimmer of another world peering through a keyhole. The last sigh of sandalwood sketches a question mark above a wisp of ash and the stick burns out at the same instant that the cosmic dissolution is completed.

To light a new universe, all you need to do is take out another one.

14. SACREDNESS*

Something still exists in India that guarantees the duration of civilizations, and when forgotten, it hastens their end: the meaning of mystery and the sacred from which we have freed ourselves. Only the obtuse ignorance of principles and symbols joined with the obscure suicidal willingness lurking in its veins, can still let the West consider itself an adult since its evacuation of the mystery—at a time when the growing immensity of this mystery is proclaimed by science; and its destruction of the sacred—whose disappearance leads to the familiar ecological, cultural and psychic calamities.

The loss of this double meaning drags man to his downfall because the mystery and the sacred live in man: within him, one and the other are the intuition of his depth and dignity, the sentiment of the immutable, the majestic, the formidable, the infinite. Comparatively, they are the souvenir of the Absolute that came to perfume existence; they prevent mediocrity and sordidness, teach the value of each gesture and each word, and respect for each object. Before starting each meal, the Hindu presents an offering, which is already a mastery of the senses. He apologizes to the earth before plowing a furrow that will injure it and kill thousands of creatures. He calls for inspiration before writing (even if just a letter) in order to prepare himself mentally for writing fairly. I was watching one of them very carefully fold the pelt of a panther. He spoke to me about his appreciation of it: it protected him from the nocturnal cold, supported him when he meditated. It offered him unselfish aid: how could he simply heap this instrument of salvation into a corner?

The Westerner who no longer prays to God would find it truly demeaning to pray to the tree he plans to assassinate. And yet, the tree is venerated as the image of the cosmos: the trunk characterizes the axis of the world, the branches, the universe that gravitates around it; the image of Brahman, which, as stated in the *Veda*, "occupies the center of the world, is surrounded by all the gods as the branches surround the trunk"; in short, the image of man uniting heaven and earth in his verticality. For man to so fiercely and

* From *The Pathways of Passion*, 21.

unrelentingly persecute His Lordship the Tree, how much hatred must he have accumulated against the world, against God, against his brothers, against himself; a hatred that can only be fabricated by the individual of a world that is *too* civilized, and who sees ruin as a necessity! I have never witnessed the destruction of forests here; I have even seen the road circumvent age-old trees. I suspect that the Hindu who must cut one down—and this must be done according to astrologically exact moments—still wishes good luck to the genie who lives in it and offers him the same prayer as in the past: "May the god who lives in this tree depart (the *yaksha*, the vegetal entity) and let us not bear the blame for having forced him out!"

But where I most clearly perceive the difference between the East and the West is where it should be the least perceptible: in the spiritual. By cheapening the supernatural or simply poetic elements and replacing them with ideological prattling or vain sentimentality, by imposing the worship of the administrative rigidity of the terrestrial city, the West pretends to make God "accessible to all," and in fact, closes the door on him. On the contrary—the *puja*—exactly like the Byzantine liturgy closing the "royal doors" of the iconostasis—encircles itself with reverential precautions and at certain times screens from view the image of the divinity, drawing the curtain, these eyelids of the altar, in front of it. The *puja* spares no effort for the sounds, fragrances and colors for purifying the senses, and invites the entire body to participate in the festival of the spirit. The Divine only allows the speculation of His actual presence as He is mysteriously veiled, as He delicately allows Himself to be seen, desired. Tossed as nourishment to the stark white of false obviousness, He retracts, He no longer exists.

Perhaps in defiance of memory, but also with the vulgar absence of any sense of secrecy, the West has increasingly entrusted everything it could to the written word; to the point where someone's remarks are only taken into consideration if they are duly documented on paper. Our defiance of spoken matters has resulted in the mutual defiance of one another and consequently we have cheerfully lost the highest revelations that were always conveyed by word of mouth. In the East, written words vanish into thin air while spoken words remain. One still strolls in the gardens of Orality. Even though the volume of Hindu Scriptures is several times that of the Bible, huge continents of words from the beginning of the ages exist alongside the body of solidified doctrines that are destined to traverse the darkest periods of the Dark Age with their anonymity; better concealed because they are deeper, because they are more dangerous also, and about which no one knows anything; except for the disciple whose master gives him some parcels of this learning that personally concern him.

Even written texts are nostalgic for the time when they were spoken, for the state where these guardians of supreme truths were still as immaterial, invisible and intangible as the Spirit they portray; they do not take up any space, do not lend themselves to any commentary, that is to say, to any inception of cerebral processing. They are still entrusted to recitation as if to return them to their original verbality, and also so as to avoid any deviation or betrayal. Also, their memorization is done in a curious manner that I readily believe is protohistoric. In the Tiruvannamalai Temple, I saw twelve-year-old brahmans learning the *Veda* by heart—with the heart—and, I must say, by gorge—with the gorge, because before wanting to *understand*, the simplicity of *learning* is required. Therefore, they recite each hymn forward then backward, by pronouncing the first syllable, then the second, by repeating the second, then the first, continuing onto the third, returning back to the first two, going down to the fourth, and so on and so forth, in a series of meticulous advances and retreats, slow conquests and incessant recapitulations; syllable after syllable, phoneme after phoneme, they manage to permanently engrave themselves with each verse until they have learned thousands of them! This mnemotechnical method, which paradoxically develops automatic reflexes rather than hampering them, furthers learning with the help of physical swaying and develops a veritable laryngo-oral memory; the doctrine is not learned mentally, but is incorporated into the entire being. This recalls the way of monastical chanting where repeating the same words gathers together the spirit and the voice for penetrating the essence of what they name rather than their intellectual meaning. While watching these young brahmans, I said to myself that it was almost how Christ "learned" the Torah: Palestinian pedagogy recognized the priority of the oral over the written, practiced similar body movements and similar impregnations of the *Targum* by emphasizing repetitive echoes.

How can the value and significance of repetition be understood by a Westerner possessed by the need for accrued speed and continual changes due to his own dissatisfaction, pregnant instability and anguish, and who instead of seeing in these sonorous meditations an exercise in concentration and deepening, a source of appeasement, or a time for putting things in order and holy sleep, only sees another occasion for yawning? To say that I had been spellbound by the *bhajan*s would be holding myself to an easy and inexact formula. Instead, I was seized by a double synthesis: the one of action (because singing is an action) and the one of contemplation (because one sings the divine Names); the one of the multiple (the inflections of the voice and the nuance of rhythms change each time) and of unity (the same *mantra* is continuously repeated). The West has completely forgotten that repeating over and over, repeating a divine Name over and over, is to identify oneself with this Name and consequently to God himself since, as Ramakrishna said, "God and his Name are identical." The West has collected loads of the last refuse of litanies and has thrown them into the great cleansing fires in its need for periodically refusing the sacred. On the other hand, how I love to rediscover the *mantra* and all its radiance in the Hesychastic "Prayer of the Heart," this *japa-yoga* of Christianity, both one and the other corresponding to a veritable manducation of the Word!

It is true that the West has not forgotten that the repetition of one thing intensifies its presence and efficiency, and that it has found replacement products that are better attuned to its nature: advertising campaigns and political slogans. Here the complete subversive conspiracy of an epic is surprised in its cold and cynical organization. What are the most basic political slogans, the deliverance of advertising's jargon, if not the parodies of sacramental words and *mantras*—with exactly the opposite effects: the explosion of hatred, the blaze of appetites?

The same is true of both auditive and visual resources. The same parallel can be established on the one hand between rosaces, icons and mandalas, and on the other between commercial advertising or caricatures that present the features, but not the faces of a lower humanity. Thus, the West has imperceptibly become an immense counter liturgy based on everything that is capable of destroying beauty, closing off all chances of elevation, of excelling. The *Kali Yuga* is not only the time when there is no longer anything but problems without solutions, nor the time when the sacred ceases to exist. It is the time when everything that fundamentally opposes the spiritual passes itself off as spiritual. And it succeeds. The *Kali Yuga* strikes the hour when "the chosen themselves are seduced." Such a quotation from the *Emerald Tablet* brings this out: "Everything that is down below is like everything that is up above, but upside down."

Attention and rigor are exactly what is unwanted by the dispersion and superficiality of such a world. They do, however, preside over the reading of the Holy Scriptures, or rather their psalmody. The Vedic psalmody is sung with concern for the exact pronunciation of a language whose words are still the things they represent. One single error committed and everything must be started over for fear of violating the integrality of the text, and by consequence, of troubling the harmony of the cosmic ocean; because this simple drop, subtly diluted, will gradually contaminate it completely, and its poison will eat away at the shores of the universe. This is what the guardians of tradition knew and know. Yet modern science has discovered that certain resonances pollute with the remote action of one vibration over another. The example is given of the sonorous repercussion following an atomic explosion in a faraway lake; this led to the pollution of the sea's water. From the time when dragons spoke, Vritra, defying the king of the gods, dealt with Indrashatru, "Conqueror of Indra"; but mispronouncing the words, he said "Conquered by Indra," and this led to his downfall. We know what is revealed by our *lapsus* lingo; it is commonly known that they can also deteriorate our internal economy.

India's loyalty is devoted less to the past—in which it is only sterilely conservative—than to certain primordial, unalterable and transtemporal principles that have originated in something other than autonomous reason. With tiny deviations and minute betrayals, these misunderstood then forgotten principles have led humanity to the present inextricable situation, to a growing servitude and an intensification of means of destruction, even if the official ideologies try to substantiate the contrary. This uninterrupted continuity, which is bathed in eternity, will always astound the West who is plunged into the course of History, that is to say, into a time that is cut off from its roots, made up of a chaotic succession of events and cracks.

One of the strongest threads of this continuity is found in Sanskrit, a language that has remained unchanged for the past three thousand years and is still spoken and written. It is as if the

West still used Homeric vocabulary and syntax and wrote in the language of Agamemnon. Likewise, for Chinese in China, notwithstanding its revolution, this linguistic fixedness got the better of all the surface transformations; and, for the same reason, I am not sure that what Valéry said about the death of civilizations[1] is applicable to these two countries with nevertheless diverging destinations.

Fixedness does not mean being at a standstill. It can be the guarantee of stability and, as demonstrated, even ferment for vitality. For example, and again unlike us, whereas the Bible has been completed once and for all, I was surprised to learn that new texts are regularly added to the existing scriptural corpus and enrich the *Smriti* with successive developments; it is as if the recent biblical editions had been complemented with the Dead Sea Scrolls or the visions of Anne Catherine Emmerich. Thus, in the eighteenth century, the *Dharma-Shastra*, including some that go back to the Vedic times, were added to the previous ones. Only an infinite respect for the sacred can authorize such boldness or familiarity with it.

I also wonder if our distinction between the sacred and the profane is not the fruit of the dualist tree. Instead, I see that here the sacred impregnates India all the way to the profane, and better yet, that the profane does not exist. This is why certain explosive mixtures just do not exist for Hindus, for whom the lyricism of incantations is not at all bothered by the humming of sewing machines in temples. Undoubtedly, it is also why Hinduism has never needed to be organized into a Church that is the holder of peremptory dogmas authoritatively dealt out, the distributor of anathema, and obsessed with heresy. Here is plenary tolerance! Hinduism has been content to proclaim human diversity, freedom of difference, and subjective reality; it has not split everything into error and truth, but it has discerned an entire scale of evaluations that come closer and closer to the truth; it has digested the religions, systems, "points of view," in keeping spiritual practice as a priority over speculations and theological mental calculations. Neither has it turned saintliness into an *inferiority complex*, nor has it hidden the existence of the "liberated while living" behind a shameful illness: even today, anyone can visit them, listen to their teachings, live however one pleases. The skeptic simply has to go to India to see the sages, as well as the tigers, strolling in their natural state.

[1] Translator's Note: Paul Valéry: "We later civilizations ... we too know that we are mortal" (*The Crisis of the Mind*, 1919).

15. WHAT HAVE WE COME LOOKING FOR?*

What have we come looking for? Everything we have lost or forgotten, everything that has been hidden or stolen from us.

First of all, the way to be less unhappy. You're thinking that I am alluding to the concentration of misery and illnesses that transform India into a 1,269,346 square mile esplanade similar to the one in Lourdes. It is true that in the game of comparison the whining Westerner is instantaneously overjoyed with his lot in life. But the spectacle is so familiar to us that soon we won't even notice it. It is the weight, the shackles of our cerebral activity that I am thinking of. We have realized that overly intellectual activity only leads to the barren juggling of ideas, inexorable desiccation and disenchantment, and does not resolve any problems but incites new ones, multiplies and sharpens them, embrangles the approach to truth, excludes all certitudes and condemns to torment. So, some of us, at least, have decided to get out of this vicious circle of dichotomies and dialectics, tried to throw much of the cumbersome learning overboard, to crack the mental ceiling that separates the worlds where crucifixions are founded.

In India, we learn how to unlearn.

She teaches us a form of archaic synthetic thinking where each symbol, each myth conceals an overlapping of meanings that unveil their richness to the extent of each individual's maturation, whereas the mind of platitude desperately collides with the panes of glass of literalism. This thought includes man in the visible and invisible, personal and cosmic totality, makes him see the inside of things and makes him see things from the inside. The traditional Easterner has not cut himself off from his gods, his genies, his ancestors, that is to say, he has not cut himself off from nature nor from himself: a happy man because he is *connected.*

She also reveals to us that the options and opinions that we believed to be opposites and for which we were capable of fighting for to death are in reality the additional or successive aspects of a diversified whole, the facets of one diamond seen from different

---

* From *The Pathways of Passion*, 29.

but equally admirable angles. With the same stroke, she opens the oasis of tolerance.

She shows us that real life and practical experience should precede abstract speculations, seductive theories with their flashy style and demonstration, but that destroy themselves mutually in heroic scuffling in the empyrean of reason; and that, instead of striving in vain to prove, for example, the existence or inexistence of God, it is much better to realize the Self at the core of oneself. The "atheists" then discover that, indeed, God does exist, the "believers," that he is not at all what they imagined. Thus, in India, we are also in quest of the techniques of interiorization.

Interiorization does not eliminate the sensory or thinking activity of the *manas*, of the physical brain; it is happy to suspend it or replace it in a more intricate ensemble, by bringing it to the limits of its attributions, which make it inept at apprehending Transcendence. It works in parallel at developing a special organ, powerful in every man, known to every tradition, but that our educational system has abandoned to atrophy: *buddhi*, the seat of superior intuition, whose lightning burns antinomies, illuminates the dens of "mysteries," grants access to the planes of these subtle realities that the *manas*, which fails at this, finds easier to deny. For thousands of years, myriads of men have absorbed an intemporal Wisdom that concerns the eternal human and whose main principle suggests above all the awakening of this organ of superior perception, opening wide the Eye of Shiva.

We have also come here to look for the feminine and oriental side of our being, to frolic among the irrational elements excluded from decorum by planned training deliberately indifferent to the arts and culture of the imponderable; training whose only goal is to create docile citizens, conform them to bureaucratic rigidity, productivity and consumerism, partial and divided against themselves, therefore among themselves, and coached to kill the poet because he is unlike them. India, on the contrary, throws us into the world of a "fantastic realism," the depths of which, in spite of the rationalist influences that stealthily invade it, she does not abandon. I am not overly surprised that not so long ago, people still prosecuted so called inanimate objects. Science has palpated the absence of water-tightness between the existing conglomerates of solidary molecules, traversed by the same fluids of a multi-degree conscious. On an extremely fine level, the same complicity comes into play between a stone teeming with internal whirlwinds and the murderer who flings it, and an equestrian and his mount. I am also not surprised that in a country where no barriers have been erected between bordering continents of drifting spaces, time is not more tightly restricted in its common categories. It is poured over undifferentiated layers, escapes dials, has secret rendezvous with eternity: each one of the clocks on the four towers of New Delhi's train station indicates a different time.

India is a place of interferences selected among the officially recorded and the unexplainable. Mischievous, elusive, the cosmic Game steals the robes from Reason, while it basks in the crystal of an Apollonian rigor, in a reassuring clarity that thinks it has foreseen everything. It exchanges weird winks with logicians who will not admit that the framework of the universe, carved by divine hands, chafes on their syllogisms or can escape the planes of their system, which would like to square off mystery. In the south of Ceylon—"the best island in the world," Marco Polo said, because Adam came from there—rises the peak that sports his name, that can only be ascended with the help of chains. No one has ever been able to explain why its shadow is always projected parallel to itself instead of spreading over the surrounding valleys. Geometricians do not get into Heaven.

We still see peasants who, by wiping their brow, rid themselves of their woes by flinging them off the back of their hand onto the wings of some charm destined for the neighboring land. That is why the hills in India have terrible migraines. What is to be said of the one who sleeps, gently lying on a bed of nails, like the Sybarites on rose petals, and for whom d'Aubigné seems to have written the verse: "The feathers of his bed, some sharp needles"? What is to be said of these great hypnotic manipulators, capable of walking barefoot across burning embers, of renewing the freshness of a wilted flower, of bringing a dead bird back to life, or of reiterating the multiplication of loaves of bread? What could the famous rope-trick be, where the fakir, having thrown a rope into the air on which a young boy climbs, joins him there, disappears into thin air, and as the celestial butcher, drops the bloody limbs of his victim to the ground, before finally setting the poor dismembered boy back on his feet again? "Memory of a mystical ascent," commented Mircea Eliade, of a "magic flight" marking a rupture in the levels, followed by a dismembering and a resurrection whose shamanic origin has been proven. But this is hardly the dissection of the phenomenon, it is only the paraphrase. Perhaps, as a figurative illusion in the universal Illusion, it does not exist any more than the reflected mirrors in a hall of mirrors.

Magic? Marvelous? Naïvety? This is what we are hungry for. Everything is too good to be true. We would like to fly along the forbidden edges of the miraculous, revive the unusual around us and within us. Thus, we do not go to India just for finding the profile of a mentality, which is equally a full face, or for reaching out to our dejected affectivity; we are starting out in search of our unconscious, of the one who knows what we do not know, and to whom we can ask the most indiscrete questions about ourselves. India renews our awareness of the mysterious signs that, invisibly connected to one another, design in our inner firmaments figures that are as strange as the lines joining the stars together; she hands us over to the premonitory blinkings, stark synchronicities, everything that parapsychology has patiently rediscovered and recognized as its own; a parapsychology where the Greek prefix denoting marginality fades away to be replaced by the *para* Sanskrit that translates the "uppermost" of things: a psychology that is no longer parallel to admitted knowledge, but goes beyond official psychology—a *supreme* psychology.

With one finger, India lifts the flagstone concealing the spiraled pits of fantasizing, where dreams, the fluid statues of our anima, open their seaweed mouths, speechlessly sending their messages, back and forth between our own riverbanks. Not only does she use dreams as introspective gondolas, she also knows the secret of properly traveling in complete lucidity in the land of satin, using the mastery of self-controlled breathing articulated with the gong of the OM to render the dreamer active in the bosom of passivity.

India takes us back to the instincts, including liberating us before attempting to go any farther, to daydreaming, delirium—fantasia of the imaginary—to the moving improvisations challenged by our society with a scowl of principle. So, having just barely arrived, over the hullabaloo of antitheses and the ditch of differences that never completely die, we feel at home here. Not only does India give freedom to freedoms, but in the kaleidoscope of her images, of her figures, there are always several that correspond to us. The *Holi* festival, where the crowd sprays itself with colored liquid, is the burlesque projection of our concave carnivals. Amidst all these heads dripping wet with paint, we recognize our own through the confetti of the conscious, and discover that the masks they are wearing resemble us even more than our own faces.

That's why more and more of us visit India—this vast underbelly under an open sky; an ever more irresistible India as one gets acquainted with her, because still more surprising; an India against which, I concede, the weak risk being shattered. They say that the Temple of the Sun, in Konarak, was built by a magician who imprisoned a demon there; a demon who called the ships to him only to be smashed there. The iron poles seen there are still considered to be magnets creating a fake magnetic pole. When approaching the Indian Sun, be careful not to *lose your wits* by sinking into the temptations from which you cannot resurface. Once these obstacles have been overcome, India enthralls, astonishes, exasperates as well; India exhausts, inspires, disconcerts, but over all, more and more, she seduces, circumvents, bewitches: India is an enveloping country.

I know: the real treasure is hidden in the house, "behind the stove," explains an old Hassidic tale; it is always nearby, in the intimacy of our heart: what good is it to run all over the world? You will quote the *Tao te Ching*: "Without ever leaving the house, one knows the universe"; and yet: "The farther one goes, the less one knows." However, it is only at the end of a long and pious journey that you will know the way and where the treasure lies; and it is frequently a stranger, a man of a different tongue, of another tradition, who reveals the exact topography to us.

Traveling in India is therefore the greatest favor you can do for yourself; it requires nothing except a bit of English, a little bit of money, the least amount of luggage, but demands a sound interior attitude, which is neither that of a mocking tourist nor a laughable conqueror, but that of the pilgrim or supplicant. It is not about coming here to judge from above, compare, condemn, curse the food, the din, the disorder, the waste of time and energy, curse the climate or the castes, deplore the administrative stiffness, the lack of reaction to physical suffering, denounce the filth and corruption; it is about becoming a beggar in the land of beggars. If we progress with an unhampered spirit, are ready for the ordeals, equal in joy and sorrow, India will give us much more than anything promised in travel agency brochures, more than everything we dared or not to expect from her. India only reveals herself to us when we leave our arrogance at the doorstep with our sandals.

Will so many pilgrimages to the source end up transforming the European's intelligence, his approach to problems, his sensitivity, his behavior? Will the water he brings home with him completely leak out of his suitcases when he opens them? Of all the thousands of pilgrims, it seems unbelievable that none of them have brought to the march of the West anything that is susceptible to slowly modifying the aspect of certain fields. These annual stampedes tend to remind us of the Greeks' visits to the initiates from Egypt, or Rome's sojourns among the Athenian philosophers to acquire the wisdom he lacked. As a matter of fact, the East has already penetrated us everywhere—a possibility for us to re-become what we were in our highest moments, to recover an identity: our civilization has forgotten that it, too, was eastern. Prepare for a lot of waste, enormous deviations; but I am sure that a few seeds, a few possibilities will dig their way through to us. So, it is likely that a new civilization will be inaugurated, one capable of harmonizing masculine and feminine, reason and intuition, conscious and unconscious, reconciling by the highest and thus regenerating the two halves of the planet.

You have read in the *Svetashvatara Upanishad* the parable about the two birds: in a tree, image of the world, one is eating fruit and the other one is watching him eat. Numerous commentaries garland this parable. But it appears to me that if the two birds represent the migrating soul and the liberated soul, it can be said—since these texts apply to all levels—that they also symbolize the two halves of ourselves, and consequently, the two parts of the world: the West dedicated to Action, Having and Becoming, the East, open to Contemplation and the Being. Classic and succinct distinction whose appropriateness only imperfectly follows the details of the two profiles, but is not any less significant at the level of respective "vocations." "East is East," said Kipling, who had not yet pierced the common core of humanity. That reminds me of the Gospels in Latin: *Est est*, "That which is, is." Not only have I relished the pleasure of aloes wood; I have found a confirmation, taken precisely from the "language of the birds." L'Est *is*. L'Est (in the English sense of the East) is the country of Being. This is undoubtedly why it can be said without any clinking of words that the Occident is interested in the "accident" and that Asia obviously favors "Aseity."[1]

---

[1] Translator's Note: The play on words in this passage stems from *est*, third person present of the Latin verb *sum* (to be), and *est*, third person present of the French verb *être* (to be). *L'Est* is French for the East.

16. ABOUT THE SPIRITUAL MASTER*

If an entire pyramid of fortunes exists, ranging from the multitude of underprivileged to the tiny number of millionaires, passing through the diversity of "average incomes," an entire range of *states of consciousness* also exists. These extend below wakefulness, dreams and deep sleep to end up in diabolical worlds as well as extending above in a wide variety of "planes," "climates," ontological lands, multiple states of being, and dimensions carrying a knowledge that is no longer mental, instinctive or emotional, but intellective and linked to the Heart as the core of individuality, to the Overmind and the Supramental, and to the "Cosmic Consciousness." The fulfillment of these states leads to Liberation. But as easy as it is to represent the pyramid of *Having*, which is measurable and can be calculated, it is equally as difficult to imagine the pyramid of *Being* with its infinitely more subtle, invisible and elusive nature, and whose existence is therefore more easily denied. It is up to the spiritual master to give the explanation of such a mystery.

The master is the man who has covered all the "spiritual hierarchies," is a participant in the universal Intellect, in the "Supraconscious," and in the undefined upward extension of the consciousness. Before him, we think of the "Spiritual Guardians" of Heraclitus—the *Egregoroi* living in "a world that is shared"; of the thirty-six Righteous men in the *Talmud*—the *Lamed Vav*—for whom prayer, it is said, keeps the world from crumbling; of the "People from the Cave" in the Koran—the *Ahl al-khaf*, who are waiting for the "Great Resurrection"; of all those guardians of the sacred Flame, ambassadors of the Soul of the World, who, at the very heart of humanity constitute an "esoteric humanity," an invisible community of Witnesses and Living. The spiritual master who has naturally renounced his name, his possessions, his ties and his ego has thus gained in inner richness; the Spirit has taken him over, has extended him to its size, has made him a being of the here and now, of everywhere and always. The spiritual master is our contemporary, but he is also a contemporary with the Primordial Age. Passing from

---

* From *Art, Gnosis, and Alchemy*, III, 1.

the "Lower Waters" to the "Upper Waters," from the formal to the informal, from *tamas*, the blinding dust of the multiple, to *sattva*, the being of truth, he has materialized the fullness of the divine level at the human level; he is the evidence that man holds the possibility to restore within himself, and therefore around him, the heavenly institution.

We would like to be able to define the spiritual master: he escapes our dictionaries. Only some *distinguishing marks* can attempt to depict him from the outside. First of all, his very refusal of the title of master: no veritable guru pretends as much; but those who appreciate his words consult him and are satisfied, create the master, make him and establish him in legitimacy. The grain of his soul is smoother. His gaze is a testament to the states he has reached; capable of drastically changing an entire life forever. His knowledge is direct: no doubt he can ignore many things intellectually;[1] but, once something is exposed, he is capable of immediately situating it in its entirety, of detecting its origins, of analyzing its development, of predicting the outcomes. His vision immediately recognizes the flaws of the soul by the stories it tells, the faults in an armor that is often heavy. His fundamental simplicity makes him indifferent to social conventions, to the circumstances of the moment, to the judgments that others make regarding him. The most famous example of this way of being is al-Khidr, disconcerting, even scandalous in the eyes of Moses in the Koran. This Noble Voyager is the one who destroys all certainties, whose behavior is a perpetual challenge to habitual and conformist moral standards, whose ambiguity is disturbing, and who attracts reprobation while hiding the greatest wisdom. Like the "Green One," the spiritual master is sometimes the only one who is troubled when others are clear; but troubled because he carries deep down the complexity of the things within, while the others are clear because they are unaware and live on the surface, simplistic and not simple. The path is sometimes placed above ethics (which doesn't prevent one, however, from living each day by destroying the lives of others). Yuan-Wu doesn't hesitate to affirm that "the veritable man has every right to leave with the

---

[1] Sri Ramana Maharshi: "I have not read anything. My knowledge is limited to what I learned up until the age of fourteen. I have neither read the *Bhagavad Gita*, nor studied the numerous commentaries written about it. All my studies have been done in my past births, and I have been satisfied with that."

farmer's ox or to take food away from the starving." No doubt, Eastern hyperbolism should not be taken literally; the distance existing between the man who is liberated from everything, as one will say, and the man who behaves hypocritically for fear of being misjudged isn't emphasized any less. The spiritual master is equally indifferent to the poverty and the luxury in which he is forced to live, to the affluence and rarity of disciples. His simplicity makes him flee all ostentation, all effect, never imposing his opinion. His contagious inner force inspires the wish to savor God, inaugurates the "itching wings" that Plato spoke of, is the stimulator of triggering energy, and maintains fervor.[2] His joy, entirely within, radiates through his laugh, like that of Swami Ramdas, gifted with this virtue of youthfulness that made him resemble the "small child" of the Gospels, able to answer the most difficult metaphysical questions like child's play.

It is equally possible to say what the master is not by using the apophatic method. He is not an "analyst" for if he takes care of what happens in the soul, he makes the disciple pass from "psychic" to "pneumatic," and this, not according to a therapeutic perspective that views the subject in his relation to the analyst, but in a mystical dimension opening into the Self. He is not a "consciousness director" because he is not located at the moral level of exoterists, but beyond the ethical dualities that he reconciles and the religious confessions he transcends. He is not a "master thinker" either because he teaches instead how to unlearn, to "vomit his intelligence," said Lao-tzu, to surpass the mental state and the dialectic games to reach the union of the opposites. Before the spiritual master, questions evaporate in the smoke of their pointlessness. From that moment on, there are *no more* questions, not because the world is absurd and the sky empty, like in the cases of existential philosophies, but because there aren't *any* questions: there is only one answer, and this answer is none other than the master in person. He is no more of an *Avatara*, because, contrary to divine Incarnation,

---

[2] This force, which is the one that lives in the divine Incarnation, can even extend beyond the physical form; thus Christ's question: "Who touched my clothes?" (Mark 5:30). One will also think of this commentary from the *I Ching*: "If man, thanks to extreme concentration, raises and strengthens his inner nature, currents of objective and mysterious forces will emanate from him; then, the effects he produces will come from his own unconscious and mysteriously act upon the unconscious of others."

the spiritual instructor leaves the earthly state to integrate the Divine, and in so doing becomes the place of synergy between the human effort that reaches for Grace and Grace that descends toward him; he is not the revelation of a religion, but he transmits, gives life to and makes this religion concrete. However, like an *Avatara,* he remains among men in order to instruct them, to help them become aware of the transmuting energies and to liberate them; and this, in the spirit of compassion and sacrificial devotion.

The spiritual master is connected to an initiatory lineage—the *silsilah* of Sufism, the "golden chain" of Eastern Christianity. Icon of the Real, central pole, referential axis, meeting point between faith and gnosis, vehicle of intellection, the spiritual master is the extreme example of a flawless and limitless consecration, of total and irreversible commitment. This man without *karma*, this "liberated while living," is a blessing for the community that is lucky enough to possess him, is a providential moment where the Absolute shows up through a tiny part of himself: a human being; but a being who is humble enough to contain the Whole, insignificant enough in appearance to become an obvious sign, who is sufficiently bare and hollowed out—in the sense of Pauline *kenosis*—to let fulfillment establish itself inside him, express itself through him, spread itself to those who welcome his word. He is the inspiration to all men that allows them to get on with business. Within him, the Archetypes converge: Absolute, Love, Truth, and the concomitant virtues: humility, as awareness of limits and the elimination of the ego; charity, as in self-sacrifice; truthfulness, as in the accomplishment of Truth. The spiritual master is a miniaturized theophany; therefore, the projection of the Infinite in the finite. And it is precisely because he falls within the *Infinite* that it is impossible to *define* him.

*

*　*

The science of the master and the master are one, because the latter teaches less with what he *knows* than with what he *is*; he is this integrated science, made of essence and presence; and therefore, defining this science is hardly possible. At the most, one can approach it, describe it with some of its external aspects, its pedagogical modalities by knowing that it is nothing other than the man-ifestation of the eternal *Sophia* in an impersonal personality.

At first, it can refuse to disclose itself, putting the intention of the disciple to the test. Those who come to consult Pippalada find themselves sent home with instructions to live a year "in asceticism, chastity and faith"; and then, each one will ask the sage only one question.[3] Certain spirituals have been seen cursing visitors, insult-ing them, chasing them away. Among the *Hassidim*, this was com-mon practice for one Rabbi Baruch of Medzebozh. Among the Pneumatophores of the Egyptian Desert, Abba Arsenius did not act any differently.[4] Nor did Nan Tsuan, who, among the Chinese Buddhists, threatened intruders with "a very sharp hatchet."

Initiation is the transmission of a spiritual force, performed according to variable modalities in diverse traditions, but relying on the same principle. The illuminated conscious of the initiator pen-etrates the obscured conscious of those who can be initiated, awak-ens their "vital force." Initiation is generally backed up with the transmission of a sacramental or mantric formula containing the Name of a divinity with whom the initiate will little by little identify himself.

On the long road that follows, the one of a sublime Adventure, the master will help the disciple carry out a reversal of himself, help him see himself as he is, and not as he believed he was, help him "un-identify" himself with the lies, prejudices, and automatic reflex-es that clasp him in a borrowed personality, help him predict the consequences of his actions, objectivize the dualities that torment him because they are not integrated, and forsake the infant state to acquire the adult state. For this task, the master will rely on his own charisma that comes from "scanning the heart," the *kardiognosia* of the Hesychasts, and from the "judgment of the spirits," the *diakrisis.* He will welcome the disciple in his destitution, giving him no orders, thus preventing him from disobeying. He will offer him sug-gestions more than advice, neither saying nor doing anything that

---

[3] *Prasna Upanishad,* I, 1-2. The twenty-four years of apprenticeship that Lao-chang forced on Lieh-tzu are compared: a duration that did not prevent, however, the *work* from beginning at the point of reaching Liberation (*Le vrai Classique du Vide parfait,* IV, 6).

[4] *Apophthegms from the Fathers of the Desert:* "When you learn where Arsenius is, don't go near!"

might discourage the disciple, and avoid any attempt to hold him back should he want to quit. He won't give him a "secret," but instead will indicate a direction, orienting him toward this *East* that has been within him for all eternity, informing him more of what he has forgotten than of what he ignores. From the world that imprisons the disciple, he will make a world that liberates him; from passions and instincts, he will make the levers that heighten the disciple to his true identity.

On a more technical level, the master will guide the disciple through the exercises of inner exploration, meditation and concentration, enlighten him about the experiences he will have, warn him about the illusions and psychic dangers he will encounter along the way, help him pass from awakening to awakening and from "beginnings to beginnings," until the first shores of the Divine arise. Slow and patient work, entailing a certain solitude, because all work done on oneself is inevitably secret, and as such, isolates; but it is meaningful and liberating work, and in the end the only work that is worth the effort of attempting because it uncovers other worlds and something unrestricted will always remain; in comparison, everything else carries the seal of mockery.

Moreover, it will be revealed that the Paradise one hopes to reach passes by its opposite. Not only will the guide be able to test the disciple's fortitude by seemingly forgetting him or momentarily abandoning him to his "dark nights," to his "acedia," but the disciple will see his complexes intensified, opposition appear, movements of revolt or hopelessness alternate with moments of loving veneration: all false attitudes, but definitely marking the distance that exists between the master's level and that of the disciple.[5]

Concerning the evolution of the latter, we must not forget that it does not occur in a straight line, but is made up of advances and retreats, of progress and setbacks. This is a fundamental law: every time one moves up a degree, something happens to cause a descent to a corresponding degree. Each summit corresponds to an abyss; this is what Pascal understood in the problem of the angel and the beast. But we don't descend any lower than we climbed; and so, if

---

[5] From which come the words of Rabbi Nahman of Bratzlaw: "We are nothing in this world; that is why this world cannot tolerate us"; and: "You are seated around me, I am seated amidst you, and I feel alone."

we rise a little higher each time, we are sure to descend a little less each time. In order to rise, the descent must be accepted; to be forever married to Heaven, we must accept being momentarily engaged to Hell.

The disciple can do anything to the master: slander him, even condemn him to drink hemlock. The only thing he cannot do is cheat; indeed, he often reproaches the master for this often intolerable ban. The latter, however, by imperturbably letting all hate roll off him, fashions, transforms the soul of the disciple; or more exactly, he helps him give himself a soul, become a being in his own right, let the unsuspected virtualities stir within him. In this way, the veritable dimension of instruction reveals itself little by little as being the one of unconditional, unrestricted Love that attracts multitudes of the sometimes illiterate humble, as well as the small cohort of scholars from the East and the West. The spiritual master is part of these "Perfect" of whom Isaac the Syrian declared: "If they were sent to the flames out of love for the human race ten times a day, they would feel that it wasn't enough."

An unhealthy curiosity enjoys inquiring about the "powers" of the master; even if his sacrifice is total, he wouldn't know how to use them (one was recently surprised by this in connection with an arm cancer) or know how to resort to any "gift of miracles." The only real miracle is that a man can lead beings as rebellious and opaque as humans to Liberation, that he can arouse the awakening to the Absolute and the desire to renounce all desire—that is to say all fears—to obtain *enstasy*[6] for which the master is the example and the place, supreme Peace, at the threshold of the eternal Present. At this point, the master is nothing other than the Self of the disciple, the mirror in which the disciple can see himself in the final stage of his evolution; he is the enlightened, awakened, unified disciple.

The science of the master inevitably corresponds to the science of the disciple. We won't go as far as asking him to have the forty-eight qualities that the *Talmud* requires of the *Torah* student.[7] At first, we will only ask him not to boast about being an "initiate," by

---

[6] Translator's Note: A word created by Mircea Eliade from the Latin *en-stasis*, meaning the inner form of "ecstasy."

[7] *Talmud*, "The Fathers," chapter VI: the era asked much more of men who could also give much more.

reminding him that initiation is only the "beginning" of the course (*initium*). Later, he must know how to obey the master for everything, with plenary confidence, similar to "the corpse in the hands of the washer," according to Islam. This unconditional duty destroys egotistical willpower. No doubt, the actual mentality, filled with hypercritical reason and systemized skepticism, can scarcely rise to this level of behavior,[8] but this behavior at the level of the master and of the disciple, each of whom are genuine, is the condition, the *sine qua non* of genuine commitment. Finally, he must show proof of his discretion, that is to say, speak neither in public nor in private of his relationship with the master, of his experiments and their results, nor mention the name of his master, "for fear of disgracing him," according to a Hindu saying.

Unlike the fake master, the veritable master does not exploit the naïvety of the disciple, nor does he suck the blood of his mind; he makes him acquire his autonomy, makes him bow to other teachers. From the moment the disciple has assimilated the teaching that he had been in search of, and when the instructor becomes an obstacle, the severance inevitably occurs. This explains the often misunderstood phrase: "If you meet Buddha, kill him!" In reality, it is not so much a rupture but rather a matter of the disciple integrating the master's essence, a final union beyond time and space, not of two people—two masks—or two personalities—two "egos"—but of the Self with the Self, resulting in the disappearance of all the dualism of human relations. Jalal ad-Din Rumi sings, "The celestial cavalier approaches, then rides away, but the dust of his gallop lingers."

*

*　*

The master uses different pedagogical methods for understanding the doctrine that he is teaching and for it to be lived experimentally.

Without a doubt, "orality," the traditional language par excellence, is still practiced in certain enclaves in Asia. Socrates,

---

[8] We've heard the witticism that really isn't one in spite of its oversimplicity: in the East, when a master appears, we bow down at his feet, even if he is a fake master; in the West, we crucify him, even if he is a real master.

Confucius and Ramakrishna did not write anything; Christ only drew a few signs in the sand, perhaps wanting to show by this that spoken words remain and that written work is swept away. However, for the current cyclical phase, writing is the most adapted means of transmission; and it is perfectly justified, so long as the truths of initiation are faithfully passed on. This is why the letters of direction rank first among the pedagogical methods: for example, the ones from Madame Guyon to Fénelon, those from Sri Aurobindo or Sheikh ad-Darqawi to their disciples. If these letters were originally of an individual nature, the universality contained in them allows for later reading by others: their confidential content has been released with time. When Montaigne, speaking as a humanist, says that "every man carries the entire form of the human condition within him," he is only reproducing a truth that is common to all traditional teaching.

Contrary to modern thinking's taste for abstraction, traditional teaching voluntarily resorts to symbols in their double function of warping (because they don't say the whole truth, but suggest it with analogy), and disclosure (such as a tear opening up to the other side of reality). These are symbols taken into account by simple edifying stories for translating truths of a higher order, according to the law where the microcosm reflects the macrocosm and where there isn't any radical opposition between substance and spirit. The Hebrew tradition is familiar with the *Haggada*, the poetic or mischievous tale that the *Tzaddikim* are fond of; Christianity uses parables, whose different interpretations are spread by hermeneutics, as Islam does with the *Modakara*, while the Indo-European region— India, Persia, Hellas—prefers myths.

As much as exotericism uses dialectics to convince and passion to disturb in its sermons or tracts, esotericism sees eloquence make fun of eloquence, the Word stand in for discourse, individual interviews replace windy homilies, sayings substitute sentences, and apophthegms nourish the very substance of teaching. So, the aphorisms of the *Tao te Ching*, rhymed and rhythmed formulas, condensed from all the Taoist wisdom.[9] The anchorites from the Desert

---

[9] The opposite may be true. Meister Eckhart's sermons abound in esoteric elements, as well as Hui-neng's *Platform Sutra*; and the Platonic dialogues go to great lengths to show the final powerlessness of dialectics.

gave the visitor a "word of salvation" (*rhema*), bearer of a transfiguring charismatic energy that he could meditate on for the rest of his
life: "See your brother, see your god" (Abba Apollon); "Stay where
you won't harm your brothers" (Abba Poemen); "Man goes to judgment in the condition in which he is found" (Abba Sisoes). These
"words" can have a prophetic aspect that seems to directly concern
us. "A time will come where men are crazy, and when they meet
someone who isn't crazy, they'll say to him: 'You're talking nonsense.' And that, just because he isn't like them" (Abba Antony).

The same nature of abrupt conciseness with its biting brevity is
found everywhere. Ramana Maharshi liked sending the questioner
back to his question so that he could perceive the inconsistency for
himself; he answered with another interrogation: "Who is asking
this question?" thus inviting the questioner to ask himself: "Who am
I?"—the answer being: "I am not a transient, illusory ego with which
I briefly identified myself out of ignorance, but the supreme
Brahman who is never born and will never die...." The Maharishi
also excelled at harmonizing a paradox with humor. To the disciple
who complained that he had completely sacrificed himself to God
without having received any kindness, he asked: "If you had given
yourself entirely to God, who would have survived to notice the
absence of kindness?"

In Zen, the *roshi* works at reducing the mental state to hopelessness, at bursting the ties to the reasoning mind, at breaking down
dialectic architecture; he doesn't even allow himself to teach anything, starting with Buddhism; because explaining a metaphysical
truth with language would obviously falsify it, to say the least. Rather
it is a matter of discovering the Truth for oneself by becoming it.
The *mondo* and the *koan* allow going beyond logic and overcoming
the tyranny of concepts. The process created by the absurd, the
mental dead-end, reveals the very vanity of all questions. "What is
Buddha?"—"The hedge at the back of the yard." In a unitarian
vision of the world, any answer is just as valuable as another. The
questioner is none other than Buddha; his only mistake is that he
doesn't know it!

Brutality and humiliation are also part of spiritual pedagogy,
especially on dry paths. In response to a question asked, the *roshi*
screams, slaps, or leaves with his sandals on his head. Marpa, the
Tibetan master of Milarepa, has his disciple successively build and
demolish several stone towers until he is exhausted, has confronted

the absurd, desired suicide. Contrary to what an insipid religion would have one believe, this method of severity is not unknown to Christianity. Any monk who always wants to be right sees his spiritual father force him to recite the *Pater* by saying: "May *my* willpower be done!" Any other who wishes to move into a cave by pretending to be an anchorite is obliged to prostrate himself before his brothers.

The master does not pass on everything he has received or accomplished; or anything more than the disciple has already sensed or perceived, nothing whose density would be intolerable. It is said that the instructor only teaches one tenth of what he knows, like air is only one tenth of ether. Rabbi Nahman, previously quoted, said: "All of my teachings are just introductions...." Moreover, he does not reveal a secret so much, but instead helps the disciple to discover his own inner secret; more than teaching, he helps with a fundamental experiment, the acceleration of maturation, the provoking of an awakening: the coincidence of the being with a transcendent reality. The *rhemata* of the Fathers of the Desert "flows from a silence that participates in the mysteries of the coming century," says Isaac the Syrian. Driving the force of those who utter them, they recall the descent of the *Shekhinah*, the "real Presence," or the transforming virtue of the *mantras* of initiation.

But the supreme method is still the silent presence of the master, sober, radiant and serene. "The supreme word is to say nothing," and "The one who speaks knows nothing, the one who knows does not speak" (Lao-tzu). Stripped of all parasitic resonance, such a word is the equivalent at the level of speaking to "non-intervention" (*wu-wei*) at the level of taking action. It is the word of one Saint Seraphim of Sarov, from whom emanated a dispensing force of peace and joy; the word of one Sheikh Ali as-Susi whose theurgical power let him silently respond to each one of the *fuqara* who came before him. Hearing the anxiety expressed by one Tzu-kung asking: "If you do not speak, what will we have to pass on?" K'ung-tzu (Confucius) replies, "Does Heaven speak?" To this is linked the attitude of Christ who remained silent before Pilate when the Roman governor interrogated him about the Truth. This is the Truth that expresses itself; it is obvious to see for anyone with eyes; it doesn't need a lawyer to defend it, an interpreter to translate it and distort it. What's more, it cannot be expressed in human language, whose structure it bursts. Finally, the gulf that may exist between the truth and the one who carelessly asks is such that it is better for him not to know what the truth is: its vacuity and its splendor would crush him. This concern with protecting another may equally explain Christ's discretion about such a subject. This "precaution" may be one of the main justifications of esotericism and the rule of secrecy: it is a matter of protecting at the same time, both the immature mind of the non-initiated and the knowledge itself from any misinterpretation and betrayal. Still yet another viewpoint expressed by Chuang-tzu, but which concerns a category of beings who have already evolved, is that if silence alone doesn't harm the Truth, it doesn't harm the disciple either; because unlike the word, which no matter how it proceeds, always alters the Truth but also infringes on the autonomy of the one who receives it, silence alone scrupulously respects the autonomy of the disciple and his "free-thinking."

Better than any discourse, the silence of the one who has achieved inner unity transmits an irreplaceable vibration, irradiates a transfiguring presence. His apparent vacuity is this real fulfillment that allows for the "heart-to-heart"—the Far East *ishin-denshin*—to which one opens up without hesitation, with complete surrender that isn't passiveness, but a leap toward efficient love. A silence superior to all other forms of teaching, to the point where one Abba Pambo declares: "If they are not edified by my silence, they won't be by my words either." One is reminded of Valéry's verses—this agnostic who abounds with Gnostic findings:

> Each atom of silence
> Is the chance of one ripe fruit....

Here, silence should be considered in an infinity of golden dots, flowers in the orchards of the Supramental, offering itself beforehand to the manducation of the disciple: feast of the inaudible, the Eucharist of the Unheard-of accompanied with a reverential contemplation of the master as an image of the Divine he reflects with all his being. Seated before him, the disciple integrates the features of the transfigured sage. Such is the meaning of *darshan* in Hinduism: to contemplate the guru is to contemplate the Divine, receive his blessing. The idea is found in Eastern Christianity where the monk abstains from questioning Abba Antony, who is surprised by this: "The only thing I need, Father, is to see you." Contemplated with the Heart's Eye, the *pater pneumatikos* reveals the original face.

In it, Logos shows through and is manifested as the one who prints "the shape of his future advent" in the icon.

*

* *

In the end, what is the spiritual master? The indispensable source of energy needed by the disciple. In his *Mathnawi*, Jalal ad-Din Rumi implores one not to take this path alone: one needs to be connected to the Force from above. Even if, as is sometimes the case, the master does not come forward; as in al-Hallaj's "Being of Light" guiding Attar, or al-Khidr, the prophet in the green coat, inspiring Ibn Arabi. In that case, one can talk about the "inner master" who, in each being, is none other than the divine *"I"* waiting to be set free by our goodwill. In Hinduism, he is *Sadguru*, the archetype and sum of all the teachers; he is the "invisible master" to whom Kabir dedicates his devotion; he is the only master Christ recognizes as the only real one: God Himself.

Whatever the face of the spiritual master, whatever his method of teaching, the purpose of his role is to teach the disciple how to know himself in order to know the universe. The Delphic saying comes to light here and is echoed in Islam: "He who knows his soul knows the Lord," in Hinduism: "Become who you are," in Christianity: "The Kingdom of Heaven is within you," and all the traditions. The master is the guide to real self-knowledge found in the acquisition and actualization of Wisdom at the crucial point where everything converges and mixes the totality into the unity of their essence: the supreme point that is to the metaphysical world what the head is to the body, the "nerve center" to the organism, the "weak point" to the cathedral; *ligature*, the unique concordance that bundles together all the beams of the Real; the place where all the opposites reconcile, where the sage takes up residence, he who, having renounced all possessions and glory, having stopped projecting and identifying himself with everything that isn't Him, can drink without becoming drunk, conform to the established order without being a lunatic, take a cantankerous wife and turn her into an *upaguru*.

To know oneself is to know all the gods as well, in accordance with the equivalence of the microcosm and macrocosm: these same forces formed man and the universe; the individual *Purusa* is the replica of the cosmic *Purusa*. This explains the assertion: "I only know myself as I know the gods, and I only know the gods as I know myself." In man, the mouth and the Word correspond to Fire; the nostrils and Breathing to the Wind; the eyes and intellective Vision to the Sun; the ears and Hearing to spatial Fields; the skin and hair, antennae for the subtle world, to Plants; the Heart and the Spirit living there to the Moon; the navel and Inhaling to Death; Sex and the Seed of life to the Waters.

Because modern Western man no longer knows himself, he no longer knows the gods; and by no longer knowing them he denies their existence. But by denying the gods, such a man denies himself, since he is what the gods are. The entire drama of existentialist reasoning is contained in these two propositions. Modern man simply dies from the ignorance he has of himself and that he maintains like a preposterous hearth; ignorance that would like to dissimulate the accumulation of learnings and actions and alone lets the real presence of the master be warded off and dissolved. Self-knowledge is the most direct, the most intimate expression of the Truth. Modern man simply dies from no longer hearing it proclaimed, because only the spiritual master can do this competently. And the latter has been killed before even having been recognized and heard. Yet, "It is with the Truth that the earth carries beings, with Truth that the sun rises, with Truth that the wind blows, with Truth that the waters flow" (*Narada-smriti*, I).

The master, let's say, has been killed.

A peculiar feature of ignorance is the refusal of knowledge and the disposal of it all the more willingly with impunity. While waiting to destroy himself in a vast collective holocaust, man has already been found guilty of at least four murders whose blood has splashed up on him from century to century. First, the murder of the Father, by proclaiming universal and mandatory atheism and affirming solely "Human Rights" against the Rights of God. Then, the murder of the Son, which corresponds to the previous one and is prefigured by the blow of the lance that pierced Christ's flank; thus the "theology of the death of God."[10] By way of consequence, the murder of Mother Nature, victim of the willpower of strength, pollution and

---

[10] A theology that relies on the fallacious syllogism: "Jesus Christ was God; he died on the cross; therefore, God died in Jesus Christ."

the loss of the meaning of holiness. With this triple murder, man is already a patricide, a fratricide, a matricide and an orphan. But there is a fourth one, more discreet and also tragic: the murder of the spiritual master, be it voluntary, as in the case of Socrates, or involuntary, as when the disciple twists the forces of the master to take them over for himself, makes him shoulder the responsibility of errors that are really his own, stones him with conscious or unconscious attacks. Whether he is killed by a human hand or soul, the master dies for the ones he loves.

Yet, as Eckhart says, "He who wants to be what he should be must stop being what he is," that is to say, an assassin. The real difficulty for such a radical change is that the absence of spiritual masters seems to completely compromise any possibility of change. A solution, however, can serve here as either a compromise or, between a situation that no longer exists and another one that is unacceptable, as the "third term."

Beforehand, it must be recognized that if there are no spiritual masters today, it is no doubt because the mediocrity of "today" could scarcely tolerate them: these *gurus*, these "men who carry weight," would be too heavy for the times, as are the saint, the hero, the genius, any strong personality, any diverse man. And yet, no era can survive without some form of *guidance*. Indeed, today it seems that the one who corresponds to our era would be another type of individual who is none other than the psychotherapist. He is assuredly beneath the spiritual master, who he doesn't pretend to equal even if he is supposed to have overcome his own problems, resolved his neuroses; but our era itself is very much beneath the ages of high spirituality. It can only absorb homeopathic doses of wisdom. Even before leaving for sovereign altitudes, one must be in the state and the frame of mind of men embarking on such a journey; in short, work one's way up to the basic form of realization; and for that, first become aware of one's inner conflicts, untangle them and get over them. Such work cannot be done without the help of psychological analysis.

Still, this must be connected to a resolutely *spiritual* dimension—which seems to be the case of "depth psychology." This offers the greatest chance for a person who is suffering to clarify his problems by first taking care of the lower degrees of the psyche, of the "little self" (the *alpatman*) according to Hinduism, before reaching the "Great Self" (the *mahatman*). Knowing oneself in such a light requires first admitting the two levels without falling into the all too frequent confusion between the psychic and the spiritual, and to gradually stop identifying oneself with the former in order to come closer to the latter with the revivification of creative energy.[11]

---

[11] This duality of levels is allusively found in Plato who distinguishes, like the Upanishad, an "immortal spirit" and a "mortal soul" (*Phaedo*, 67-68; *Meno*, 81) and in the Gospel: "Whosoever will come after me, let him deny himself" (Mark 8:34): vivifying negation, the opposite of suicidal negation denounced above. Likewise, to be a disciple of Christ, one must "hate even one's own soul" (Luke 14:26). Egyptian wisdom had already distinguished the "heart" *hati*: the volitive, instinctive and affective psyche, and *Ab*, the "heart of the Heart."

IV

Spiritual Ecology

17. THE TREE*

Who among us has never seen, abandoned on a beach, a piece of driftwood, a piece of castaway debris whose fantastic forms conjure up images of some sort of beached monster, a visitor from some fabulous land? Intrigued, we look at this part of ourselves that we once were or fear being. Yet, it is just an approximate symbol, aborted, a symbol in its most basic form.

Since the beginning of time this equation has been recognized: the tree equals man; only with more sinews sculpted here, more leafy curves there. Our vocabulary serves as a reminder of this when we speak of the trunk, the roots, the heart, speak of an old man who is still green. Here, India gambols in the river of speculative connections.[1] The tree that is cut down also moans; and it has nothing to do with romantic sentimentality: the record of its death indicates a real spasm. The creation of both man and a tree takes place on three levels: the chthonic world where the roots grow deep (from the imaginary and the subconscious), the heavenly world where the foliage shoots upward (from the imaginal and the supraconscious), and the intermediary world, the trunk (from the mental state and the conscious).

Ancient beliefs want us to have been born from the tree, which is itself the son of the primordial Man. Which Australian tribe doesn't claim to be descended from a ficus or a mimosa? Which people, when swinging an axe, wouldn't fear wounding the young girl sleeping in the sacred alder, the daughter of the Phaëthon sisters, who Ovid called "metamorphosis"? According to Mircea Eliade, "Man is only a brief appearance of a new vegetal mode." The Fathers of the Church identify Christ with the *arbor fructifera*, the cross with a shoot of the Savior Tree of the Garden (and this is why we still "touch wood" to ward off misfortune). When the blind man restored to sight sees for the first time, he declares, "I see men as trees walking."[2] From resemblance to identification, there is only a hairline

* From *Art, Gnosis, and Alchemy*, I, 5.

[1] For example, in the *Brihad-aranyaka Upanishad*, III, 9,28: there are analogies between hair and leaves, skin and bark, flesh and splinters, blood and sap, tendons and sapwood, bone marrow and core. Added to this are arms and branches.

[2] Mark, 7:24. A text that may have inspired Shakespeare, in *Macbeth*, V, 4—the allusion to the Birnam Wood walking toward Dunsinane.

separation, the one that separates the tree from its bark: "I am Oak," declares Taliesin, the Celtic bard. Up until modern times, the tree and the hero died together. The cremation of the corpse and the logs are one and the same: the ashes, now mixed together, are full of fertilizing properties.

Like the leaves of an aspen, these images, which are still outside of man, are gently rolled up by the lightest breeze and offer many inner landscapes. The tree that Nabuchadnezzar, the king who lost his reason, saw in his dream refers to him, denounces an ego so overdeveloped that it behaves as the Self. Under the pressure of the trunk granting a new ring of growth, the bark is stripped away, representing the "bark" that keeps man from seeing and being. The illuminated Christmas Tree of our various childhoods, if it reiterates and perpetuates the heavenly Tree, first reveals the spectral image of the subtle body with its energetic dots, its flickering starry vibrations, and its psychic ribbons, then the *chakra* that the *kundalini* snake crosses to reach the crown of the head, which shaped like a lotus with a thousand petals or a star with five points, assembles all the polarities of ecstatic consciousness. Such representations of the Tree of Jesse recall the three Sephirotic branches wantonly entwined like the three arteries in Hindu anatomy and in the floral intertwining of the *nadi* that became the "tinsel" on the Christmas Tree.

Of all the men that a tree could resemble, the man who is fulfilled is the one it most resembles. Having descended from its mountain or forest homelands, laden with fundamental essence, the tree is a spiritual master living among us, except in our public parks where our indifference to it only serves to intensify its exile; it is perhaps the last master we have left.

It is a spiritual master, undoubtedly with its beauty: by worshiping the cherry trees in bloom, the Japanese worship that which attests to a purity approaching beatitude. It is one with its upright center that suggests rectitude and the respect of pledges to the natural order of things. It is one with its immobility that speaks of inner peace, balance gained, the symmetrical placing of the components of life; but also with its mobility: the branches are the *mudra* of the vegetable kingdom; their almost aquatic swaying teaches the suppleness of a sacred dance that follows the circumstances rather than colliding with them. It is one with its longevity, guarantor of wisdom:

we've always been familiar with the elm or linden, cousins of the twisted sequoias, exhausted by parasitic moss, nonetheless pressing up against their thirty-five centuries of existential experience or creeping along on their crutches, and the bristlecone pines, born in the days of Abraham. It is one with the absence of an "ego": if vegetal matter is not inanimate or insensitive, the tree, in "the childlike innocence of the original essence" as described in the *I Ching*, is unaware of itself; or rather its consciousness is not limited to an ego. Lupasco spoke of a "potential energetic reality," which in a reverse analogy, refers to the "impersonality" of the liberated while living.

It is also a spiritual master by its method of teaching: sometimes with the rustling of the Dodona oaks shaken by the wind all the way down to the chiming of their tiniest leaves, and dispensers of oracles; sometimes with silence—"uninterrupted eloquence," said the Maharishi—that has no need for oratory effects because it states the obvious, the exemplary presence of the one who knows, and remains silent, as Abba Pambo before the archbishop of Alexandria or Christ before Pilate: silence that accentuates even more so the omnipresent Logos, as the ideograms of bare branches only "*infine*"[3] the sky. It is also one with its greenery: one might say it wears the color of God, which rubs off on those who associate with Him. Every tree is more or less akin to the tree Rumi writes about in his *Maktubat*, the one whose name was ignored by all, but as soon as someone stood in its shade, their hearts felt "happy and green." It would be unmistakably identified as the "Green One" in the Koranic tradition: al-Khidr closely resembles Merlin, the anchorite of Broceliande, and the Mercury of alchemists, which is exalted as "blessed greening power" (*benedicta viriditas*). Here, green means the source of all life, the reassuring vital force, but also the fantastic unpredictable destiny, capable of tricking us into undergoing great trials and who knows so much more than we do: it is "in the secret of the gods" of the forest.

It is a spiritual master especially by its unified double nature; its verticality links it to the male principle: cutting down a tree is castration, as shown in the legend of Atys. But it also bears fruit: this

---

[3] Translator's Note: The author has coined the word *infine* to mean "amplify" or "open up," as opposed to the word *define* which encloses the meaning of a word into its definition.

maternity links it to the female principle. Thus the Trimurti is sometimes represented in the form of a tree that has three suns for children.[4] These fruits must be gathered to obtain immortality; thus the
Golden Apples from the Garden of Hesperides. For Islam, cedars
show these two principles excellently with their beauty and majestic
traits. The tree reconciles other opposites: the water carried by its
phloem, the earth that nourishes it, the air it breathes, the fire started by rubbing it. In it, movement and immobility, one and multiples
are united. It changes faces yet still remains the same, illustrating
the old Chinese adage that says "transformation is immutability." Its
aerial and underground aspects give it a double nature; the sap cir-
culating throughout endows it with a certain "essence" (and in
Sanskrit *rasa* means one and the other). Around the "Upright
Woods," the *kien-mou*, anything that stands perfectly erect should
not cast a shadow; all the contrasts are reabsorbed in the Unity. That
being the case, the tree is no longer just the protector of the meditating Buddha; it is itself the Awakener and the arborescent and unitive Illumination that concentrates spiritual energy within to diffuse
them on a worldwide scale.

Who doesn't have a secret preference for a maple, sycamore, or
trembling acacia tree? Which seeker of *être* (being) doesn't have his
hêtre (beech tree)? In one special tree alone and in no other, we
always find, to our surprise, the qualities and virtues that we are
dying to have: that one is our ideal father, the one we'd love to be
like! And if it isn't our intellectual master—it refrains from being
that!—it is certainly our master for prayer and flowering.

*

*　　*

If, in leaving the human microcosmic levels, we now rise to the
macrocosmic levels, the tree reveals itself to us as the basic central
axis around which revolve all the storms and stars, the cycle of phenomena, and the dreams of all creatures.

---

[4] In Latin, the gender of *arbor* is feminine: the tree is the mother of fruit; while
declining to the form of masculine words: she is a mother who impregnates herself. We note that the poet is himself androgynous, but reciprocally. *Poeta* is masculine: the poet is a man but declines to the form of feminine words: a man linked
to the *anima* as the inner woman.

Here, the *Axis Mundi* no longer indicates only the directions in space or the seasons of man, the convergence of synergy between the ascetic effort from below and Grace leaning toward an encounter; it is the backbone of the cosmos where telluric and Uranian marrows mix, the scale of metamorphoses where saps and resins elaborate the implosion of a patient concentrated force that is none other than the creative force of *All That*. Within it, the divine energetic Circuit reveals itself, the incessant, free, and profuse circulation of rising and descending *dynameis*. At the center of the "Invariable Middle," the tree is the Mediator, whose spherical foliage fills the canopy of the Sky and whose roots inhabit the labyrinths of the Earth. Image of the universe, the enormous is its motto. Its growth reaches delirious proportions as it abounds with meaning. The magic tree planted in front of the Prophet's Palace is so huge that it would take a century for a galloping horse to come out from under its shadow. Emerging with great effort from the nocturnal depths, Yggdrasil, the huge world ash tree, for which the Germanic Irmensul is the doublet, covers the Earth completely; the clouds are its leaves, the stars its fruit.

This cosmic state could borrow its language from sexuality. The tree that comes from the womb of the Great Goddess, in Mohenjo-Daro, announces the lotus (Brahma) born from the center of the Non-manifest (Vishnu). Naturally related to this is the Tree of Jesse, ancestor of our genealogies, that displays in Isaiah the continuation of the entire line of the kings of Judah, as well as the alchemists' *arbor philosophica*, taking the place of the large sex of a man (the *Materia prima*).

The central axis and the two cosmic currents are found in the Spindle of Necessity that Plato assimilates to a diamond pillar, an image of both the invisible and immutable. In the Tibetan version it is a thunderbolt (*vajra*) that crosses the world and illuminates it in a flash, and whose six branches indicate the double power of creation and destruction. Sufism resorts to the same symbolism when it speaks of the tree of "Intellect" covering the hierarchy of the worlds: thus, the branches and the leaves correspond to the differentiations of the Spirit in the multiple states of existence.

As the descending movement of the Spirit and the spreading of the universe, the tree is content with and prefers being inverted. In this case it is *Ashvattha*, the "imperishable pipal" of the *Bhagavad*

Gita.[5] Its roots plunge into the supreme Brahman; its buds correspond to the objects of the senses; its branches,—the five elements—nourished by fundamental tendencies (*guna*), refer to the
world that is displayed. Between its roots that spread over the sup-
raphysical level and its branches that spread over the material
world, man wanders until the moment when, with the sword of
indifference, he severs the bonds of all desire to attain Liberation.

Receptacle of the sacred, support for divine appearances, the
tree exalts the numinous. What the lion is to the animal kingdom,
the oak is to the vegetable kingdom. Heracles' club is made from its
wood; and we know that in Latin, *robur* means both "strength" and
"oak." The tree is not only an archetypical expression of strength—
the most obvious one—but also one of grace, harmony, generosity,
growth, and love. Masterpiece of the universal substance, the eternal Being uplifted,—who, having been created before the luminar-
ies, beasts and man, denotes, contrary to the evolutionary vision, its
highly spiritual specificity—the tree wears Divine names like ontological phylacteries, provocative trophies. All the way to its leafy
depths, a tempestuous voice; to the tips of its twigs, transparent
mass, ecstatic vigor, pronunciation of Logos, theophany. At the very
top, the imperceptible pendular *momentum* measures the instants
that make up eternity. Is it astonishing that one Joachim of Floris,
in his *Liber figurarum*, read through the Tree of the Apocalypse the
Age of the Father, the "Law" of the Old Testament, the Age of the
Son, the "Faith" of the New, and the Age of the Holy Ghost, the
eschatological reconciliation between the Gentiles and the Jews? It
is the only real vision where the "meaning of History" is not a race
to the chasms, but instead a deepening and growing interiorization
of the love story between God and humanity.

In Hindu mythology, *Ashvattha* means "station" or "residence of
the Horse"; the Horse designates the Sun as the spiritual principle,
fruit of the World Tree. In biblical mythology, the same World Tree,
the same fruit of life. As long as Adam nourishes himself from it, he
is one with the One, at the lips of beatitude. But what starts out as a
metaphysical fairy tale turns into a detective story. Why all the
crimes, bloodbaths, scourges, and death? The guilty party is none

[5] *Bhagavad Gita*, XV, 1-4. See also *Rig Veda*, I, 24, 7, and *Katha Upanishad*, VI, I. The
tree is called *nyagrodha*, "crossing toward the bottom," *Aitareya Brahmana*, VII, 30,
and *Satapatha Brahmana*, XII, 2, 7, 3.

other than the investigator. To his amazement, the existence of a second tree reveals itself: the tree of the Science of good and evil, the tree of Duality, which Adam was not allowed to taste. By transgressing the order, man cut himself off from the Unity. Henceforth, he would live in separation; his conscience would become intermittent and fragmented, his being, cancerous multiplicity. Rigor would succeed Grace. From the moment that the Adversary of the One would be man's inspiration for the dualistic sin, the Tree of Life—the divine and invigorating Spirit—would become inaccessible to him. In myths it is located in the far reaches of the earth, in the depths of the oceans, on the top of some mountain. Monsters guard it, the *Cherubim* armed with flamboyant double-edged swords.... Son of the desert, Islam mentions the "jujube tree of the limit," the *Sidrat al-Muntaha*, that marks the threshold of the unknowable, the farthest borders that even the souls nearest to God cannot cross without being shred to pieces by the thorns.

What could have turned into a final tragedy subsides in the light of reconciliation; the dialectic of the two rivals fades and blends. Identified with the Tree of Life, the Cross is made from the wood of Duality: after having been the instrument of the Fall, the latter becomes the instrument of Salvation. The Tree of *Sephiroth*—the "metaphysical Numerations," the "Processions" of the Divinity, its "eyes" and "lamps"—also gathers together the two trees of Mercy and Justice, reunited in the center column where the two tendencies are in balance. In the same way, the Cross of Christ is placed on Golgotha between the crosses of the good and the bad thieves.

In the *Zohar*, the Tree of Life that "spreads from top to bottom"—and also belongs to the family of the "inverted"—is called the "Tree of Light." In this way it is akin to the burning bush that rekindles itself, and to Vanaspati, the "Lord of the Trees," identified with the god Agni. Finally, although in a different context, the Koran speaks of a "blessed tree" (filled with spiritual influence), an olive tree whose oil keeps the light of a lamp (Allah himself) alive, in contrast to the "accursed tree." Suhrawardi sees in the former "the intellective imagination" that works on "the imaginal," in contrast to "the imaginary" that remains in the sensory and illusionary world, while at the same time misrepresenting it. This would evoke another war; in reality, it is just the consequence of the first one: the imaginary is only one of a thousand aspects of the original Fall.

*

*   *

All peoples have devoted a cult to the tree; not the tree as such, but because of the psychological, sapiential, and metaphysical realities of which this "candelabra of darkness" is the bearer. If, once again according to Mircea Eliade, the *Whole* exists within each *significant fragment*, "it is not because the law of 'participation' is true, it is because every significant fragment *repeats* the Whole."

All the more so when the fragment multiplies, when the tree commits this excrescence: the forest. Dwelling place for the elemental and the hamadryads, bandits and hermits, blessed solitude, place of chivalrous and mystic initiation, image of the soul surprised by its tormented depths, reflection of simplicity that has branched out from ontological principles, this "adventure-filled forest," enchantment of the medieval Geste, is still a tree; but an immensified tree.

18.   THE BIRD[*]

Anyone who says tree, says sky, anyone who says tree and sky says bird. The tree is the temple for which the nest is the sanctuary. As for the bird, it is the symbol par excellence, in as far as every symbol is the key to an initiatory truth: figuratively, the bird is very much a key, the one that opens the chasms above. Inseparable from the tree, perched on the top, the stork communicates the presiding spiritual principle of alchemic Work. Another perspective: while the tree expresses cosmic totality, the bird expresses the celestial and feminine aspect, as the snake expresses the terrestrial and masculine aspect.

But in as much as the massiveness of one suggests a global nature that is indivisible, the smallness of the other will prompt detailed exploration.

The bird's *plumage* is the first to call us: tiny chromatic theophany, a miniature rainbow. Anyone who has seen the wedding finery of the Great Emerald Bird of Paradise (quite a spectacle!), would crown it the orchid of the kingdom of bird-sellers, as Malcolm de Chazal who saw the wings as petals.

With their colors, birds extract from the invisible the vibratory frequencies belonging to the texture of the universe. While their overlapping trajectories give concrete expression to the lines of force that hem in the whole with the energetic netting, guarantor of its coherency, these colors materialize or suggest—astonishing stained glass windows of the cosmic cathedral—latent colors reigning over other planes, revealing some of the dust of divine Energy, magnified by thousands, captured and brought back among us by some supramental magnifying glass.

Alchemy seized the symbolism of these colors. The black of the crow and the blackbird manifest the advances of darkness, *Nigredo*, as the whiteness of the dove, *Albedo* signifies awakening and light; and the red of the purple heron—"the cinnabar bird" (*tan-niao*) for the Taoist—*Rubedo*, the realization of the Philosopher's Stone, symbolized elsewhere by the sun. But elsewhere is here. As for the "pea-

---

[*] From *Art, Gnosis, and Alchemy*, I, 6.

cock's tail," the alchemic *cauda pavonis*, it symbolizes the union of all the colors in an image of totality that leads to white. The eagle's feathers imitate the rays of this sun and are the signature of spiritual investiture for the American Indian. As for the more rustic goose feathers, the memory of the Calamus tracing the destinies of the world on the secret Table will remain in their axial quality for a long time to come; this doesn't avoid perpetuating the ritualistic nature of writing where the scribe becomes the imitator of the Demiurge, his faithful secretary or his innocent rival.

Birds are fragments of intelligible Knowledge to the eye, as their *songs* are fragments of the Music of the spheres to the ear, scattered rainfall from the Grand Oratorio of the world; they are God's Morse code.

If the bird gives texture to the immobile with its flight, to eternity with its dazzling speed, to the vacuum with its plumage, it gives full value to silence with its singing. "Bird crying, the mountain silence deepens" notes the poem from the *Zenrin*. Night watchman-awakener, it arouses the sun: the cock beckons Amaterasu out of her cave. In his summons there is a solar stridency, something metallic, quarrelsome: the former is a helmeted chant, that makes the pun *gallus*, cock, and *Gallus*, Gaulois, not quite so unfounded.[1] But which chant is not praise for the Creator as well? Saint Francis preaching to "our brothers the little birds" asks them to "always try hard to praise God."

These chants also symbolize the "verbal seeds"—the *bija-mantra* of Hinduism—eternal entities located behind articulated syllables. The modulated repetition of the same notes recalls the fervent short prayer of esoteric traditions. Like the "non-sensical *mantra*"[2] of India, they undoubtedly have nothing of an intellectual sense to offer, but they have the power to hammer out an elementary truth, and according to some, a therapeutic value. As for the "language of the birds," the Islamic tradition understands it here as supreme knowledge, before becoming the title of the famous work by Farid

---

[1] The Chinese have a similar play on words with *ki*, "cock" and *ki*, "good omen." (Translator's Note: the French cockerel is the emblem of the French fighting spirit.)

[2] Translator's Note: The syllables of this *mantra*, which has no intellectual signification, are chosen for the vibrations they create rather than for any particular meaning.

ad-Din Attar, the *Mantiq at-Tayr*, woven from significant puns. The "swan's song" is a variation of it in its prophetic modality.

But which bird doesn't sing simply for the pleasure of singing, enthusiast of generous acts? And so the nightingale, in the twilight velvet: he strives for nothing less than perfection *for God*; and so the lark, invisible high up in altitude—the zenith replaces him in song!— "synthesis of a flight and a song," writes Bachelard in *Air and Dreams*.

Flight, precisely in its lightness, is the bird's most meaningful characteristic. Plato says in the *Phaedrus* that "among all the corporeal elements, it is the wing that is most akin to the divine." The twinship of the wings marks the complementarity of two solidary efforts, exalting the soul toward its first kingdom. Attached to the heels of Hermes, they reconcile the top and the bottom, depriving gravity of its excess of curses.

Rarely at rest, the bird illustrates the fact that, in the universe, everything is ever-changing because living. It incomparably embodies the Shiva dance of the atoms; its velocity is conquered only by thought.[3] The shaman practices magic flight by imitating the bird— and being of age—as already expressed by the drawings of Altamira, reuniting that which man, in the beginning, knew how to do: rejoin the bosom of the world by rising up into the sky. A voyage that doesn't imply space travel—that is for astronauts—but instead an ecstatic comprehension of things, rising to the planets of within, the construction of the Self: Daedalus, the architect, escapes bondage, blindness, by gluing feathers to his arms; Vishvakarma does his architectural work by flapping his feather-covered arms. It is in this sense one must understand the yogi power of flight (*laghiman*), or Mohammed's winged flight during his sleep, the Taoist flight to the Isles of the Blessed. A beyond that is more a state of being than a place; the place to which the Egyptian falcon, who is himself the symbol of the soul of the dead, soars.

In flight, the bird leaves no scratches in the air that immediately closes up on the wake behind it, replacing it in an instant. The *Mahabharata* remarks: "We never see any trace of a bird's passage." We understand: nothing that is born and dies leaves a vestige after itself; the very illusionary "ego" must disappear into errors and truth, objects of the senses, desires (even the desire for the

3 "Intelligence (*manas*) is faster than the bird," declares the *Rig Veda*, VI, 9, 5.

Supreme), *karma*, must dissolve in the existential atmosphere. Before and after the ephemeral silent route, nothing leads us to suspect that a bird ever existed: nothing other than the sky exists, nothing other than He exists!

It happens, sometimes, that a flight of birds leaves a negative value behind: in that case it means fantasies, idealization, mental vagabonding, evanescence of daydreams, these "bad thoughts" that Ramakrishna talks about. This is the alchemic "volatile," Mercury, that needs to be fixed into reality in the first phases of the opus: the bird that was in the sun (*sol*) comes to land on the ground (*solum*). The ostrich, which doesn't fly but runs, represents the union between the fixed and the volatile. In *Atalante fugitive*, the wings of the crow will have been clipped in the same sense. Taking root in chthonian energy is the only thing that will allow the "influence of the stars" to be welcomed.

Inseparable from the theme of flight is the theme of migration.

Majestic whiteness crumbling, flapping its wings from north to south, Apollo's swan carries the solar god to the polar place, toward the springtime of knowledge, to this land of Hyperboreans where frozen opposites harmonize—this "transparent glacier of flights unknown"—where the "motionless Mover" collects and transcends fragmented flights. Brother of Lohengrin's swan; brother of the flamingo or the wild goose serving as Varuna's mount. Likewise, Garuda, the "winged Word," made from the words of the triple *Veda*, transports man to other worlds. Faster than lightning: its cruising speed; birds who are as much the representation of *Atman*, the spiritual principle joining with other "climates," or the absolute Center from which there is no return. Perilous undertaking from elsewhere: in Attar's poem, quoted before, thirty birds out of the thousands of "poor nothings," guided by the hoopoe, manage to cross the seven Valleys to reach Simurgh, the Phoenix, the divine Essence in its indescribable splendor.

It isn't only the shimmering line of migrating birds that suggests the golden chain of the initiated, the mystic lineage where each one, son of the founding "Seer," is perfectly individuated, but where all, established in a permanent and fundamental totality, transmit the password to each other, sharing the immemorial secret.

*

*   *

The bird teaches wisdom to humans.

Its lightness translates the art of transmuting heaviness into its opposite. In some Muslim texts, Christ gives flight to the sparrows he modeled in clay. One might conclude that this physical lightness is an unawareness, a belief that all birds are "bird brains." In fact, it illustrates the greatest of faith; not unlike the wild lily, the bird "neither plants nor harvests": it follows destiny. In the same way, *Buddha's Law Among the Birds* shows that the cuckoo's apparent immoralism (Avalokiteshvara) signifies its detachment from family duties.

The bird's fragileness, joined with its smallness, inspires the image of the *spiritual* lost in the material world whose brutality gets the better of it. But it is exactly this creature, the most unnoticed here below, that is the greatest up above: as such, it is the model of God's servant, of the soul who is in this world without being here, and who, like the turtledove, lives hidden in a hollow in the rocks.

As a true Taoist (and even more authentic because it doesn't know that it is!), the bird demonstrates how to make something good come of evil; as the seagull or the buzzard floating on air currents instead of fighting against the wind, using an opposing force to their advantage. Or when the peacock, according to the old belief, gives such brilliance to its plumage by incorporating the venom of the snakes it kills! And in still another way, the bird excels at the reconciliation of opposites. We alluded to the couple of wings in love; but flight—going out into the world, the image of action and appearance—alternates with stopping—the retreat, the image of the mental assembly that the heron, king of the yogis, practices in an exemplary fashion. Alternating or coinciding: the hawk, with wings spread, nailed to the sky, *hovers*: peasant image of the Spirit. A bird's step speaks of incarnation, its flight, of deification. Furthermore, what happens when it swims? It unites the four elements. In the famous parable of the birds, all the exegetes know that the one who tastes the fruit designates the *jivatman* engaged in action, and the one who looks at it with a contemplative soul, the unconditional Atman.[4]

---

[4] *Mundaka Upanishad*, III, I, 1: "Two birds, inseparably united companions, live in the same tree. One eats the tree's fruit, the other looks at it without eating it." A slightly different version exists in the *Svetashvatara Upanishad*, IV, 6.

These aspects confer a mysterious kind of knowledge upon the bird. Which Holy Spirit for animals guides the swallow for thousands of miles back to its village, helps it to recognize its perch and its nest? Unerring instinct detected in all the homing pigeons that correct their flight patterns according to the sun's position...! Transferred to an inner level, this knowledge will be once again symbolized by the peacock, who was Argos. The peacock is the "all-seeing" gnostic (*panoptes*), thanks to the ocelli of its tail feathers when spread. When considering it, we think of the "four beasts" of Revelation, each one bearing six wings constellated with eyes, repetitions of the Tetramorph of Ezekiel.

Such wisdom doesn't hesitate at the threshold of supreme sacrifice. In the Hindu epic, Jatayu offers his life in order to keep Ravana, the devil, from kidnapping Sita. In the Christian bestiary, the pelican nourishes its babies by opening its belly (and there is no need here for the scientifically proven vomiting of predigested fish!). Figure of the Redeemer, the pelican shares its flesh and blood with men. This intimate part of the bird is the capacity of death itself nourished by immortality. This is the meaning of the Phoenix—the *bennou* of Egypt—who, every hundred years, is reborn from its ashes.

Seminal projections from the Light, resonant sparks from parallel worlds, still scattered touches of a haggard tapestry, errant gems of the future, we would like to imagine that contrary to the misshapen limbs searching, in the Empedoclean vision, to be united by chance encounters, all these prophetic seeds symbolized by birds prefigure instead their harmonization in a vast floating mosaic, in anticipation of the eternal century. From Cloud Cuckoo Land to Celestial Jerusalem, the difference is some rustling of wings, the difference that separates the oriole's trill from its implementation in Messiaen's composition. We would like to see in birds' flight— "dawn exalted just as a flock of doves"—the ritualistic launching of oracular pieces by a hand hidden behind the foliage. We just have to wait for them to land to observe the lines that will join their footprints in the sand of memory and provide the soothsayers' insight with figures as curious as those linking the stars. In China, the inspiration for written characters came from birds' footprints that were copied by a minister under Huang Ti. Invaded by their presence, the sky becomes the materialized "field of possibilities," the *templum* of omens where what is going to happen here below has already taken place somewhere in another stratum of time. The Greek *ornis* means both "bird" and "omen"—just as in French the word *cygne* (swan) can also be written *signe* (sign). Which is also what the Koranic adage means: "Every man has a bird around his neck."

Emissary of the gods, destiny's telegram, the bird, in its philanthropy, brings a cloud-covered mountain of myths, the beverage of life, to man. Two doves "caressing the ether of their song" guide Enea to the essential Tree, the warning of the Italian sanctuary. A dove had already brought a branch to Noah as evidence; and also a dove who anticipates the Angel and the Annunciation. The assimilation of the bird to the angel happens quite naturally; it opens onto a new image, that of the higher states of the being, whose language is precisely that of the "guardian-angels" (*angelloi*): poetry, solar speech, *Syriac* and chanted. Birds consequently appear as the *intermediary bodies* between us and the different ontological levels of the supramental sphere: Wisdom, Knowledge, Love, Harmony, Liberty. These are what designate, in the wild mustard seed—the Kingdom of Heaven—the sparrows that come to land there. As for the eagle, he sets his sight on the sun: he has a direct perception of Intellectivity. In the language of the birds, the term could be related to *aigle,* meaning "radiance" in Greek.[5] (Then, *gaus* means "cow" in Sanskrit, but "luminous ray" in the figurative sense.) In its Olympian richness, it unites the "fullness" of its gliding and the "exaltation" of its flight, symbolizing Logos as will the Rokh bird (*al-Ruh,* "the transcendent Spirit").

If, as Novalis writes, "the tree is a flowering flame," we could say that the bird is a flying flame. This is nearly the form with which Saint Thomas adorns angels; Elijah, the prophet, climbs to Heaven in a chariot of fire; this fire which is nothing more than ether in this case, the *akasha,* abode of the original Sound, chalice of the theophanies, cavern of visitations, the in-between world where earthlings and the heavenly meet, the latter bringing news from Elsewhere to the former, and as such deserving of the reverential welcome and the salutation of men.

If the tree begets a forest, the bird lays an egg.

The symbolism of the egg is first of all cosmologic: it concerns the

---

[5] Translator's Note: *aigle* also means "eagle" in French.

universe. All traditions evoke the same Ovule, a certain waterline on the primitive Ocean, a certain brooding by the royal swan for which Leda is a prototype. Image of universal potentiality, it delimits the world by its form, prepares the polarization of the Androgyne by splitting. Its shell furnishes Earth, the solid base, material basis of creation; the egg white, Water, the flowing and humid element, the unifying intermediary, and also the Moon; the yolk, Fire, the invigorating and subtle fluid, and the Sun; finally, the seed, Air, the initial central vibration, containing the whole egg that contains the whole world. The egg is only a point in the universe, the smallest in nature, but it is a point that is the Whole: the "golden embryo" of Hinduism.

The symbolism of the egg is also alchemical: it concerns the human microcosm. Corresponding to the different constituents are the Self (the seed), the intellective spirit (the yolk), the psychomental body (the egg white), the physical envelope (the shell). Both the container and the contents, the philosophical Egg also designates the "raw material" enclosed in the athanor, from which the "chick" hatches, mercurial energy, the liberated soul. The egg must be opened with a sharp double-edged sword, that is to say, divided into its elements to recreate the *Chaos* from which *Tao* will be born. This sword heals by wounding; it is the ray of consciousness that breaks and discriminates, gives access to more than itself: to a conscious that is knowledge.

The richness of significance and the intensity of life of which the egg is bearer perhaps better justifies the respect with which the Pythagoreans, in their vegetarianism, worshiped it; this explains the custom of Easter Eggs, whose meaning is scarcely understood, but which, heavy with a secret knowledge, persist in falling, once a year, from the sky into the gardens of atheism—without breaking!

*

* *

Ornithological symbolism is inseparable from dendromorph symbolism. We have only detected some of the traits. Enough, nonetheless, to perceive its complexity. We can easily correlate, in an *archaic* perspective, feathers and leaves, wings and branches, feet and roots, eggs and fruit. Certain Persian stylizations go as far as to confuse the face of one with the profile of the other. The tree and the bird unite together in the coherence of a *learning*, in a perfect circulation of meaning, where all the planes are connected together and integrated.

Beyond their respective identity and common unity, one and other *name God*. From it, they retain the force and the grace, the irradiant verticality, the elusive omnipresence. But the crushing masts of one refuse the material to which it testifies, thus translating by successive gaps the immateriality of the Spirit, while the humility of the other not only recalls the exquisite poverty of the Divine, but proclaims the relationship of the azure blue sky to humus. By naming God, they *say man*. But if the tree shows him what he is, the bird suggests to him what he should be, just as the mirror reflects the image of his real face, when the icon informs him about the face he should become. One and the other are enlighteners of our deep and outer, immediate and perennial reality.

The contemplation of such symbols is not only self-revealing; it is purification, asceticism of the eyes, a meeting of the beauty where the essence is incorporated. It also provokes perpetual wonder, a calm stupor before intelligence, delicacy, the power of things created, the exaltation of an equanimous child discovering that every symbol is poetry. It sharpens the attention and the perspicacity of sight; it results in the awakening, in the discrimination, and the memory of what is to come. The man who contemplates this is endowed with the power of Athena's bird in the sacred olive tree: to see in the night.

19. THE HARMONICS OF UNITY*

As soon as Transcendence—this "hidden treasure" that was hoping to be unburied—emerges on its own and spreads over the contingency, it comes into perspective, condemns itself to limitations, and splits up into series of proliferating contraries. The separating agent that gives the cosmic substance its discontinuous nature signs the gap existing between the Principle and Manifestation. The differentiations arising from the original unique Prototype are these "couples of opposites," these "polarities" cropping up through diversified combinations of elements and energies, creating the gradation of contrasts, the accentuation of dissonance. All the spiritual traditions testify to what is, in fact, just the logical and ineluctable consequence of the disassociation of the One from himself.

But there are two ways of viewing the field of dualities: one consists of seeing divergent and contradictory forces in the "poles"; the other of seeing convergent and complementary forces there. In other words, contraries may be seen as irreconcilable and this perspective leads to modern dualism, which is already seeded in the Christian radicalism that opposes God and the Devil,[1] or they are seen as reconcilable because they are never really separated as in Eastern non-dualism. Here lies all the ambiguity of the contingency, which either allows for scissions to grow and intensify until reality is pulverized, or for them to be overstepped and reintegrated into the supreme Unity.

The man of today has adopted the first of these attitudes, condemning himself to an accrued number of social, racial, political and administrative barriers, religious and intellectual fragmentations, and an increasing complexity that is either broken into anarchic arborescences or artificially maintained in the corset of restrictive measures; and for which the paroxysm, materialized in atomic fission, leads one to believe that the ultimate phase of disjunction from the Principle has been reached. Such demarcations (concrete walls or invisible fences) not only render life intolera-

---

* From *Return to the Essential*, Conclusion.
[1] *Diabolos* comes from *diaballein*, "throw from one side to the other," "separate," "disunite," "divert," and consequently, "slander."

ble—think of the many novels that have chosen incommunicability or loneliness in a crowd for a theme! They also incite permanent and unsolvable conflicts that have been promoted to the rank of normalities that one must adapt to in order to survive. They secrete a climate of hostility and competition that, in the long run, is more sterilizing than stimulating. Yet, it is a fact of life that the deeper one descends into the animal kingdom, the more the behavioral models appear rigid and compartmentalized. On the other hand, the more someone is "cultivated," "civilized," and as a consequence less subject to the pressure of primitive affects, the more he acquires flexibility and availability, the vocation for change, and an open-mindedness toward others.

Torn between contradictions that have become incoherent, modern man can no longer do anything else than submit to them without understanding them or be revolted without changing them. In any case, the only religion left for him is Hazard.[2] However, some discreet hints should lead him to suspect the existence of another order, that of universality. Hasn't he seen growing in his garden, strange exotic plants that he didn't sow, and whose seeds, notwithstanding Customs and borders, had fallen from the wings of a plane soaring up from the antipode? Hasn't he read in society pages the touching examples of conjugal osmosis, poorly hidden behind the mask of complementary neurosis: "He couldn't go on after the death of his octogenarian wife"? And hasn't he ever wondered in which myriad relations his thousands of ancestors are to be found, if through the tangle of genealogical branches, he should ever go back several centuries into his double ancestry? If the Iron Curtain was the atheist version of the iconostasis, the iconostasis itself separates the nave from the sanctuary less than it links Earth to Heaven: the "Holy Gates" guarantee the passage, the icons prepare for the identification. But more than all these examples, the initiatic teachings from Heraclitus to Lao-tzu, to Shankara, from al-Hallaj to Christ, are here to confirm the primacy of union over division, of the One over the multiple.

Only the restoration of such pre-excellence is capable of extracting man from the suicidal situation he has committed himself to.

[2] The words of Ecclesiastes 9:1 can be applied in advance to such an individual: "No man knoweth either love or hatred by all that is before them," and the Koran 92:4, "In truth, all your tendencies are divergent."

*

*   *

The peoples of tradition have always known that man is not isolated from the cosmos, that he is both an integral part and center of it. Everyone who feels a sense of belonging to the family of beasts, trees, and elements also respects and feels a great collaboration with Mother Nature, and has no desire to dominate her.

Ether is this "mercurial oil," this "binder" that harmonizes elements together, contributes to flexibility, unites the top and the bottom, the inner and the outer, eases the sliding of particles over each other, around us and in us. The Fathers of the Church, including Dionysius the Areopagite, extol the "attraction" that holds things together, that creates lively tension from contradictions. For the Chinese, the Tao of Heaven, the Tao of the Earth and the one of Man are the harmonics needed for perfect "spontaneity" and "continuity,"—"the greatest law of the world," according to Lieh-tzu—opening, in perfect balance, communication between the other and me. "The sky, the earth and I have the same roots," declares Seng-chao; "the ten thousand beings and I come from the same substance." "By being both the leaf and the wind" one enters the cosmic dance, the *lila* of Hinduism, the Platonic *paideia*—which is ornamented and brought to life by divine gratuitousness.[3] Even more, man—the microcosm—potentially carries the archetypes of the macrocosm within himself; the body and the spirit of man attract the substances of the universe by reproducing the structures. The Sufi adage: "The universe is a big man and man is a little universe," is expressed in a multitude of languages in the choir of traditions.

In its own way, contemporary science corroborates this intuition when it detects the thermonuclear cinder of the supernova that exploded six billion years ago in our blood's iron. Even more so, man potentially carries within himself the archetypes of the microcosm; and the entire spiritual world is manifested in the physical world. "This one exists in that one with essences, that one exists in this one with symbols, and the entire work of both is one."[4]

---

[3] See Alan Watts, *The Book: On the Taboo Against Knowing Who You Are*, IV, "The World is Your Body," (New York, 1966) and *Nature, Man and Woman*, I, 3, "The Art of Feeling."

[4] Maximus the Confessor, *Mystagogy*, 2.

If in so many "legends"—that is to say in "what you *should* read"—
the gods like themselves in animal clothing, man can likewise dis-
mount from a totem pole or identify himself with a symbolic animal.
The Shaman understands the "language of the birds." In terms that
were already Rousseau-like, Chuang-tzu praises the time when
"humans lived fraternally with animals and belonged to the family
of the ten thousand beings." Such was the native behavior of creatures before barriers were put up, arbitrarily penning them in and
pitting them against each other. Certain wise men could be born of
a flower or grass. By studying "vegetal sensitivity," Jagadas Chunder
Bose detected unusual affinities between man and plants; in particular, we know that plants have a well-developed maternal instinct,
that they suffer when there is suffering nearby, and that they are
happy when approached by someone who likes them. His research
on diverse molecular phenomena proved the existence of a common general property in all living or organic forms of matter. This
absence of hiatus between the kingdoms concerns them even to the
most concentrated degrees, and demonstrates that the Greeks
could have established their origin in stones.[5] If the man of today,
barded with indifference and for whom "anything-other-than-him-
self doesn't exist," has few chances of regaining the state and the
smooth flow of beginnings, the gift of interference, and the *flexibility* that would assure the inner tranquility and the "identity principle" of all things made sensitive to the heart by the absence of the
"ego" and by being present in the present, it is at least possible to
celebrate episodic encounters with nature. This is attempted by
those who, while on vacation, act like clandestine lovers, meeting up
with and merging with nature as soon as they can.

Relearning the art of relationships touches other realms of life.
Let's risk giving a few suggestions here.

It would be salutary, at the social level, to avoid the undefined
fragmentation of city living and its fractional *distractive* enticements:
fragmentation that "divides and conquers," and as a consequence
destroys the soul; salutary to escape both self-destructive isolation—
"it isn't good for man to be alone"—and simple and artificial

---

[5] In the post-Diluvian episode of Deucalion and Pyra, from the play on words *laas*,
"stone" and *laos*, "people."

groups, reassuring caricatures of "spirit families," of "intermediary powers" and of "human communion"; salutary to set aside rapid and general alternatives such as "left and right," and other neurotic dissociations of the same genre. Likewise, at the moral level, it would be a matter of not falling into the trap of "good and bad," by being aware of the relative and fluctuating character of these notions and by remembering that the virtuous one is not so much the one who practices good behavior and ignores the bad, but is the one who maintains the balance between one and the other and draws from the latter's positive charges. Evil is not so much the contrary of good but rather one of its inferior or "ill" degrees. Lastly, because each being is subject to different and differently dosed "tendencies," ethics cannot be a single structure uniformly imposed on all.

As for the inevitable and "blessed suffering," the only fair attitude is the unrestricted *Yes*, the conscious experience of one's emotions, the adherence to a Will that is higher than the ego's. To follow it rather than oppose it, either for the sake of obedience (the religious way) or by equanimity (the sapiential way), is to experience life as it is, and not as one wishes it would be; to become one with the Whole, which *also* implies suffering, to become the Whole.[6]

At the mental level, the unitive attitude can only reject the reign of the *doxai*, "opinions," "prejudices," limited and sectarian "options," any system confined to itself, outside of which there would not be any safety. The existence of international languages such as music, mathematics, or genetics, the recourse to a certain "interdisciplinarity" may already suggest another conception of intellectual relationships. Obviously, this exclusivism should not be replaced with amalgams whose goal is nothing other than the alteration of ever partial truths. One of the great ravages of the unilaterality of the spirit is whichever field it operates in, its strategy always consists of retaining only the positive aspects that it approves of (or the ones that suit it), and the negative aspects of that which it condemns. In this respect, it can never hold any hope for durable and

---

[6] See, for example, Meister Eckhart, *Sermons*, I, 30: "If one thing can make them happy, and another sad, they aren't fair.... You should be steady and firm, that is to say similar in joy and in pain, in happiness and unhappiness." This evangelic stoicism is close to the *Bhagavad Gita*, II, 38; VI, 7; XIV, 24, etc.

satisfying solutions, but only a permanent aggressiveness between the parties present, and in the end the establishment of an intellectual hell.

This intellectual hell originates in Cartesian dualism, heir to Hebrew and Greek dualisms, when the former separates too distinctly the Creator and Creation, and the latter, the world of Ideas and the world of shapes. Such dualism has managed to hypostatize Reason as the only organ of knowledge and measure of each man. The East opportunely reminds us that above Reason, Intuition is the place wherein the conflicts between the rational and irrational, intelligence and the senses are abolished. It reminds us of what all "opinions" have in common: they are partial, based on erroneous or relative perceptions that are only valuable for the one stating them. Indeed, the properties of things are *both* identical and non-identical, homogeneous and heterogeneous; the only veritable solution is found in the "logic of the contradictory." The different "points of view," or *darshanas* in Hinduism, are introduced as more additional visions of a Truth perceived from different angles that complete and fertilize each other without affecting the doctrinal entirety. Only the acceptance of diverse "points of view" allows the consideration of the largest number possible of the different facets of a question or levels of a problem, and guarantees the chances of true tolerance. This is what allowed Ramakrishna to declare: "I accept everything: the supraconscious state, the awakened state, dreams, deep sleep, Brahman, *jiva*, creation; I accept all of that as varied manifestations of the Supreme Being; without which, his integral worth would be diminished. Thus, I accept both the Absolute and the manifestation."[7] All the mystic traditions insist on the idea of the unity of life, of the interdependence of its manifestations and cycles, of the universal interconnection of phenomena. Taoism especially insists on the notion of "fluctuations," resumed by Prigogine in modern science. The *I Ching* is based on the fact that *yes* and *no* continuously follow and replace each other.

Following Westerners, but also Christian Kabbalists and German Romantics—the "philosophers of nature"—holistic thinking rediscovers the same paths: it encompasses and surpasses more than it

---

[7] In a different but similar language, Dogen says, "Even at midnight, daybreak is present; even at the break of day, it is night."

divides and excludes. Once again, it includes the phenomena *and* the Absolute, the multiple *and* the One, the illusionary *and* the Real, sense *and* intuition, nature *and* culture, curses *and* blessings, nuclear fire *and* the Burning Bush.... Abellio's "intellectual yoga" falls within this perspective. The law of the "included third" and the simultaneous states of semi-actualization and semi-potentiation, espoused by Lupasco, also fall within this. Systemic thinking rediscovers that antagonisms are complementary, that the entire universe, in its microscopic and macroscopic aspects, is where these never-ending transmutations of a unique energy, of ever more complex attractions and repulsions occur. It results in the unification of the contradictory aspects of Reality: continuous-discontinuous, separable-inseparable, living-nonliving, permanent-impermanent. It reveals that all phenomena are of a communicative and interactive nature.

*

*　*

That man cannot reconcile himself with his surroundings until he has first reconciled with himself is an obvious truth. The human soul is not only *twofold*, but also multiple, scattered, dispersed. The dissociative and discordant states of the psyche, dual personalities, extreme specializations, and the rupture with the outside world put modern man, despoiled of all transcendent references, in exactly the opposite situation of a unified man.

The alchemical undertaking, as carried out and adapted by "depth psychology," first helps internal contradictions emerge to the conscious, to accept them for what they are, and to integrate them; then, to unite with the feminine inner personality (the *anima*)—because if according to the Taoist formula, "knowing masculinity" is worthwhile, "adhering to femininity" is better.[8] Next follows the realization of the Self, or at least its attempt through individuation, to re-become, at the end of the "coincidence of the opposites," the total Man, the Osiris who beforehand was dismembered. This endeavor of patience allows man to knock down the

---

[8] *Tao te Ching,* XXVIII. Naturally, for a woman, the goal is to bring the *animus* to the conscious.

screen between the conscious and unconscious, and to turn his cross into a center for convergence and reunification instead of using it as an instrument of torture for stretching man in the four directions.

The individual soul and body are not separated; this is proven by the "somatizations" or the suffering from agony.[9] Likewise, in a latent manner, each psyche contains the rest of humanity. This is revealed by all analysis and the discontinuation of projections, as well as by dreams from a transpersonal unconscious. At this same level it becomes possible to surprise the most secret links bonding all beings together without their knowing it. This veritable "mystical participation" guarantees alone the right to be different, as opposed to the massing that drowns the personality in the anonymous, vestibule of the worst servitudes. Listening to the "ancestral memory" will reveal some similar structural dispositions, some archetypes common to the whole of humanity, actualized in the form of symbols, mandalas, ideas, or sentiments. This is the only place where, without indecency, the evoking of an authentic "fraternity" beyond all superficial cosmopolitanism or circumstantial camaraderie is allowed.

The strength of this relationship is such that it assures the harmony between societies that, despite being neighbors, ignore each other. This is the meaning that should be given to the parable of the inhabitants of bordering countries who enjoyed hearing their barking dogs and crowing roosters without ever feeling the need to visit each other.[10] It wasn't indifference, egoism, or suspicion that inspired this as-for-myself attitude (as in the case of those inhabitants living near the river that was the border, who were denounced by Pascal). It was a communion by the highest order, in the sound judgment of non-action and of the Tao, essence of all real social contracts. Each one being in concordance with himself was consequently in concordance with everyone else without needing any special external manifestations.[11]

---

[9] St. Justin: "Since these two components, when separated, do not in any way constitute man, it must be said that only the unity formed by their union deserves to be called a man" (*Fragments*, chap. VIII).

[10] *Tao te Ching*, LXXX.

[11] This was also the inner state of the Thelemites imagined by Rabelais. This ideal society is connected to Heraclitus' "world of the enlightened" and the "communion of the Buddhas" or "saints." In these diverse examples, beings are united by a state of supraconsciousness, where the will of each one is abolished in a unanimous and superior will.

Furthermore, the complementarity of matter and the psyche reveals the energetic expression of a Totality that is spread over the subtle levels. Matter and psyche appear as two aspects of a reality that is one and the same; the psyche being defined as a quality of the matter, the latter as the concrete aspect of the psyche. Therefore, substance and conscience blend, are made up of the same elements. When any archetype becomes especially activated in the unconscious, the synchronistic phenomenon is present for marking the connection between the internal or oneiric events, and the others, external and correspondent to them. The unity is visible, to the world and to the Being, revealing the *Unus Mundus* of medieval authors, the continuum of the Chinese, that Jung resumes in his *Mysterium Coniunctionis* as the sum of all the "primordial causes" that is identified with divine Wisdom. This vision is hardly far from the vision of certain physicists who conceive the material universe as the double of a spiritual universe that is infinitely more vast and original, that could be related some day to the Buddha *acintya*—the "unthinkable," the "inconceivable"—matrix containing in itself the possibility of all the other "points of view" that have not yet occurred on the plane of mental formulation.[12]

At the very heart of the matter recent explorations have revealed other conciliations, such as the one of waves and corpuscles, in which one aspect or another prevails according to the situation. The "inseparability" of phenomena illustrates the fact that although very distant, these phenomena can act among themselves as if there was no distance between them. It makes you wonder whether, at a certain level of the Real, instantaneous relationships exist between all the points in the universe. The acknowledged absence of separation between the observer and the object being observed, the psychic "collapse" that takes place at the level of observation and interpretation of the phenomenon signals and underscores the role of interferences: subject and object vibrate with the same electrons. For modern science as for ancient cosmology, the world, just like man, is this *and* that. So, the particles are both destructible and indestructible; matter is both continuous and discontinuous; energy and matter are different faces of an identical phenomenon;

---

[12] "If the spirit lives peacefully within the One, the dueling views will disappear by themselves," declares Seng-ts'an (*Hsin-Hsin-Ming*, 5).

space and time become the quadri-dimensional space-time *continuum*. The atomic theory even manages to go beyond the opposites of existence-inexistence, because the particle, model of probability, ends up being neither present nor absent. This rejoins the "quantum *koan*" familiar to Frithjof Capra, and lets us say that if God is not French, he has every chance of being Japanese!

As the *Dharmadhatu* of Mahayana Buddhism, which represents the universe as an immense group of crystals where each one reflects the others, the unifying regard rediscovers once again a cosmos where all the events are interdependent, an organic Whole, woven with exchanges.

*
*   *

The imbrications displayed by psycho-physical planes are only the shadow of the spiritual planes for which the sage is our truest image. He is in fact, "free from the pairs of opposites," the *dvandva*—hot-cold, pleasure-pain, praise-blame, victory-defeat, honor-dishonor—and bearer of the knowledge that consists of seeing in beings and things the expression of the unique and indivisible Being. He is the one who achieves perfect equanimity between the inner and the outer, the relative and the absolute, good and evil, *Samsara* and *Nirvana*. He is the one who "loves his neighbor as himself," because he is this neighbor, and the latter—angel or serpent—is himself.[13] He is the one who joins within himself the two seas, fresh water and seawater, that are the celestial and terrestrial worlds; the one who achieves the identity of the individual (*jiva*) and of the universal Soul (*Purusa*), and, if he is Hindu, he can say with Shankara: "I am Shiva," or if Christian, with Meister Eckhart: "The eye that I see God with and the eye that God sees me with are one and the same."

The divergences between theologians and the differences in degrees between divine messages can be counted; it is nonetheless true that there are obvious similarities between Christianity's "iconic man," Hinduism's "liberated while living," the "burning man" in

---

[13] To the Evangelical precept will be added Ramakrishna's words: "None is other than you." The sage of Dakshinesvar illustrated this in concrete terms the day he saw a farmer beating an ox and his back began to bleed. This explains the connection with the stigmata of the saints in Western Christianity.

192

the Kabbalah, the Great Vehicle's "Awakened," Sufism's "man of light," and Taoism's "transcendent man." While the roads differ, they do not diverge; spiritual fulfillment is at the end: the fulfillment of the highest human potentialities in the same ascending movement, the manifestation of a sovereign vocation, *deification.* Through time and space, in spite of the differences in mentalities, languages, and spiritual techniques, such men have transcended the realm of forms and appearances, have passed from the multiple to the One, from the particular to the universal, from obscurity to light.

Just as there is no absolute separation between the demons and the gods—Prajapati, their father, could not distinguish between the *deva*s and *asuras*—and just as demons can serve men while at the same time appearing hostile, there isn't any more of an absolute separation between the gods and men, on whom the gods can play cruel tricks. The Vedic *rishi*s identified themselves with the invoked god to the point of taking his name; and with their devotion and austerity, the ascetics acquire powers that make them equal to Indra. As for the Supreme Being, he enters the sidereal night that separates him from the human condition to clothe himself with the latter by becoming incarnate; his only goal is to let man recover the divine state. Eastern Christianity evokes the notion of "synergy" and the collaboration between man and God to continually create the world. With his habitual boldness, Meister Eckhart assures that truly perceiving the omnipresence of God would allow receiving communion with the Body of Christ with unconsecrated bread.

The totality of the Real is composed of an undefined group of "planes" and multiple "states" of being, none of which is absolutely material or immaterial, but all of which are made from vibratory differences. "Noumena," "Gods," and "Archetypes" constitute what could be called the structures of the Essence, the architecture of the Invisible that props up, supports, and provides the framework for the manifested world, in the unity of a systemic thinking that is refound within each theology. Thus, in the enunciation of the Trinity, Basil of Caesarea and Maximus the Confessor show that *three* is not a number: the divine Persons are not added up, they exist in each other. There is a circulation of Unity, *perichoresis*, where each Person only exists by its relationship to the others. "Even if the

Divinity, which is beyond all, is celebrated by us as Trinity and as Unity, it is neither the three nor the one that we consider to be numbers."[14]

The fusion without confusion of the divine planes attests in Hinduism that the "three thousand and three gods" are one in the same God, that the Ishvara of dualities and the Supreme Brahman are not totally distinct. God is personal as he is impersonal; he manifests himself in the theophanies, but he is also "undifferentiated." In the Kabbalah, each *Sephirah* contains the impulse of its opposite contribution; in each one, the other *Sephiroth* are implicated, all of which become integrated in the One that is but one. The Spirit is transcendent to everything: therefore, it is the *Ein Soph*; but it circulates throughout all: it manifests itself through the *Sephiroth*, it lives inside everything and is immanent and omnipresent as the true Presence, the *Shekhinah*. The Spirit is at the same time above, that is to say, beyond categories and accidents, limitations and forms, and, with divine Energies, it influences the web of created things. In the same manner, the "divine Qualities" of Sufism and the "uncreated Energies" of Orthodoxy are distinct from the Essence, while at the same time they cannot be detached from it.

Any integrated polarity can only be so by a third term, the reconciling *tertium*, to which the traditions clearly and implicitly refer. It would be easy to evoke the triads that populate the cosmological, mystical, and metaphysical spheres, such as the sacrificial Victim, the Sacrificer, and the Sacrifice; the Loved One, the Lover, and Love; or yet, the Known, the Knower, and Knowledge. Easy to recall as well that in Hebraic esotericism, the two organizing Principles of created Existence, Rigor (*Din*) and Mercy (*Hesed*), become synthesized in the "mediatory Column" (*Tiphereth*). Easy in short, to multiply the scriptural quotations. Thus, for us to be able to hold onto two traditions seemingly very far apart, Christianity says: "The One starts off because of its fulfillment; two is overstepped because divinity is beyond all opposition; perfection is accomplished in three, who is the first to surpass the composition of two." And Taoism says:

---

[14] Maximus the Confessor, *On Divine Names*, 13. Likewise, Basil of Caesarea, *Treatise on the Holy Ghost*, 18: "We do not count by addition, by starting at Unity to end up at plurality." The qualified notion of numbers, which belonged to the Pythagoreans and the Chinese, as well, was transposed for Christianity.

"Tao begets the One, the One begets the two, the two begets three."
While syncretism is the arbitrary and hasty connection of apparent
resemblances between religions, even adds by that to confused
thinking as it caricatures universality, synthesis proceeds by unifying
convergences and concentric radiances in the core of the Unity. In
a more colorful way, syncretism may be portrayed as plucking the
petals (the exoteric aspects) off several flowers (the religions) to
make up an artificial and deceptive bouquet, whereas synthesis
gathers pollen (esotericism) to make honey. Synthesis refers to the
premier origin of the different religions, going back to the supreme
principle that is anterior and common to all of them: the *Sanatana
Dharma* of the Hindus, which has remained integral and unchanged
through cyclical perpetuity, or even, the kingdom of Melchizedek,
corresponding to the "primordial Tradition." This, we have seen, is
the direct emanation from the point of invariability where the mentally formulated divergences and limitations of a theological nature
are dissolved. It is the place of supreme Reconciliation. From this
area, the "gift of languages," which finds its infrahuman parody in
the Tower of Babel, is unfurled. We remember, as a matter of fact,
that "in the beginning, all men formed a unique people and had
the same language," but Babel came to consecrate the multiplication and confusion of languages, consecrating in this way those of
the diverse religions: separated from each other because separated
from their origins, they became reciprocally incomprehensible. We
know that inversely, Pentecost reestablished the comprehension of
languages among men "filled with the Holy Ghost." This first figu-
ration of the Unity lost, then found, will savor its complete fulfillment at the end of time, when, according to Revelation, "the men
of all nations, all tribes, all peoples and all languages" worship the
Lamb "in a single voice."

At this level the Spirit "breathes wherever he pleases"; he who is
no more here than there and whose essence is free, spontaneous,
ubiquitous, fluid, plural. Also, at this level, each religion forms a sovereign symphony with the other ones, completing one another, presenting themselves in different manners, all of them refusing the
obtuse rigidity of institutional monolithism as well as the whining of
a shattered multiplicity, so as to fuse together without becoming
confused in the Unity; the Unity that is filled with the people of the
possible, scintillating with diversity like a palace with walls of
beveled mirrors, where the inside and the outside, the top and the

bottom, gnosis and faith are in the Whole. Here is where all the mystics gather together to drink the same wine from the same goblet; here it is possible to comprehend the words of Ibn Arabi: "My heart can take any shape. It is a prairie for gazelles, a monastery for Christian monks, a temple for idols, the Ka'aba for pilgrims, the tables for the Torah, and the Koran. I profess the religion of Love, and whatever direction its camels take, Love is my religion and my faith."[15]

*
*   *

Do we really need to point out that with the contingent world being the reflection of the "Order from above," the rejection of this "Order"—because man is free to conform to it or dismiss it—can only lead to the destruction of the reflection itself without affecting the "Order" at all? The only solution is in accepting this obvious fact and rediscovering this "Order," which is the one of the Unity.

Since there is a "Unity of Essence," the horizontal involvement of the created in the created is completed and perfected in the vertical involvement of the particular in the Universal, of the creature in the Creator, of the human in the Divine. Such universality not only allows for the "lowering of customs barriers": it is the surest guarantee of taking root; it maintains the stimulating and saving ambiguity that makes mathematicians suspect that two parallel lines will eventually meet somewhere, and wonder if the sage is a man or a butterfly; it creates compensatory equilibrium, repeated alternations, which draw their permanence from their fragility, and from their fresh start, their newness; it is what casts transcendence into the world. If anything is marked with the seal of universality, it is first and foremost the universe surrounding us, that penetrates us and that we are. It is incumbent on the new generations to set off on the quest, by remembering the ancient watchword: *Contraria sunt complementa*. It is here that the reversal of the outlook, the recovering of an inclusive and concordant being become possible again; here that *the return to the Essential consists essentially in a return to Unity*.

---

[15] *Tarjuman al-ashwaq*, XI. In a stronger apophatic tonality, Jalal ad-Din Rumi says in his *Diwan*: "I am neither Christian nor Jew, neither Zoroastrian nor Muslim; I am neither from the East nor the West, neither from the earth nor the sea.... only One I seek, only One I know, only One I see, only One I name."

Recovering Unity requires first of all recovering Simplicity, the one where a mountain reappears as a mountain, where drawing water from a well becomes marvelous, where saying yes to the obvious means saying an unrestricted Yes to the Whole. Simplicity where human nature and great Nature come to meet in the light of a superior ecology; Simplicity of *daily living* relieved of the superfluous, open to the vast breath of eternal nature; who teaches that in life, density is more important than volume; that desires the creation of small communities with simple decentralized structures, where men can acknowledge and call each other, put a name to a face and enjoy conviviality. Simplicity of *intellectual living*, which discourages dialectic reasoning, book-like stacking, heavy mental machinery that, while complicating the simple, does not brighten the obscure; the establishment of a mental emptiness that assumes the fullness of paradisiac transparence where man ceases reflecting with his human thinking so he can reflect the divine Thinking within. Simplicity of *spiritual living*, free from the scaffolding of misunderstood dogmas and by that, contradictory, and free from moral and scheming hardening; once again enriched by the universal Gnosis of "absolute beginnings," where the invocation of the divine Name condenses all liturgy and theology, for which the fervent and continuous perfecting with the repetition of the same syllables, far from eroding the language, on the contrary, energizes, revives it and makes it sacred. Three simultaneous phases that make the universe once again human and suitable, where the ambiance, lifestyle, attitude, and inner practices are indissociable; three phases that are the Path.

This return to Unity is an obvious return to the Essential. And it is this return to the Essential that will make it possible for the Essential to return.

V

Philosophia Perennis

20. Approach to Esotericism[*]

First we need to determine, on the one hand, the method of apprehending Truth, or if preferred, the organ of this knowledge, and on the other hand, the language used for expressing this Truth in the least inadequate terms.

The modes of the metaphysical approach can be divided into three ways: the way of mental, didactic, and conceptual *Reason*, which speculative philosophies and rational theologies assume;[1] the way of *Faith*, which consists of believing without any pre-established proof or need for understanding, and with a spontaneous and unconditional act of membership from which exotericism originates;[2] and lastly, the way of *Gnosis*, direct, immediate, intuitive, inspired by "transcendent Intellect," and from which esotericism originates. The *intellectus* of the medieval Scholastic—equivalent to the *nous* for the Greek Fathers, to the *buddhi* in Hinduism, to the *ruh* for the Sufis—supra-individual and supra-rational by nature, uncreated in its immutable essence, but created as the first cosmic entity, resides in the soul of man and allows him to reach "The One with neither modalities nor properties." It is "the spirit's fine point," the "spark of the soul," the inalienable center, bearer of all knowledge, the human reflection of the divine Logos. It is the organ that receives the Truth and transmits it to the levels of consciousness, similar to a mirror that, reflecting the Supreme Being, does not have to demonstrate it. In it, the subject is the object, and vice versa; the reason for the obviousness of certainty, direct participation of the conscious of the Absolute. The human subject is just the veil that separates the Self from itself; in this sense it is illusion. The behavior of Intellect lets the ego be extinguished in the Self; it does not follow the meanders of reasoning, it short-circuits thinking in a spiritual flash of lightning.[3] It opens wide in wonder the eyes of the

---

[*] From *Passports for New Times*, II, 3.

[1] As the existence of God is demonstrated by Saint Anselm in *Monologion*: We have the idea of a perfect being; and yet, absolute perfection implies existence; therefore the perfect being exists.

[2] This is the *Credo quia absurdum* attributed to Augustine.

[3] The "wink" of God is symbolized by this flash of lightning (Koran, 54:50).

Apostles, witnesses of the glory of Christ on Mount Tabor;[4] it allows Arjuna to see, with the help of the "third Eye," Sri Krishna in his cosmic reality;[5] and once more, it activates the "inspiration" of *satori*, the sudden intuition born of the intemporal center, of the ray of universal Intelligence linking man to the Deity.

In contrast with simple conceptual reason, Intellect provides new distinctions between exotericism and esotericism. Although exotericism is no stranger to the *visitations* of the Intellect, its tendency is to ignore it or to confuse it with something "created." While exotericism contents itself with formal Intelligence (which often runs the risk of degenerating into intellectualism), and with discursive reason conditioned by its own objects (partial truths which mutually exclude themselves), esotericism, on the contrary, fully recognizes Intellect as informal intelligence that sustains it and makes it exist. Without a doubt, exotericism is quick to accuse the one who refers to the intellective way as "*intellectual* arrogance," confusing the two levels into one, which is its own. Yet, the "mental state" still only represents the ego, in contrast with the "heart," the center of esoteric Knowledge. Moreover, the receptiveness of the Self is correlative to the practice of "virtues," such as humility, reducer and destroyer of the ego. In this way, the reproach of arrogance disappears by itself.[6] For exotericism, there is this imperfect, impure, ephemeral but real world, and there is a God as Demiurge and Divine Person, considered only in his relationship with the created, not in His total and infinite Reality, and who annihilates everything that is not Him. On the contrary, for esotericism, this world is only a "cosmic illusion," appearance, quasi-nothingness. Lastly, while exotericism reveals the Supreme Being with the help of faith and reason, by resorting to the cataphatic theology that enumerates the different attributes or predicates of God, as do Saint Anselm or Saint Thomas,[7] esotericism reveals, on the contrary, by the intermediary of Intellect, that which corresponds to the Non-Being or

---

[4] Matt. 17:2-3; Mark 9:2-4; Luke 9:29-33.

[5] *Bhagavad Gita*, XI, 8, and following.

[6] René Guénon wrote: "It would truly be a show of singular arrogance to deny the existence of the value of individuality under the pretext that it means nothing to the Principle" (*Initiation and Spiritual Realization*).

[7] For Aquinas, the "negative way" is only a complement to the "affirmative way," or kataphatic way, tending to avoid the anthropomorphism attributed to God.

the ontological Supra-Being, the ineffable and indescribable Divinity, infinitely beyond the Supreme Being, and containing it. For this, it resorts to apophatic and antinomic theology, the "negative way" of Plotinus, Dionysius the Areopagite, Gregory Palamas, Meister Eckhart and the Vedantins: Reality is beyond all determination, qualification, or affirmation; it is supreme Impersonality and Monad.

*

* *

The method of expression used by esotericism for translating divine realities is and can only be symbolism, insofar as the symbol is the least inept for giving an explanation. In the name of the analogy between macrocosm and microcosm, and of the identity of their elements and structures, the reality of a certain order can be represented by that of a lower order, while the inverse is impossible since the symbol should be more accessible than what it represents. It allows for different superposed or interwoven interpretations, which are always coherent and complementary, equally true according to the conceivable points of view of a synthetic nature, and totalizing inasmuch as all symbols simultaneously possess both a positive and a negative pole.[8] It can be said that symbolism is the natural and universal expression of the "intelligible": natural because it lives in the nature of things, that is to say, in real analogies; universal because it is sensitive to multiple and unlimited applications in all orders of Reality.

While exotericism places itself more in the historicity of events—thus the endless sterile questions concerning the "facts" of the life of Christ and his "miracles"—esotericism, without denying the literalness of the texts, goes infinitely beyond the *basic form*, and instead of confining itself to the short-sightedness of exegesis and erudition, captures the iridescence of a symbolic reading.[9] Esotericism knows that "the letter kills" and that "the Spirit invigorates"; it

[8] For example, the Serpent in Genesis will symbolize Evil as a dividing principle born of the "tamasic" depths of the earth; the Serpent coiled around the cross will symbolize Christ the Savior.

[9] Thus, when exotericism reads, "In the beginning," it *understands*: "At the beginning of time"; esotericism *interprets*: "In the Principle" (of the eternal One).

knows from the *Zohar* that the one who "thinks the meaning of the stories in the Scriptures can only be literal is cursed." Reducing these sacred texts to this meaning is to ignore the unfathomable richness of their semantic stratifications and radiance, and in so doing, limits oneself to a platitude that relativizes these texts, reduces them to the level of profane texts, and condemns them to a decline and a weakening that sides with adverse forces.

From that moment on, when symbolism is no longer *there* to design through "mountains" and "rivers," *here* for divine elevation and majesty, the unrecognizable part of the Divine, or *there* for the current of multiple things and creatures, and reason no longer sees anything other than the geological concretions and the flow of rivers to be traced on a map, what can one still grasp from the meaning of Mount Horeb, the Sinai, and the four sources of Paradise in relation to the four "Aspects" of Yahweh, the four cardinal points, and the four elements? From that moment on when symbolism is no longer there to make one understand that "honey" and "wine" refer to the mystic gentleness and intellectual exhilaration of Fulfillment, and reason no longer sees anything other than consumer products included in a "politico-economical context," what can one still understand of Love and Knowledge? From that moment on, when symbolism is no longer there for expressing now and then the fundamental tendencies of human beings through "animals," or sometimes, with gazelles, the contemplative "stations," or with cows, the ecstatic "radiance," and reason no longer sees anything other than simple animal motifs for ornamental value, what else is one condemned to, by laughing at the "naïveness of the Scriptures," than to laugh at one's own foolishness? From that moment on, when symbolism is no longer there to show that the "characters" on stage represent the different aspects, the polarities and states of the conscious of the inner man, and reason no longer sees anything other than legendary heroes, what role can be attributed to Jacob and the Angel, to Cain and Abel, or to these "kings of Edom" who are, in the Jewish faith, none other than the "animic" demonstrations of cycles prior to *Fiat Lux?* From that moment on, when symbolism is no longer there to discern, in the fire of Hell, the "samsaric" desire to plunge once again into the cycle of birth, and reason no longer sees anything other than a furnace kindled by horned devils, what chance is there of being able to understand anything about the transmigration of psychic elements and the "combustion" that kindles the craving for the current of forms?

The hermeneutics or symbolic exegesis of the Scriptures is in every tradition. In Christianity, Dionysius the Areopagite, Saint Gregory of Nyssa, Maximus the Confessor constantly resorted to it. For Thomas Aquinas, the Holy Scriptures conceal a literal or historic sense, a moral sense, an analogical sense, and an allegorical sense.[10] Patristic literature abounds in interpretations of the same nature: the ascension of Moses recounts the different stages from the mystic to God; the Song of Songs celebrates the marriage of the soul and the Lord God. For Saint Teresa of Ávila, the "interior castles" indicate the degrees of prayer. A similar symbolism is found in *The Ascent of Mount Carmel* by Saint John of the Cross, in Dante's *Divine Comedy*, in the Treatises and Sermons by Eckhart, in the Commentaries by Saint Bonaventura or by Richard of Saint Victor. Only exotericism, allied with discursive reason, can see contradictions in the sacred texts and provide no answers in the face of atheism's allegations. These contradictions are not on the side of Truth, but on the side of human receptacles; they appear more numerous and serious as one distances oneself from Truth by the simultaneous oversight of symbolism and Intellect. The explanation for these contradictions is based on the fact that some stem from the historicity of facts, and others from their symbolism.[11]

Without excessively covering the chapter on esoteric interpretations, we will add some examples to those we have already cited here or there. The seven days in the Book of Genesis, in relation to the seven "constructive *Sephiroth*," the seven Heavens, the seven Earths, the seven Hells, the seven judgments naturally indicate an

---

[10] Dante admits, likewise, four meanings in the Scripture (*Il Convivio*, II, 1), that correspond to the ones recognized by Islamic esotericists in the Koran (*zahir, batin, hadd, muttala*).

[11] As an example, we will use two stories from the Book of Genesis; in the first one, man is created after all the other creatures; in the second, he is created before them, in the Garden of Eden. In reality, it must be understood that the first story follows the historical order of the facts: the chaos, the stars, the plants, the animals, and man; the second story follows the divine order: man is the first born, not in the temporal and chronological order but in the metaphysical order, as the synthesis of all creatures and the most perfect manifestation, the being in the highest position on the scale of created beings, as much in this world (animal, vegetable, or mineral kingdoms) as in the other (the angelic hierarchies who are not free to choose or refuse God).

unspecified duration, much more significant than a week, if one remembers that "a thousand years are a day for the Lord God."[12] Naming, as Adam did, the animals in Paradise, signifies that he acknowledges their essence, because the *name* of a being indicates who he is, in contrast with his *form*, which is linked to appearances. Forbidding man "to eat from the Tree of the Knowledge of Good and Evil" is a direct allusion to otherness, separateness, the knowledge of things in the diversity and multiplicity of their appearance, in contrast with the knowledge of things in the metaphysical unity of their essence. In fact, it is the duality symbolized by such a Tree and the revelation of the one who eats its fruit, thus leading to the state of "falling," which opposes rather than unites, separates rather than reconciles.[13] By tasting the multiple, the illusionary, the ephemeral, man destines himself to separation and death. Clemency is succeeded by Rigor, The One by scission and fragmentation, the continuous by the discontinuous, paradisiac intellectuality by mental, sensory, discursive reflection; or in Hindu terms, the *Kali Yuga* succeeds the *Satya Yuga*. In the original Paradise, Adam corresponds to the integral manifestation of *Metatron*, the "cosmic Intellect," united with Eve, who corresponds to the Personification of *Avir*, the pure and universal Substance, in the light of the "divine Presence," *Shekhinah*. They acted there as the active and enlightening Principle, and as the receptive and generating Principle. "Adam's sleep" illustrates the idea that, to achieve metaphysical Knowledge, man must die in the world of appearances. Eve is created from Adam's rib;[14] this means that woman is of the same essence as man; she represents Life (*Havah*). Adam can only reach the Knowledge of his own reality through death—"deep sleep"—his own death. From the moment when this unseparated separation becomes an actual separation, everything starts going wrong for

---

[12] The seventh day corresponds to the Sabbath, that is to say, to a day of rest, to the return of the Principle; in Hindu terms, the end of a *Manvantara*.

[13] Add to this that Adam's *dualistic* act was going to initiate the unlimited series of all the dissociations, up to and including, in the modern era, nuclear disintegration—volatilization of cosmic matter, which Oppenheimer identifies with the "work of the devil"—and in inverse analogy, cancer—this disorganized cellular proliferation within the human body.

[14] *Tsél'a* in Hebrew means "rib" but also "side," which once again cuts short any pathetic joking to which we are accustomed.

Adam and Eve, for their descendants, and for the whole of cosmic manifestation. By leaving this spiritual union, by abandoning divine Immanence in favor of "knowing each other," Man's substantial nature was stripped of its beatific Light, "denuded" in its subtle and corporeal differentiations.

The rejection of esotericism by Christians not only deprives them of the esotericism of the Old Testament, but with a logical continuation, of that of the New Testament. This gives rise to irreparable shortcomings: faced with materialistic arguments, the explanations given solely by exotericism present either a poor defense or none at all, at least in the debate concerning the historicity of Christ. Is it not a matter of wanting to deny the human existence of Christ, which by the way, is upheld by explicit and implicit evidence; but it is certain that the symbolic reading of the life and the *chanson de geste* of Christ reveals many more interpretations in its transhistoric and, so to speak, "mythical" dimension (without any pejorative nuances). The birth of the Savior will be seen as that of the Holy Infant, or of the Self, in the cavern of the heart. The arrival of the Three Kings will reveal the manifestation of the three "supreme functions" which are those of Agarttha as the initiatic hierarchy and receptacle of the primordial Tradition. The Cross will be, on the one hand, the Realization of "Universal Man," as the perfect communion of the totality of the states of a being, in the sense of "ampleness" (that is to say a certain degree of determined existence, according to the integral extension of individuality in its different modalities), and in the sense of "exaltation" (that is to say in the hierarchical superposition of the multiple states of a being); it will be, on the other hand and at the same time, the image of the union of complementaries, corresponding to the primordial "Androgyne," and of the "resolution of the opposites" in perfect balance and in the supreme Emptiness. According to the same point of view, the "end of the world" will be interpreted in the sense of the goal that the universe strives for: consequently, it is a question of achievement, of a transfiguration, of a passage from the physical mode to the spiritual mode.

These few lines suffice to show that the *demythologizing* inaugurated by modernistic Christianity, which does not have the slightest idea of symbolism, deprives itself of such riches and broadened points of view. In this way, only a literal interpretation, and therefore solely exoteric, of the Gospel authorizes a *socialist* reading of the Christlike message. Undoubtedly, it is not a matter of denying the "social doctrine" of the Church, any more than making Christ the spokesman of the "rich" against the "poor": that would be falling into a dualism contrary to the other and just as erroneous. In fact, if God is not French, He is not of any particular class either: He does not address the citizens of the terrestrial City, or potential voters, or "the most disadvantaged socio-professional categories"; He addresses all beings who, each and every one, reflect Him here below with a touching awkwardness, and represent Him in their own way, invariably in a fledgling manner.

Having said this, we might emphasize that, even in the literal sense, the texts must not make Christ out to be the defender of the proletariat and working masses. When the Three Kings present the Holy Infant with gifts of gold, frankincense and myrrh, it is not clear how this homage to the East—which is a noteworthy Indo-European element at the very heart of the Semitic context—would exclude material riches. At the other extremity of his terrestrial course, when the body of Christ is requested for burial, it is a "rich man," Joseph of Arimathaea, member of the Sanhedrin, who comes to beg Pilate for it, whereas the multitude had demanded the liberation of Barabbas and the crucifixion of Christ. It may be asked how Christ showed himself to be truly "charitable" when, tempted by Satan, he refused to turn stones into bread, refusing in this way to solve the economic problem and wipe "the sweat from the brow"; or again, when he teaches that "man shall not live by bread alone, but by every word that proceedeth out of the mouth of God"—even though this bread is described as "supra-essential" and is not assimilated here to material nourishment, but to the Eucharist.[15] How does Christ show himself to be truly "charitable" when accepting the "very precious perfume" that a woman pours over his head? In answer to those who become indignant due to this "waste" and think that the profit from the sale of the perfume should have been given to the poor, he replies: "For ye have the poor always with you."[16] How does Christ

[15] The Latin text mentions the "daily bread"—*panem cotidianum* (Matt. 6:11), and the "supra-essential bread"—*panem supersubstantialem* (Luke 11:3), even though the Greek text only mentions this last one—*ton arton épiousion*.

[16] Matt. 26:11. This doesn't mean that one should remain insensitive to human distress: "Thou shalt open thy hand wide to thy brother, to thy needy, and to thy poor" (Deut. 15:11), which is not easy if one believes the story of the young notable (Matt. 19:22).

show himself to be truly "charitable" in the parable of the winemakers, where the laborers who worked one hour receive the same salary as those who worked all day;[17] or in the parable of the lost sheep, where for one sheep alone, the good priest abandons the entire flock?[18]

On the other hand, the esoteric approach to the Gospel would permit coming to the deepest meanings, and would certainly have nothing more to do with any ideological interpretation. Here again, several examples will be sufficient. The massacre of the innocents, presented as humble victims of the dominant class, would have been understood to be, in reality, the killing of the innumerable fake "egos" of man, in order to let the Self appear in the form of the Holy Infant. The Miracle at Cana would not only transform water into wine—the wine of the workers—but would manifest the metamorphosis of humanity, or of exotericism, into the wine of divine Knowledge, esotericism, as blood, fire, and secret. The return of Christ as a thief would not assimilate the latter to the dropouts forced to steal in order to survive, but would allow the understanding that Christ will return again at night—at the "end of time"—when people will have forgotten about it. The resurrection of the dead would no longer be interpreted as the awakening of the proletariat, to correspond to the manifestation of the "glorious body"—the *sambhoga-kaya* in Buddhism—at the end of a cyclical revolution.[19] As for Christ expelling the merchants assimilated with "capitalists" from the temple, one would read that such an action targets not so much the merchants as the animals they sell for sac-

---

[17] Matt. 20:1-16. The meaning of the parable becomes quite clear if, in leaving behind the literal sense for the symbolic sense, one understands: 1) that the eleventh-hour worker indicates the one who has converted to God in the last moments of his life; and 2) that this worker represents the humanity of late, saved by achieving the "tenth of the Law."

[18] Matt. 28:12-14. The meaning of the parable is clear, if one understands, on the symbolic level that, in order to save humanity (the lost sheep), Christ momentarily abandons all cosmic manifestation (the other ninety-nine sheep) by incarnating himself here below: exemplary pre-eminence of the singular over the collective.

[19] The symbolism of jewels may be remembered on this occasion when, far from manifesting the insolent luxury of the Church (even if it would later fall into the trap), they are supposed to exteriorize and materialize the body of glory and its subtle centers. Likewise, it is too often forgotten that if Christ was crowned with "thorns," he was also crowned with "diamonds," the word *skamir* in Hebrew having both of these meanings.

rifice: by chasing them out, Christ announces an even better sacrifice, his own. The fact that Christ had been a carpenter does not assimilate him to a man of the people: not only is he of royal blood through his ancestor David, without even evoking his divine ascendance through Abraham, but if, as the "man Jesus," he sets girders—probable announcement of his own cross—as God, he symbolically arranges the cosmic framework, that is to say the universal manifestation.[20] Finally, if "Paradise belongs to the violent," that does not mean that it belongs to those who, in the name of the proletarian revolution, shed the blood of others rather than their own (contrary to Christ), but to those who, by asceticism, renunciation, purification of themselves, and by vigils, fasting, prayers, and penitence, deserve access to the Kingdom of Heaven.

*

*   *

If, as we have just seen, symbolism truly does exist in Christianity and thus guarantees it an esoteric dimension, do we need to add that it exists just as much, to say the least, in all traditions? One guesses the considerable interior enrichment derived from studying it if we look at it from the perspective of a doctrinal formation. Here again, a limited number of examples, waiting to be broadened and borrowed exclusively from Sufism and Hinduism, will be sufficient.

Sufism abounds in symbolic readings of the Koranic verses and the *ahadith*, or words attributed to the Prophet. What can be understood of any of them if they are taken literally? Will anything other than the fables born of imaginative brains be seen? So, the tradition teaches that God first created the Calamus (*Qalam*), the Guarded Tablet (*Lawh al-mahfuz*), and the Throne (*Arsh*); the Ink (*Midad*) flowed from the Calamus and drew the Letters (*Huruf*), thus writing the destiny of the creatures. Fifty thousand years later, God created the Heavens and the Earth. Five Archangels (*Mala'ikatu*) surround his Throne, which sits on the Waters: *ar-Ruh, Jibra'il, Mika'il, Israfil,* and *Izra'il.* Only the esoteric interpretation will provide satisfactory commentaries that can be summarized as follows: the Calamus is

---

[20] *Hyle* in Greek means both "tree" and "matter," and consequently "substance," in the philosophical sense of the term. As a cosmic carpenter, Christ can be assimilated to the *Vishvakarma* in Hinduism, "the Spirit of universal Construction."

the "first divine autodetermination" with the idea of Creation, the Principle of universal manifestation; the Tablet indicates the universal Possibility formed by the "Names" (*Asma*) or the divine "Aspects," the "Substance," both naturing and natured Nature; the Throne corresponds to the immutable Transcendence, to the informal Manifestation, to the ontological Principle; the Ink, to the initial and undifferentiated possibility of manifestation; the Letters, to the undefined differentiation of the Ink in creatures, starting with their prototypes. The fifty thousand years symbolically indicate the incommensurability between the principial order and the manifested order, and the transcendence of the Calamus and the Tablet in comparison with the result of their "common action"; the Heavens and the Earth signify, likewise, informal manifestation and formal manifestation; the Waters are the cosmic possibilities; the Archangels, the divine "functions": *ar-Ruh* is the "Spirit," the Creator Principle that manifests Light; *Mika'il*, the Lord of rain and harvest; and *Israfil*, Lord of Resurrection; *Jibra'il* is the Lord of Revelation; *Izra'il*, Lord of Death.[21] In numerous esoteric Islamic texts, one symbol returns frequently. It is the one of the Veil (*Hijab*), which indicates the mystery surrounding Divinity, the cosmic Illusion that hides Him from looks while also revealing Him, filtering as such the divine Light, which Quintessence (*Lubab*) contrasts with, as the interior contrasts with the exterior. A certain *hadith* by Seyyidna Muhammed, which mentions "women, perfume and prayer made worthy of love," will be interpreted in this way: women translate the formal projection of Interiority, spiritual company; perfume, the informal qualities or beauties; prayer, the link between divine Interiority and divine Exteriority.

A poem such as the *Khamriyya* by Omar Ibn al-Farid is an eloquent example of this kind of broadening. "Ecstasy" will symbolize the state of beatitude born from the contemplation of the veritable Existence outside of the futile and illusionary world; likewise, the "taverns" will be the divine Names and Attributes, or even the

---

[21] For further details, see *Dimensions of Islam*, the chapter "*An-Nur*," by Frithjof Schuon. The author establishes relationships between the Calamus and *Purusa* in Hinduism; the Guarded Tablet and *Prakriti-Vikriti*; the Throne and *Buddhi*; *ar-Ruh* and Brahma; *Mika'il-Israfil* and two important aspects of Vishnu: substance and spiritual life; *Jibra'il*, and two important aspects of Shiva: the return to the Principle and destruction.

assemblies of "people of the divine sciences," the "torch" will be the radiance of Light, the "fawn," the degree of radiation from the Beloved, the "beauty mark," the Unity of universal Existence. In his *Mantiq at-Tayr*, Farid ad-Din Attar will likewise evoke the "seven Valleys" of the ego to indicate the Search (for God), Love, Knowledge, Detachment, Unity, Astonishment, Annihilation.

Likewise, one sees the *Brahma Sutra* in Hinduism give rise to interpretations of a symbolic nature by the successors of Shankaracharya, as the Dialogues by Plato had done with the Neoplatonists. Along the same line of ideas, one would cite the different interpretations of the *Bhagavad Gita*, which followed one another from Shankara to Aurobindo, according to new intellectual standards and without altering orthodoxy. As a matter of fact, they translate at the same time, both the multiple resources of symbolism in the sacred texts and their inexhaustible riches. It seems that as God slowly reveals himself through time, these texts only reveal the diverse aspects of their contents to successive generations little by little. With the abundance and the complexity of its myths, Hinduism lends itself especially to this kind of deciphering. Such myths can be read at different levels, from that of the human soul to the worlds of the gods and they lend themselves to ritualistic, moral, psychological, cosmogonic, philosophical, and yogic (according to four main types of *yoga*) interpretations. Sri Aurobindo, going beyond the methods of university philology to consult the original archetypes, interprets the war stories and pastoral scenes of the *Veda* as the phenomena and procedures of inner life: the battle between the forces of Light and Darkness, Death and Immortality. The *rishi* Angiras are the ones who bring the (spiritual) Dawn, win Truth; they are the "powers of Agni" (the divine Force); they conflict with Panis, the powers of obscuration, enemies of the supra-conscious Truth. They create Sacrifice, which grants a superior existence. They capture the "Cows," that is to say the enlightening truths of Knowledge, and the "horses," the forces of Dawn. *Soma* (immortal Joy), and the Word (the inspired language that expresses the Truth), help the Angiras in their work. Indra (the enlightened Mental state), accompanied by Sarama, the dog (Intuition), discovers the Cows and frees them.[22]

---

[22] Sri Aurobindo, *The Secret of the Veda.*

We think these examples offer a sufficient sampling of the symbolic attitude to anyone wishing to learn doctrinally and give himself the framework needed when facing the surge of organized subversion. Following this preliminary work, the one who knows how to take the Apocalypse for its true meaning will then need to attend the "unveiling" of different points of the esoteric doctrine and explore the methods of practical realization in order to find the ones most suitable for him.

21. Answers to Some Questions*

"Why is it," one will ask, "that supreme Truth has been fragmented into several religions?" A text in the colorful style of India says, "Knowledge is one, as is the color of milk," but "doctrines are multiple, as are the colors of the coats of cows." Besides the cyclical decline that always distances itself even further from the One by tending towards the multiple, at least two reasons can explain the phenomenon. The first is that any form, any verbalizing restricts, erodes, relativizes the Absolute. Neither vocabularies, nor man's logic are capable of expressing the divine Totality; this explains its explosion and scattering through different Messages. Frithjof Schuon writes: "Absolute Truth is only found beyond all possible expressions; these expressions, as such, would not know how to allege the attributes of this Truth; their relative distancing in relation to the latter is expressed by their differentiation and their multiplicity which obviously limits them." It is a widely known tradition that if God manifested himself entirely all at once, He would reduce the universe to ashes.[1] Thus, all religions are true since they contain elements of Truth, but all of them are partial to the extent that they do not explicitly express the totality of this Truth. None of them are vast enough to account for, on their own, the divine Vastness.

The second reason is that in order to be accepted, Truth is forced to diversify itself by keeping with the times and places, according to the diversity of human receptacles, attitudes, tendencies, spiritual needs of the people it addresses, their ability to comprehend, the requirements and emergencies of the cosmic moment, the general influences of the earth's atmosphere. To use a suggestive image, one might say that the Divine, desiring to describe Himself to humanity, slowly reveals His aspects in the same way that a kaleidoscope, with its colored fragments, offers ever changing designs to the eye. He is the supreme Diamond whose facets will be captured by every tradition, while completely reflecting Him.[2] Thus,

---

* From *Passports for New Times*, III, 1.

[1] "For no man shall see me, and live" (Exod. 33:20). The Koran says likewise that "no sight can reach Him," and the *Chuang-tzu*, that "neither sight nor hearing can reach the Principle."

[2] Translator's Note: As with a diamond which turns under the light, at any one time, some facets will reflect completely while others reflect less. Each of the traditions reflects Him completely although in their different ways.

Christianity will insist more specifically on Love and Incarnation, Islam on divine Unity, Submission, and Generosity, Buddhism on Emptiness, Suffering, and Impermanence, Hinduism on Sacrifice, the distinction of the Real from Illusion, Taoism and Zen on Purity and Simplicity.

Concerning the contradictions that exotericism does not explain and that atheism greatly takes advantage of, we would like to add this. These false questions that the man of the *Kali Yuga* cannot avoid encountering on his path, only exist, in fact, at the level of formal crystallizations, distorting refractions, due to the insufficiency of human language. The theological points of view are only the detailing of the metaphysical point of view; they are the result of affective and mental exotericism.[3] The contradictions they include are reduced at the esoteric level. Let's offer some examples.

Is there only one God, as some religions affirm, or several, as affirmed by others?—First, it must be understood that the first ones insist on the Unity of the Spirit, while the others appear more sensitive to the different aspects or manifestations of the unique Principle. Hinduism has thirty million gods, but over them all, it proclaims only one; the Supreme Brahma, "the One second to none"; inversely, Judaism talks about *Elohim*, the *Sephiroth*, angelic hierarchies, that Christianity considers to be its own, by adding the Three Persons of the Trinity and the "uncreated Energies" (that it calls "gods"). However, Islam enumerates the unfathomable list of "Qualities" and "divine Names."

Is the world real or unreal?—Religious exotericism proves to be unilateral by affirming the reality of the world in the face of the reality of God. Esotericism will respond, depending on the case, by "yes" or "no" or by "yes and no" or even by "neither yes nor no" but without any Pharisaism. The world is real to the extent that it is the causal, effective, and substantial manifestation of a Principle. Anything perceived by a subject is obviously existent; external objects are as such the matter for cognition. "Non-being" (in the

[3] Geometric symbolism facilitates comprehending that the different traditional ways are comparable to the radiuses of the same circle that unites them at one same point: as the radiuses approach the center, they also approach each other. The center is Intellect; their coming together corresponds to esotericism. To the degree that the radiuses extend toward the perimeter, they distance themselves from the center and at the same time from each other; this distancing and divergence corresponds to exotericism.

sense of "nothingness") can never appear as an objective fact of experience given its internal contradiction. However, the world is unreal in relation to the Absolute, within which it disappears with all the distinctions and limitations woven by Illusion, the magician of appearances. The phenomenal world is unreal to the extent that only the permanent and infinite Absolute is real, and that the world is not the Absolute, but only one of its aspects. In short, if it is not real, the world is not totally unreal either. Real to the extent that the effect (creation) preexists in the cause (the Principle), it is unreal to the extent that the effect is only a manifestation of the cause. Illusion is at the origin of an illusionary world, but by being at the origin of it, it creates it. The world comes neither from pure nothingness, nor true reality; it possesses a relative reality: it *is* not, it *exists* as "*un apparaître de l'Être*" (an appearance of the Supreme Being), according to the penetrating expression of Jean d'Encausse.

Are there several Divine Incarnations or only one?—Each religion proclaims its founder as unique, but there are several religions, therefore, several founders. Christ is unique and he said it as Logos, but the Logos that is unique can also manifest Himself in diverse ways. Either He becomes "Flesh" as in Christianity—and it is perhaps as such that his sacrifice is the greatest, and that this religion benefits from a certain preeminence—or "Law" as in Judaism or Buddhism, "Book" in Islam, "*Avatara*" in Hinduism. Moreover, the latter establishes subtle distinctions between the main *Avataras*, and between these and the minor or partial *Avataras*, sometimes described as *Vibhuti*, everyone who contributes to the enrichment or the clarifying of the *Sophia perennis* as inspired commentators. In this way an entire range of "Messengers" exists, each bearing a varying and differentiating percentage of "Spirit." But the content of the Message is always the same, regardless of the diversity of the languages used or of those who speak it. Therefore, Christianity says that by Incarnation, "God became man so that man becomes God." Hinduism says that "*Atma* becomes *Maya* (in the human form) so that *Maya* (humanity) becomes *Atma*." Islam says that the Real, which expresses the unitarian testimony (the *Shahadah*), descends into the "perishable," becoming the Koran so that the "perishable" can return to the "Face of the Lord of the Worlds." Buddhism says that *Nirvana* manifests itself in the *Samsara* by the intermediary of Buddha Amitabha, so that the *Samsara*—the illusionary, the impermanent—becomes in turn *Nirvana*—the extinction of that which is not.

Is there one life for each man or is there a transmigration of the soul?—As for the preceding questions, one can respond: both, according to the envisaged point of view. There is a unique life to the degree that the "ego" disappears at the moment of bodily death; there is transmigration to the degree that the unpurified psychic elements and the formation of diverse adventitious "personalities" seek physical supports. The central being, for which everything will be different in the new life, transmigrates alone, because the Infinite as such, is never repeated. Something from anterior energies and predominant elements may reappear under new conditions, but completely reblended into new combinations of elements. What is reincarnated will be the personality's most fundamental tendency of a moment—not the existential events, the intellectual capacities, the vital movements, the "distinctive traits" or the "particular qualities" of a person—by definition, unique in his genre—but the very essence of being.[4]

Not only can the so-called "contradictions" between religions be resolved on the esoteric level, but these religions present numerous equivalent examples at this level as well. Once again we will cite some examples borrowed from Hinduism and Christianity, two traditions that are apparently quite distinct from one another. What Aristotle and Saint Thomas said of the "Motionless Mover" as a Principle of all inactive action is close to *Purusa* who is identified in India with the Supreme Brahma and declared inactive because his activity is nonessential but relative to his states of manifestation. At the very center of universal rotation, represented by the Svastika, which symbolizes at the same time the four elements, the four directions in space, and the four cosmic cycles, is *Agni*, the immobile point in the rotational movement, to which *Agnus*, the cosmic Lamb at the source of the four rivers of Paradise, will be compared. The

---

[4] Note that Hinduism, which teaches transmigration, interprets it symbolically (except at the level of common religion) by seeing within it a succession of changes of state up until the final Liberation. By pretending not to abolish the Hebrew tradition, Christ implicitly admits the *ghilgoul* that it talks about and that strongly resembles the migration of souls. As said in the *Zohar* (I, 187 b), "The Holy One plants souls here below. If they take root (in the Realization): fine. If not, He tears them out, even several times, and replants them until they take root."

informal manifestation is the direct reflection of the Creator Principle—*Purusa*—in the cosmic substance—*Prakriti*, reflection of manifested divine Intelligence—*Buddhi*. The supreme Unity has no aspects; it is the super-essential Non-Being, the Matrix of the Archetypes that Christianity talks about, the equivalent in the Vedanta of the *Nirguna Brahma* ("unqualified"), as the *Saguna Brahma* ("qualified") is of the Supreme Being. The Water that the Spirit blows on during Creation symbolizes the potential and plastic principle of forms. *Prakriti* corresponds to Water, as *Purusa* does to the Spirit.

The Angels in the Judeo-Christian tradition indicate the informal states of manifestation; they are the principial determinations, the eternal causes of created things, the possible "aspects" of divine Essence. They correspond to the *Deva* in the Hindu tradition.[5] The battle between the two groups allows the cosmic activity to take place through the different phases of expansion and retention, perpetually oscillating between the polarities of the multiple and the One. The Serpent in the Book of Genesis corresponds to *Shesha*, symbol of the Indefinability of the universal Existence. It appears, coiled around the Tree—or the Meru—under its evil aspect, the progression of the human being in the undetermined series of cycles of manifestation, the wheel of deaths and births, the *Samsara* that unwinds its unquenched round around the world. The biblical temptation distances human beings from the original central Unity, subjects them to cyclical mutations, that is to say to all the ups and downs of an adventurous life and problematic death. *Avidya*, Ignorance, separates from the One to plunge into the mirages of *Maya* and into the turbulences of lunar dust raised by Illusion, the places in which it stirs souls. "Work," the "*joug*"[6] will consist of passing from the circumference to the Center, of getting out of the "infernal" series of manifested states to return to lost Eden, the *Brahma loka*.

Although the Trinity belongs specifically to Christianity and is not to be confused with the *Trimurti* in Hinduism, it is possible, how-

---

[5] They also correspond to the Greek "gods," the Platonic "Ideas," the *Sephiroth* of Judaism, the "Divine Names," the "Qualities" of Islam, the "Divine Energies" of Orthodoxy—all Powers, personified or not, filling the "space" between the Principle from which they emanate and the manifestation they support.

[6] Translator's Note: *Joug* means yoke in French and is akin to *yoga* in Sanskrit.

ever, at this level as well, to establish certain correlations. If the Being is one, it is possible to conceive of Him as having several distinguishing aspects in certain respects. It can be said that, *mutatis mutandis*, Shiva corresponds to the first Cause, and as "Progenitor," can be linked to the Father; Vishnu is manifested as the *Avatara* and consequently plays the role attributed to the Son; as Brahma, in his power of extension and relation, plays that of the Holy Ghost. Another system of correspondences is possible starting with the ternary *Sat-Chit-Ananda*: *Sat*, the Self, the pure Being, corresponds to the Father; *Chit*, the Consciousness of the Self, is conceived as the *filial* exteriorization of *Sat*, as well as in his rapport with his unique object, *Ananda*, Beatitude; the three form a Being that is one and the same, *Atma*, considered to be above and beyond all the special conditions.

An essential identity between the Vedic Sacrifice and the Christlike Sacrifice also exists. One comes directly from the primordial Tradition, the other, from the priesthood of Melchizedek, two expressions used for intrinsically indicating the same reality. Since the beginning of the world, the immolation of the Lamb has corresponded to the Vedic sacrifice of *Purusa* living in all beings. The mother of the *Avatara* is *Maya* (which will be linked to *Maria*), image of *Prakriti*, the Earth, the *materia prima* (remarkably expressed by the "Black Virgins"), the universal Substance, Wisdom as *Theotokos*, the divine Receptiveness that allows the Father—*Purusa*— to beget the Logos—the *Avatara*. The latter, born of a virginal birth (Christ, Gautama, Krishna) is gifted with miraculous "powers" that have numerous symbolic implications and that prove a total deconditioning with respect to the laws of nature. Thus, Christ comes forward with the waves, as the primordial Yaksha, Brahma, "strides the crest of the sea," as Indra "retains the current of the waters as he pleases," as Vishnu Narayana is "The One who walks on water."

Lastly, the description of the "Kingdom of Heaven" given in the Gospels and the one that the Hindu tradition gives of *Atma* also deserve being compared. The Kingdom of Heaven is as small as a wild mustard seed, but once it has grown it becomes a tree where birds from heaven will alight. Likewise, *Atma* is similar to a millet seed, but at the same time is bigger than the earth, the atmosphere, and the sky. The growth of the tree symbolizes the development of spiritual possibilities, as the birds from heaven symbolize the superior states of the being. These can be related to two birds from another text, one of which eats a piece of fruit (it represents the individual soul engaged in action), while the other watches the first one (it represents the unconditioned Self). As for the identification of the Kingdom and *Atma*, it will be remembered that if *Atma* is said to live "in the heart" as the "internal organizer," Christ declares likewise to the Pharisees that "the Kingdom is within you." The "divine City"—*Brahmapura*—is illuminated by the radiance of *Purusa*; the Christian tradition even mentions the Light of the Lamb illuminating the "Celestial Jerusalem."[7]

Indeed some Christians are beginning to understand the interest of not only forming relationships between the Abrahamic religions, but also with qualified representatives of what were, up until recently, contemptuously called the Asian polytheisms. Even in the eighteenth century, Anne Catherine Emmerich, nevertheless, continually denouncing the "empires of darkness" and the monstrosities of idolaters, had heard Christ speaking highly of a certain just and wise King Djemschid who had ruled over India. Yet, "among his people," said Christ, "the truth had not been so darkened." It cannot be seen why, in the name of the "open-mindedness" recommended today, Christians should be drawn to an interest in profane philosophies or adverse ideologies, without being equally offered the possibility of learning about other traditions. It so happens that there is still a lot of work to be done.[8] It is quite easily admitted that as guardians of a given exotericism, the clergy continues to defy everything that is not part of that and to warn the faithful against "outside" contributions, even more harmful in that they can be very different from the orthodoxy they come from. This should even be the first duty of the Church. But as soon as Christians, by refusing other spiritual messages, welcome that which is contrary to Christianity, and campaign for Freudian psychoanalysis, Marxism, structuralism, Teilhardism, or the theology of the death of God, one has the right to say that a greater knowledge of the East would not only grant them a tolerance that is free from

---

[7] Speaking of the primordial *Purusa*, Krishna, declares in the *Bhagavad Gita* that this "place" which "is not illuminated by the sun, the moon or fire: is my supreme sojourn." As a parallel, in Revelation it is said that this city is not illuminated by the sun or the moon, but by the Glory of God.

[8] The Declaration "*Nostra Aetate*" of the Vatican II Council could recognize the validity of non-Christian religions; but errors and omissions are still made. For example, one speaks of Islam without mentioning Sufism.

fear of competition, but would also help them convert to their own religion! There are some pioneers who have discovered the true value of Hinduism without renouncing their own faith: Lanza del Vasto, disciple and propagator of Gandhi, the Le Saux Fathers, Cocagnac, Deleury, while Thomas Merton pushes forward to the East. Olivier Lacombe does not exclude the possibility of integrating Hindu elements into Christianity; he believes that "of all the Christian saints, Francis (of Assisi) is the one who seems the closest to India, and who would be voluntarily adopted as an Easterner."[9] Care should be taken to avoid omitting the efforts of Louis Massignon for a better mutual understanding between Christians and Muslims, and those of Jean Tourniac for a better understanding between Christians and Jews. The importance of a comparative study of traditions at their esoteric level cannot be emphasized enough. This will allow them a fruitful dialogue rather than an ecumenism that only skims the surface, undoubtedly full of good intentions, but stumbling over secondary subjects that from an exoteric point of view, are insurmountable obstacles or dormant conflicts, never-endingly re-begun, stirred up from both the inside and the outside, continually weakening the cause of the believers and discrediting them in the eyes of their adversaries who are the only beneficiaries of such dissensions. In this attempt at a general reconciliation at the top and the forming of a "common religious front," the work of Frithjof Schuon is by no means among the least.

---

[9] But one might add that of all the Christian gnostics, Meister Eckhart is the closest to Sri Shankaracharya.

22. THE REMEMBRANCE OF THE NAME[*]

If the philokalic universe—this "hole in transcendence" as it has been called—has been revealed in our time to the West, it is for specific timely reasons. In this sphere, more than in any other, things really do take place when they should. The remembrance of the Name first suggests special roots in both the most authentic lineage of Christianity and in the whole of all the spiritual traditions.

To pray the Prayer of the Heart is to establish communion with everyone who, at the same time, in different places and circumstances, without knowing one another, pronounces the same syllables, turns their mind toward the same pole. Likewise, it establishes a similar communion with everyone who preceded them. Faithfully repeated from one generation to another, the same sounds end up creating, at the subtle level, an uninterrupted chain beyond space and time between the supplicants of today and the theophorous Fathers from the solitudes of the Thebaid and Anatolia, from Mount Sinai and Mount Athos, the hermits from the Greek Archipelago, the martyrs going to their execution, the homeless pilgrims, the inspired peacemakers, the stylites, the "onomatodox suns," but also the obscure Alexandrian and Byzantine craftsmen, the keepers of goats, Thessaly's and Macedonia's bee shepherds, all those "in the likeness of angels," those "Trinitarian dwellings," cavern anchorites, the Holy Ghost's lips of fire, eternal Wisdom's inextinguishable torches, "companions of divine mysteries." It is this immense family that is included in the Prayer of Jesus, a disconcerting and yet fraternal family, a direct heir to the Apostles, and for whom millions of representatives have incessantly intertwined air, millions of times, for two millennium, with the Divine Name.

But by its resemblances to what corresponds to it elsewhere and everywhere, the "remembrance-invocation" is deeply rooted even more mysteriously in all of praying humanity. In fact, all the major traditions are acquainted with similar methods. Finicky or grave minds, more likely to oppose than to unite, remember to emphasize the differences, which in truth are sometimes quite notable. Hesychasm undoubtedly ignores the notion of *kundalini*, the com-

---

[*] From *Passports for New Times*, III, 5.

plicated techniques of controlled breathing; neither chants nor music accompany the invocation; there is no speculation about the quasi-magical value of uttered tones. But the points of merger are infinitely more numerous, as much at the level of principles as at that of techniques and results.

One first notices that in the Gospel of Saint John as well as in the Koran and the *Bhagavad Gita,* the first word is the one that indicates the Word, that is to say, the Name. The enunciation of the Name appears as the one of a doctrine. Saying "Jesus" will confess that Christ is God; saying "Allah" will proclaim the divine Unity; saying "Rama" or "Krishna" will state the abandon of one's own existence for that of the Lord; saying "Amitabha" will recall the doctrine of merciful redemption of all beings. Hinduism stresses the idea that the formula used—the *mantra*—conveys the cosmic Power manifested in the form of "mystic sounds." The *mantra* clarifies the essence of the vibration of a thing; it is the "verb of force," a phoneme born of the depth of the being and bearing the Name of a divinity, for whom its sonant form is a kind of manifestation of the spiritual body; consequently, it is this very divinity. Presenting themselves under the aspect of "subtle letters" or "causals," these sonorities are analogous to the Greek *logoi spermatikoi,* the Kabbalists' "letters of light," the medieval Hermeticists' "Clavicules."[1] The *mantra* makes the body and soul vibrate with its own vibrations, makes them become the Name they bear. The most important *mantra,* the monosyllable OM, known since Vedic times, identified with Brahman and all the gods, is considered to be the surest way to attain Liberation. This sacred phoneme is the quintessence of the universe, of all its elements, of all its properties, the conscious of the omnipresent Reality; it is the fundamental Syllable that the "germ-sounds" depend on, the verbal seeds that are at the origin of every aspect of the manifestation. The OM attracts our interest all the more since it is closely related to the AMIN of the Abrahamic religions and consequently to the whole of the Western world that we belong to.[2] The OM (AWM) and the AMIN (AMN) philologically

---

[1] The mantric science acting on objects as aggregates of atoms comes close to modern science working on the physical particles by modifying their vibrations and rhythms. The "unified field theory" reveals that each particle "plays its own song."

[2] It is interesting to note that AMIN comes from the Egyptian IMN, meaning "hidden," and corresponding to the god Amon: this word refers to the invisible world, lieu of the occultation of the sun, that is to say, the West.

form one and the same vocable. Each one has the value of affirmation, confirmation, first enunciation; each one is a Name of the Word.[3]

At the level of techniques, a first analogy would be found in the very attitude of the one who invokes. *Hesychia* (which is probably linked to *hesthai*, "seated") corresponds to the notion of "seat," of contemplative tranquility, meditation, pacification, of a respite in God. The Hesychast, seated on a low chair, or on the floor— "human," "humus," "humbleness" are one—as Mary listening to Christ. It is impossible to avoid linking it with the Buddhist *zazen*, destined to obtain the same sentiment of inner unity, stability, and fulfillment. "The habit of being seated," says Dogen "is the passage that leads from truth to total liberation." The Hesychast method also offers analogies with certain *asana*s of Hindu yoga—flexed position or straight position—as well as with *pranayama*, the discipline of breathing, where breathing allows for the domination of vital, mental, and psychic energy. As much can be said about concentrating on the area surrounding the heart which corresponds to the *anahata-chakra* in yogic anatomy; about the physical perception of a light that recalls the *paranjyoti*; about *hesychia* itself, which is very close to *kaivalya*, the final state of beatitude. The worshipful contemplation of the icon of Christ and the *Theotokos* originates from the same point of view as the Hindu *darshan*, the contemplation of the chosen divinity, serving as a visual support for the repetition of the Name. Consequently, there is a correspondence in the duration between the Christlike formula and the *mantra*, just as there is in space between the icon and the *mandala*.[4] Thus, to the extent that yoga can be defined as a "spiritualizing technique," it is legitimate to talk about a Christian yoga.

---

[3] OM equals: "Yes, I assent by bowing" (*Chandogya Upanishad*). This is exactly the acceptance of AMIN, translated by: "So be it." It is also said that "this syllable, OM, is the entire universe" (*Mandukya Upanishad*). To establish a parallel with Anne Catherine Emmerich: "He seems to say that with the word (AMEN), God had created the world." OM refers to the Supreme Brahman, as Yahweh is AMIN, as are Christ and Mohammed as well. We will also point out a curious connection between the Sanskrit OM and Russian OUM meaning "intellect" (*nous* in Greek).

[4] In his *Spiritual Writings*, Silouan recounts his experiences of a mystical nature, praying before the icon of the Savior and feeling as if he were invested with Grace. This would be comparable to the experience of Sri Ramakrishna praying before the image of the Divine Mother.

But the most obvious link between the different memorizations is found in the formulas they resort to. Be it for Christianity and Judaism, the ones we have indicated, or for Islam, the remembrance and the mentioning of God as the Name of the Essence embedded in the profession of faith: LA ILAHA ILLA-LLAH—"There is no God but God"—or the Indian *mantra* with the Names: KRISHNA, HARI, RAMA, or any other God or even the great Tibetan mantra OM MANI PADME HUM—"OM, the Jewel in the Lotus"—transmitted by the Bodhisattva Chenrezig or NAMU AMIDA BUTSU—"Worship paid to Amitabha Buddha"—from Japanese Buddhism, the same characteristics of conciseness, sacralization, and force are expressed, the same requirements for attention and frequency are formulated, the same effects guaranteed. A large number of Koranic verses insist upon the necessity of invoking the Name of God, and invoking it often: "Mention my Name, I will mention you"; "Remember Allah often!"; "The invocation of Allah is all important"; "Invoke Allah frequently!" The same echoes in Hinduism. Thus, Swami Ramdas: "At all times, cling to the Name of the Lord." Ma Ananda Moyi: "Remember Him in all your actions." India develops the idea that one must offer one's *japa* to the divinity one venerates. Buddhism insists on the fact that a quasi-continuous repetition of the Name creates a state of consciousness that tends to dull the mind's ordinary functions; no matter what the posture or what one does. What is required everywhere and always is a reverential attitude with respect to the Name, consistency in the exercise, the heart's sincerity. Buddha assures his disciples that they will be reborn in the Land of Bliss if they just pronounce his Name as evidence of their good faith, of their desire to be saved and of absolute confidence.[5] Swami Ramdas teaches that "the one who has unalterable faith in the Name of the Lord is saved."

At the level of the results, similar converging can be observed. *The Laws of Manu* already affirmed that "in comparison to other practiced rituals, *japa* produces an effect that is ten times greater." For Ramakrishna, "consciously or not, no matter what state we are

---

[5] D. T. Suzuki in his *Essays on Zen Buddhism* cites the words of Shinran in his *Mattosho*: "A man may have faith, but if he doesn't pronounce the Name, his faith will be of no use to him. Another may pronounce the Name in thinking solely of that, but if his faith is not deep enough, he will not be reborn."

in, if we invoke the Name of God, we will benefit from the merit of this invocation." The *mantra* reduces the difficulties. "By thinking of Me you will overcome all obstacles with the help of My Grace," Krishna tells Arjuna.[6] Sri Aurobindo writes that *mantras* can "create new subjective states within us, modify our psychic being, reveal knowledge and difficulties that we were unaware of before." Personal sanctification will gradually spread to others, as Ma Ananda Moyi says: "Those around you will also benefit from your *japa* and your meditation under the beneficial influence of your presence."

The methods of prayer that rely on repetitive formulas with a bhaktic tonality bring liquefaction to inner resistance. John Climacus evokes the one who wore tears like a wedding cloak; not at all sentimental tears, but "psychic," destined to consume carnal and spiritual arrogance. It will be associated with the *hadith*: "The one who invokes God to the point that his eyes overflow out of fear and the earth becomes flooded with tears will go unpunished by God on Resurrection Day." The remembrance of the Name even dissolves the karmic debt. The Buddhist invocation of Amitabha makes the "torturer's sword" explode into pieces, that is to say *karma*. Each syllable of the mantric formula is filled with Avalokiteshvara's power and mercy; each one of them destroys one of the six Kingdoms of impermanence.

The idea that repeating a Divine Name means appropriating its ontological essence, its holiness, and its perfection is also found in the whole of the traditions. Each time, it is a matter of *becoming the Name*. What Ibn Arabi says about *dhikr*: "It is the Same One who speaks and who listens," can be applied to every onomastic reminiscence. Founded on the doctrine of mystic reciprocity, identification with the Name provides for the disidentification of everything that is not Him. The remembrance of the Name will be the opposite of the human being's ordinary state, which is oblivion and unconsciousness; at the same time it is the oblivion of this oblivion. The quintessential prayer unites man with the Supreme Being; man realizes this even though he had never been separated. In Hinduism, *japa-yoga* provides for divine realization; Krishna affirms this with these words: "He who thinks of Me constantly, while think-

---

[6] Ramana Maharshi said the same, "Pronouncing *japa*, even if just once, provokes its own beneficial effect."

ing of nothing else, he who is completely harmonized by yoga, comes to Me easily." The repetition of the Name not only appeases doubts, but according to Ramakrishna, "God Himself is realized by the power of His own Holy Name." In Tibetan Buddhism, the formula used will be a blessing for all beings, but to the extent that the one who invokes identifies himself with it, it will also endow all the centers of consciousness with the Buddha nature. The insufficiency and dissatisfaction with the states of existence appear wearing their true colors, certain proof of Deliverance. Likewise, the Japanese *nembutsu*, deprived of all mental significance, creates a state of innocence that erases all sins, making for rebirth in the Pure Land.[7]

This collection of reasons means that the one who invokes, whoever he is and whatever be the Name, can legitimately feel connected not only to everyone who, before him, after him, and at the same time as him, invoked, will invoke, and is invoking the same name, but also to everyone who, when invoking different Names under different spiritual heavens, resort to the same manner of prayer throughout all time and places. Nothing in the invocation is more encouraging than the certainty of a totalizing, symphonic, Pentecostal unity of prayer, where each syllable of each formula is a note that adds to and perfectly blends into the immense silent murmur. This certainty will be intensified by the living testimony of everyone who "takes the Name," as they say in India, and who, by using this method, has ascended to the Divine. There is no better example of comparative onomatology than *The Way of a Pilgrim*, a delightfully refreshing document, and the poignantly sincere *In Quest of God* by Ramdas. More than any of the other learned treatises, this is the kind of reading we would like to see recommended.

*
* *

The remembrance of the Name is a precious support in modern man's daily life. Moreover, it is considered to be the spiritual

---

[7] D. T. Suzuki writes in his *Essays on Zen Buddhism*: "The believer walks with the name, he descends into the depths with him; even though he often notices that he is separated, he always remembers it and remains in his company. One day, without his really knowing how it happened, he is no longer himself, and the name is no longer with him. There is only the name, and he is the name, and the name is him; up until the moment when it all disappears."

method that most adequately corresponds to him. In short, it is the useful and indispensable preparation for the great rite of passage that is death. These are the three main aspects that must now be examined.

We'll say that the remembrance of the Name is first of all an important aid for today's man, laic in his condition and confronted with the rude clashes of this world. Nicolas Cabasilas had already dedicated *Life in Jesus Christ* to the men who had taken vows in the secular world; and Paisius Velichkovsky recommended the Prayer of Jesus to everyone. Saint Seraphim said to Motovilov: "As for the fact that you are of the laity and I am a monk, there is no need to think about that." *The Way of a Pilgrim* refers to what Saint Gregory Palamas said earlier: "We need to introduce this teaching (of perpetual prayer) to everyone, monks, the laity, the intelligent or the simple-minded, men, women, and children." Today, the desert where demons are confronted is no longer the one in Egypt, it is every place where God has been excluded: the universe that we live in. Cast without defense into a dangerous world, today's laic man finds his surest auxiliary in the Prayer of the Heart. Accessible to every human, requiring no specific qualification other than the desire to progress spiritually, it can be practiced by the weakened patient, the worker constrained to tedious work, and the intellectual, if beneath his reflection he knows how to let the remembrance murmur. It is enough for each one to determine his own form of invocation so long as the Name is included. Feasible for everyone, the Prayer of the Heart is also possible anywhere: in the bedroom or in the street, at the office, the factory, or the laboratory, in a hospital bed, a little rustic chapel, in the sordid halls of solitary confinement, or in a concentration camp—has the double meaning of this term ever been considered? The Prayer of the Heart is equally practicable under any circumstances: while doing boring housework, during especially insipid and sterile meetings, insomnia; during the anxious wait for medical or university results; at the announcement of tragic news; in the face of a sadistic police chief's yelling; at the time of burial or a cruel separation. It can even serve as the invisible tie between two friends separated by distance momentarily or forever, a meeting place known only to them, beyond space.

It is unlikely that the modern Westerner will ever attain "divine contemplations." Isaac the Syrian clearly declared: "One man out of ten thousand has the advantage (of spiritual prayer)"; and, he added, "for the mystery found beyond, it would be difficult to find one man in an entire generation who has made this acquaintance with the glory of God."[8] As such, isn't this what is asked of the modern Westerner...? But—and this will already be quite a lot—his outlook will gradually become clearer, the ferments of hate, enmity, envy will be transformed into their opposites. Dreams that are chaotic and flee from God will give way to the "meditations" sent by God; the imaginal will succeed the imaginary. The Prayer of the Heart will return to the praying figure in the "royal and universal priesthood of the laity." It is because "every laic person is the priest of his own existence; he offers in sacrifice the whole of his life and being." He makes his life a liturgy; in a laic fragmented world, filled with the uproar of prattling, he is the candelabrum of silent and unitive prayer.

Monological prayer directly affects modern man's state of mind, best corresponds to his nature. It is simple, and as a consequence can be easily retained by those beings whose memory often fails. It is easy because all it requires is conscientious repetition, calm breathing, a bit of attention and love.[9] It is concise, and for this reason applies especially to people who are always rushed, who scarcely appreciate things being uselessly dragged out. It is efficient because the psychological modifications it leads to are verifiable by men attached to tangible proof and receptive to rapid results. It neither prevents nor hinders action, something which modern man cannot suddenly discontinue, but it is superimposed there, before penetrating, since it is possible to repeat the Name while performing any activity. Thus, man will not be frustrated by his essential activities, while illicit action, negative thoughts, blasphemous words will slowly move away from him.

Silently radiant, it supports his whole existence in filigree, invigorates a lull in time. Paradoxical and rigorous, it demonstrates to

[8] This recalls the verse of the *Gita*: "Among the thousands of men, one here and there strives for perfection, and among those who strive for perfection, and attain it, one here and there will know Me in all the principle of My existence."

[9] It goes without saying that people should not be fooled by this easiness. "Spiritual achievement," wrote Frithjof Schuon, "is theoretically the easiest and practically the most difficult thing there is. The easiest: because it is sufficient to think of God; the most difficult: because human nature is the forgetfulness of God."

the one who believes he has no time for prayer that it's possible to pray all the time. It contributes to pacifying a man at war with himself and the world, victim of extreme tension and aggression, of a defeated vitality. The mortification it demands resides in the liberation of all artificial needs, of all *doping*: speed, din, diverse stimulants.[10] It is the undeviating center at the heart of the seeming and the incoherent, the immobile and stable axis around which efflorescence revolves, the changing game of circumstances, all alternative events, all this froth of illusion that shrouds the ocean of the Real. If, as Theolepte of Philadelphia says, "mundane activities imprint memories on the soul as feet leave their footprints in the snow," then the Prayer of the Heart will communicate the same united characteristic of the snow to their discontinuous aspect: the image of reconciled unity, of the irenical recovery of the Kingdom. In the middle of the current inflation of language, the monological repetition is the reduction to the lowest common denominator of all the words, the catalysis of this *logos hysterikos* which affects so many of our contemporaries, a silent pounding of the transcendence that brings the syncopated world back to the unison of its origins and with its discreet rhythms, counterbalances political and commercial slogans, the ready-made expressions of automated brains, the spasmodic panting of the industrial metropolis. By focusing his attention on one object alone, the remembrance-invocation reeducates a man whose heart, "scattered over the earth" as the *Macarian Homilies* had already noted, is even more so in the century of audio-visual enticement. In a world filigreed with dissipation and dispersal, "the rhythmic monotone repetition that lacks haste and brilliance, is a unique formula, brief but powerful due to mental representations attached to it and with the real Presence of God, brings silence to the intellect, unifies the attention at the thymic level, and in the end achieves complete concentration." In short, the Prayer of the Heart is a weapon against the suggestions assailing modern man. "In the face of temptation," advises Evagrius Ponticus, "resort to a short and vehement prayer."[11]

---

[10] The psychotherapeutic methods of Autogenic Training could have been considered as having more than an air of resemblance to the Hesychast methods, which would tend to prove that "Byzantine obscurantism" is not as incompatible with modern science as one would like to believe.

[11] Likewise, John Climacus: "Strike your adversary with the name of Jesus, there is no stronger weapon on Earth or in Heaven."

Another meeting point between the invocation of the Name and present times is the semi-secret or completely secret aspect to which a truly spiritual life is condemned. Just as the Hesychasts were said to live "below creation," likewise, one might say that today, those who devote themselves to the Prayer of the Heart live in some ways *below* modern Hell, *below* the infrastructures of the anti-Christlike reign. Having reached an era where it is allowed to assume the loss of all outside forms of worship—unless one with caricatural traces subsists for throwing people off track—where the liturgy will be celebrated more and more within man, where he will be his own monastery, every man continuing to kindle the lamp of the Prayer of the Heart within himself will be a sort of little portable Ark, destined to traverse the deluge while saving the essential. Suppose the worst situations—absolute moral and social solitude, deprivation of any book affording comfort and courage, absence of therapists for confiding one's distress, spiritual Fathers for asking help and advice, and friends for human kindness, where confessing one's faith under prohibition carries the risk of capital punishment, life imprisonment, torture, devastation in the world. The only reality that can be counted on to remain forever in spite of everything, that cannot be destroyed by any coercive measures, is the inexhaustible, invincible, adoring repetition of the Divine Name. In no way can such a prayer denounce the one who is devoted to it; it constitutes the only wealth that cannot be taken away from men by laws of restriction or retaliation, not even by catastrophic circumstances; escaping in advance any control or accounting for; establishing in "interiorized monasticism," the only secret society that is exempt from any statutes and can never be detected or betrayed.

Without going as far as the most extreme case that will not find its solution here, we would like to talk about Eucharistic deprivation. As a matter of fact, the condition of many anchorites who lived far from a church in the midst of vipers and scorpions can, *mutatis mutandis*, become that of deported or persecuted Christians, condemned to only receive for their daily gruel, the vociferations of untruthful propaganda and the sugary persuasion of a generalized mindless state. According to certain methods, monological prayer can take the place of divine manducation. The heart becomes the Chamber where the Last Supper will once again be celebrated. The Name will replace the bread (IESOUS) and the wine (CHRISTOS). In a completely inner offering, the Name will be presented to the

Father as the immolated Lamb. Its repetition will allow one's entire life to be an action of grace, doxology, a sacrament of communion; in a world where God is booed, it will be the watchman who assures a perpetuated Epiclesis.

During this rediscovery of the Prayer of the Heart, it is superfluous to say how useful and opportune it would be for disoriented Western Christians to renew ties with the Orthodox Church, guardian of this prayer. It would be another crime against the Spirit to choose to remain blind under the "lights of the holy philosophy." The entirely positive sign of the times needs to be seen in the philokalic advent, in this revelation of the last school of noticeable and accessible metaphysical realization in Christendom.

This return to its own sources demonstrates to the West that all salvation is not lost. The existence of Hesychasm, adapted without betraying the laity during this time, once again makes it possessor of its own means of liberation. Thus, perhaps in the Christian perspective, the "tenth of the Law" corresponds to the Prayer of Jesus; perhaps, for today's Christian, even deprived of any Church, the passport for modern times is the Name of "He who Comes."

As demonstrated by the traditions, the remembrance of the Name also constitutes the most appropriate spiritual mode for the man of the *Kali Yuga*. India would say that it is an *upaya*, a simple method, based on a Name as an operative theme and on an invocatory formula; it appears extremely concise and requires the minimum of outside means, which links it markedly with certain tantric methods.

The correlation between the remembrance-invocation and the cyclical conjuncture is indicated in this way in the Old Testament: "The sun shall be darkened and the moon shall bleed before the day of the Lord.... Whoever calls upon the Name of the Lord shall be saved."[12] The Gospels proclaim likewise: "Pray ye that your flight be not in winter."[13] The Islamic tradition carries on the theme by emphasizing that prayer holds the world together, even when it is

[12] The text might also be a symbolic allusion to the darkening and the "eclipse" of intellective faculties (the sun) and the massacre of the living forces of the unconscious (the moon).

[13] The fourth season of the annual cycle corresponds to the fourth Age of the cosmic era. The flight will obviously take place during the descending phase of the "Great Year."

burning everywhere. "The supreme hour," assures a *hadith*, "shall come when there is no one left on Earth to say Allah!" The Hindu wise men agree that *japa* constitutes the most adequate discipline for our time. "That which is obtained in the *Krita* Age (the Age of Gold) by meditating on Vishnu, in the *Treta* Age by offering him gifts and sacrifices, in the *Dvapara* Age, by being devoted to his form of worship, is obtained in the *Kali* Age by celebrating the praises of Hari (Vishnu)." Ramakrishna says of *japa* that it is the "*yuga yoga*," the *yoga* of the Iron Age.[14] The long rites of the preceding eras, the hard penitence cannot be assumed by the man of modern times: "Life is too short."[15] The *mantra* replaces the spiritual master. For Swami Ramdas, "the name is the Lord himself, the Guru, the Whole in everything." Ma Ananda Moyi: "For as long as you have not yet found a guru, hold on to the name (or its form) of He who attracts you the most, and pray to Him constantly so that He will reveal himself to you as the supreme guru."

What Paisius Velichkovsky did in Eastern Europe during the nineteenth century by diffusing the Prayer of the Heart among vast levels of the population, had already been done by Chaitanya in India in the sixteenth century. Driven by a premonition whose scope is better measured today, he made *japa-yoga* popular, as did Honen Shonin in Japan in the twelfth century, by presenting the *nembutsu* as the quickest and easiest means of reaching the condition of no return. Tao-ch'o declared: "In the present age, which belongs to the half-millennium after Buddha, we have to repent our sins, cultivate the virtues and pronounce the name of Buddha." Still, a modern commentator alluding to the dangers concealed in the countless distractions organized today by the world of leisure and leading to the irretrievable waste of this human life that is so difficult to obtain, wrote on the subject of *nembutsu*—but this opinion is heard in all traditions—that "a life filled with this celestial influence leaves little room for infiltration by the emissaries of Mara...." The latter is still at work, especially in places where one escapes them, in the last

---

[14] The sage of Dakshinesvar specifies that a "'violent devotion' permits taking God's citadel by storm." This can be paralleled with the image of arrows and the Evangelistic idea that heaven belongs to the violent.

[15] In the *Kali Yuga*, the only appropriate means of cutting the ties that bind us to the world is by constant repetition of the Holy Names of God, by keeping our mind fixed on Him.

reserves that have been spared the tide of terror and barbarity. The homeland of the OM MANI PADME HUM still appeared as such. Its omnipresence, according to travelers, was heard being murmured everywhere, seen inscribed everywhere. Its formula was on the lips of every pilgrim, lama, and dying man; it was perceived in the chant of the torrents, in the forests and mountains, in the frozen deserts of the high plateaux; it was seen carved in the rocks, written on prayer flags planted next to every villager's house, tents in the nomadic pastures, giant reliquaries, and on the rolls of the famous "windmills." The prevailing atmosphere in the Land of Snow was such that one felt less transported to an altitude of five thousand meters than to thousands of years uphill, in full paradisiacal primordiality. An enclave of which nothing remains because following the immense and encompassing buzzing of mantric bees came the rumbling of tanks; and not only were the monasteries destroyed, the libraries burned, the monks subjected to the most infamous treatment, but the rocks themselves that bore the OM were dynamited by the emissaries of Mara.

Lastly, the remembrance of the Name is not only preparation for the end of this world, but also for an individual life, training for the great passage. Every tradition insists on the crucial importance of the moment of death as a recapitulation of all anterior states, initial condition for the following states. All of them teach that a human being, by attraction and affinity, goes toward the levels with which he established bonds, maintained "friendships" in this life. Hell will correspond to the nonintegration of our nature's inferior fragments, as Paradise does to the superior degrees in a preformed similarity here below. All of them agree in saying that not everything perishes with death, but that something like a "flavor" remains, more or less sweet or bitter, but decisive for the voyage, depending on the dispositions in which one finds oneself *in articulo mortis*.

The repetition of the Name for the duration of the terrestrial existence also serves in a way as a general rehearsal of the most difficult hardships. In Egypt, forgetting the Name at the moment of leaving life was thought to endanger the destiny of the deceased. Islam is fond of the *hadith* which says "man will be judged according to what he was at the time of death." *Dhikr* is thought of as the best learning possible of death. The last syllable of ALLAH even merges together with the last breath of a dying man. *Dhikr* will be the companion of the deceased in the tomb, when he no longer has any property, spouse, children, or friends. Hinduism stresses the idea that one becomes the subject of his meditation at the time of death. So Krishna declares to his disciple, "the one who, upon dying, is only aware of Me, unites with My essence when he leaves his body; about this, let there be no doubt." For Ramakrishna, "since the new incarnation of a man is determined by his thoughts at the moment of death, pious exercise is absolutely necessary."[16] The nature of the last thought is obviously the result of all the preceding work, sustained and supported by the remembrance of the Divine. An entire life is barely sufficient for perfecting this thought, which also corresponds to a certain psychic atmosphere, to a collection of dispositions and orientations that is superior to the disorders of agony. Buddhism doesn't speak of *karma* in any other way; it is good to get used to the vision and names of the divinities so as to recognize them at the right time. The one who has become identified with the *mantra* can confront death in complete tranquility; as the *Bardo Thodol* assures, in the state between life and death, the noise of a thousand thunders is transformed into the melody of sacred syllables.

If Christianity seems less explicit on this subject, it nevertheless recommends the *memento mori* and the usage of onomastic praying with the same intention. It puts the one who prays in the presence of God by making him leave time and its sphere of influence, elevating him above his hopes and fears, denuding him and washing him, projecting him by this time into eternity; in this way it constitutes a death of this world and of himself, a death of death, and anticipates the rendezvous with beatitude. If, to repeat the Latin proverb, "every arrow (or every hour) wounds, the last one kills," one may say, in the perspective of jaculatory prayer, that all the arrows invigorate and the last one resuscitates. Knowing the ultimate purpose of monological prayer allows for a better understanding of the idea that pronouncing the Divine Name is a sufficient enough objective in and of itself for one human life. Praying the Hesychast prayer will therefore simultaneously vitalize the present existence and reserve a favorable outcome for the

---

[16] Hindu tradition cites the example of King Bharata who lost the fruit of his asceticism for having been too attached to a young fawn: he was reborn as a cervid, the fawn being the last image that held his attention.

future, by visualizing that death can come at any moment, that one may be too weak for long prayers, that any amnesic moment from God is irremediably lost.

We will end the consideration of remembrance-invocation here, in the hopes of having shown its interest and actuality. Naturally, there is no question of recommending such a practice outside of its traditional setting and it would be disturbing to see a Sufi resort to *nembutsu,* or a Christian dancing to Krishna. One even advises strongly against it. Nonetheless, onomastic prayer is a supplementary place of convergence of the East and the West. For the reasons we have mentioned, one can only prompt any willing man to the glorification of the Name. If the diverse dispositions discussed in this work have given us the opportunity to speak, none of them, except one, has proved itself more possible, practicable or permitted; it is assuredly monological prayer that must be chosen without a shadow of a doubt. It is the only one that can still provide this "Light without crepuscule" capable of enlightening crepuscular man.

23. CHRISTIAN ESOTERICISM AND PRIMORDIAL TRADITION*

Two kinds of ecumenisms are usually distinguished: "branches" and "roots."

The "ecumenism of branches" concerns the reconciliation of the three Christian confessions. With generous intentions, it all too often addresses the problem from the wrong end by dwelling on historical or dogmatic considerations having little interest today with respect to the seriousness of the times, and without any of the three confessions in question being thoroughly convinced of the need for making the first sacrifices. In all immediate susceptibility, it would be incumbent upon Catholicism to renounce its legalism and papal monolithism, upon Protestantism to give up its rigid moralism and open up to the monastic and supernatural dimensions, upon Orthodoxy to abandon a certain intransigence that is no longer in season.[1]

Even when concessions are made here and there, even when a harmonization is in sight, a serious danger subsists: that of the break-up and thoughtless mixture of forms for which the traditional movements pay. An excessive opening to the others increases the disorder under the cover of intercommunion, as well as developing the seeds of a dissolution of structures and a phenomenon of entropy. Similarly, an excessive withdrawal encourages a lack of growth, vitality, and flexibility, imprisons in ritualism and fossilization, turns the sanctuary into a "laundered sepulcher." In one case or the other, the absence of balance and moderation creates a risk of death. Rather than wanting to sew the too disparate points of view together, it would be undoubtedly wiser to consider that beyond the outdated disputes, the differences of mentalities and temperaments—Latin, Germanic, and Slavic to simplify—constitute

---

* From *Return to the Essential*, III, 3.

[1] We know these schematizations may be excessive. There are very different, if not opposing, tendencies in the bosom of the Reformed Church, including, since recently, a contemplative tendency. The Roman Church has become more flexible and decentralized, though a firm authority is justified in the dissolution phases. As for the Byzantine Church, its defiance with regard to Western Christians is explained by its minority position and its legitimate fear of being absorbed. Its internal dissentions do it great harm.

and inspire the diverse visages of a Church that is one and the same, whose true unity is not at the level of rites and theologies, which are tributary to these same differences, but at the level of an identical core which is none other than Christian esotericism.[2]

The "ecumenism of roots" concerns the meeting of religions growing from the same tree; as it happens, the three Semitic religions. A meeting that, from certain aspects, presents serious difficulties, especially at the level of the Divine Unity that seems disturbed by the Incarnation of the Son, but which under other aspects and paradoxically, seems more readily feasible: the same metaphysical elements of Super-Being, Being, and Manifestation, the same eschatological elements concerning the "ultimate ends" of man and the world, the same mystical elements of the realization are found, through changing imageries, in the Torah, the Gospels, and the Koran. Judaism refers to Abraham by Isaac and Jacob, as does Islam by Ishmael, while Christianity refers to Abraham and to Melchizedek, which explains its special role with regard to the two others. If the major element is moved—the Super-Being in Judaism, the Divine Unity in Islam, the Trinity in Christianity—if the essential priorities equally differ, such as Gnosis or Rigor in Islam and Judaism, Mystic and Mercy in Christianity, the three religions unite in the conceptions of a unique and transcendent God, of the macrocosm and microcosm.

We can, however, imagine a third ecumenism, which would be the one of "flowers," of an infinitely more delicate order, where each of the three religions considered—in the same way that flowers are the result of subtle elaborations and the convergence of slow and secret previous maturations—would reveal its hidden goods with the movements that preceded them and from which they are derived, or the even more distant ones that they encountered and that enriched them with their contributions. In this way, step by step, Judaism would be put in touch with Ancient Greece and Mesopotamia, as Christianity with Greece and India, and Islam with Iran and China.

---

[2] On the notion of "Christian esotericism," we refer to two essential authors: F. Schuon, *The Transcendent Unity of Religions* (1st ed.), chapters VIII and IX, and S. H. Nasr, *Knowledge and the Sacred*, chapter 1.

The "ecumenism of flowers" is not limited to a defined geographic region, nor to a precise historic era; it embraces the totality of existing spiritual forms and by that constitutes the veritable reconciliation for which the two others are just the preambles. It constitutes it even more so in that this somewhat horizontal meeting is superimposed on a vertical meeting where borrowing and influences cease. All these revelations proceed from a transhuman plane, from a supra-conscious or supermental center, unique in any case, and which are themselves just terrestrial refractions.

Jung showed that at the psychological level, there are two kinds of unconscious that he qualified as personal and collective. The first one refers to each individual's particular patrimony; the second one to the inner subjacent patrimony, common to all of humanity. Likewise, at the spiritual level, by turning these terms in the direction of the supra-conscious and the transconscious, we can establish that if exotericism corresponds to the conscious, the esotericism of one's own religion will correspond to the personal unconscious; and to the collective unconscious, the esotericism that is common to the whole of religions, which will be called indiscriminately Universal Esotericism, *philosophia perennis*, or Primordial Tradition. As the archetypical dreams unite the heart of every man to the universe of symbols and myths belonging to all civilizations, we can say that at the level of Universal Esotericism, beyond the level of particularisms and dogmatic oppositions, the different traditions communicate with each other implicitly. At this level of intimacy, they reveal their common quintessence, the Spirit that originally animates them in the nudity anterior to all clothing, and that allows the introduction, even at the cost of agonizing revisions, and perhaps even thanks to them, of an entire system of equations where the *Adam Qadmon*, the *Purusa*, and the *Chen-jen*, where the pre-eternal *Shekhinah*, the *Theotokos*, *Shakti*, Demeter, and Kwan-yin, where Merlin and al-Khidr, Dionysos and Shiva are more than just distant cousins: a system of equations that is a system of evidences.

This first comparison inspires us with another one. We know that scientists today are leaning more and more toward a systemic vision of the world, seeing in it an indivisible whole for which the diverse components are essentially relationships. Consequently, the universe appears as a unitary whole, composed of relatively separate and distinct parts, but which vanish at the level of subatomic particles, and are only definable in their interconnections. We might even say, *mutatis mutandis,* that Universal Esotericism is the systemic vision of the Spiritual, linking together these religions (whose main role is to link together[3]), and tracing between their different doctrinal points, over the artificial demarcations, henceforth abolished, an entire network of lines similar to those linking together the stars. For Universal Esotericism, the veritable reality is a whole made up of several revelations communicating with each other at the keenest level, that of "transcendent Intellect." We might even complete the comparison by adding that, as in David Bohm's theory of the so-called "implicate" or "enveloped" order, where each part of the hologram contains the whole, each religion, similarly, contains, implicates the others. Each one, however, favors some aspects to the detriment of certain others; and it doesn't take much more for these differences in the degrees of *insistence* to create the belief that the religions are radically opposed to each other.

We are mistaken besides in believing that Christianity wanted to oust other religions for good. It undoubtedly felt tempted more than once in its phase of conquering expansion, at that time moved less by the action of the Holy Spirit than by what Camus calls "European arrogance." But these vague hegemonic impulses pertain to the instances of exotericism and sooner or later collide with territorial limits. Christ himself proclaims "in my Father's house there are many mansions," and "they shall come from the east, the west, the north and the south, and shall sit down in the kingdom of God." Among the interpretations of these verses, there is one that is quite significant: the plurality of mansions corresponds to that of the paradises obtained at the end of different posthumous evolutions, which are related to the diversity of the spiritual paths. As for the East, which is alluded to, it seems difficult to restrict it to Palestine. For the Easterners who did not receive his message, Christ recognizes implicitly the legitimacy of their own tradition, its possibility for their "redemption" and to appear at the messianic wedding banquet. That "the wind bloweth where it listeth" is to be taken in a similar meaning: the spirit's gratuitousness of action is such that men of God exist in all the forms of spirituality.

---

[3] Translator's Note: From a play on words in the original French text: *"reliant ensemble les religions dont le rôle principal est lui-même de relier...."* This is based on the Latin roots of religion: *religere* meaning to "bring together" and *religare,* to "assemble" (See also the Translator's Note on this point at Chapter 7, fn. 8 [p. 88]).

The acceptation of the latter by Christianity is found mentioned in numerous written texts, some examples of which we will give. Justin, in his *Apology*: "Everyone who has lived according to the Logos is Christian, even if they passed themselves off as atheists, as Socrates, Heraclitus and their kind among the Greeks." Origen, in his *Commentary on the Gospel of John*: "The Word became man at the end of time, it became Jesus Christ; but before this visible coming of flesh, he was already, without being man, the mediator of humans." Irenaeus of Lyons, *Against the Heresies*: "There is only one unique Father God, and his Word is forever present in humanity, although with diverse dispositions and multiform workings, saving since the commencement those who have been saved, that is to say those who love God and who, according to their time, follow the Word." And later, "Christ did not come for those alone, who starting with the Emperor Tiber, believed in him, and the Father did not use his providence only in favor of men who live now, but in favor of all men who, without exception, from the commencement, according to their abilities and those of their time, feared and loved God, practiced justice and kindness toward their neighbor, desired to see Christ and hear his voice." All religions, and even all cultures, have received a "visit from the Word." The latter, according to Maximus the Confessor, appeared in three ways at the time, which are like as many degrees of "incorporation": considered as theophany in the cosmos; in the wisdoms included in the core of the Holy Scriptures; in the assumed Incarnation of the Son of God. More precisely informed, Nicolas of Cusa could say that "the revelations are multiple"; he sees dogma and ritual as partial truths. "Through the diversity of Divine Names, it is You who they name, for as You are, as You live, unknown and ineffable."

This kind of affirmation regularly punctuates the history of Christianity. Even if they are rarely quoted and heard, they explicitly tell the validity of the non-Christian traditions, and by way of consequence, recognize the inspiration inhabiting them, the orthodoxy of their instruction, the saintliness of their representatives. If Saint Paul wants us to refuse the messages that do not come from Christ, it is not because they are all necessarily untrue, but because the message of Christ, as much by its content as by its expression, is the most adapted to the Westerners of the time and their descendents. These same affirmations admit perfectly that the Word can reveal itself on several occasions during human history—which relates to the question of the *Avataras*, or "Divine Descents" in Hinduism. These, we know, distinguish between the major *Avataras*, or plenary Incarnations of the Divine, and the minor *Avataras*, or partial Incarnations. Christ, who is identified with the Logos and was "before Abraham was," obviously belongs to the first category, from the jnanic point of view, with its constant concern for putting into perspective *in divinis* the manifestations of the Absolute with regard to the Absolute itself. He will even be placed above the avaritic series according to the bhaktic point of view, insisting on the fact that "God became man" only once, and once for all time.

It should be noted, however, that Christianity is not alone in insisting on the notion of a personal God: Vishnuism, Amidism, and Buddhism do so as well. Also, favoring such a way does not necessarily lead to condemning the way of the impersonal God just because it does not offer any human mediator between man and Heaven, as in Judaism, Islam, and Zen. The worshipers of God have not forgiven the successors of Plato and Shankaracharya for wanting to attain this "unknown God," even though he would make himself known.[4] They want all human types to be like their own—affectionate, emotional, proselyte—without thinking that others could in the past, can still today, although in diminishing numbers, realize the Divine by their own means. Christ appeared at the critical and *crucial* moment where the cyclical degeneracy made the ways of "God within" dangerous or impracticable. He certainly did not descend into Hades to save the pagans that couldn't have known him, but the ones who turned away from all spirituality.

To assume that the Incarnation of Christ has nothing in common with the *Avataras* may be an act of faith worthy of respect and justified by the unconditional love devoted to the divinity of one's choice and in response to his love; it may also be an easy way to ignore what is being said and done on the other side of the river. Overall, unlike the *Avatara* who haunt the "cosmic religions" and appear every time humanity needs them, while at the same time remaining more or less blurred in the mists of the mythological, Christ would mark the intrusion of God in History. This neglects

---

[4] According to Saint Paul, this is what he did by incarnating himself in the person of Christ, but it is not what he did if we consider that the "unknown God" of the Athenians is and remains forever the Super-Being.

that such an intrusion had begun much earlier: with Abraham to say the least. Moreover, to support this perspective, which plunges the centuries preceding the coming of Christ into the shadows of ignorance, fatally reduces the Christian tradition to historicism; it results in an evolutionary and progressive vision of humanity, based on the impossible dialogue between Christians and atheists, on technology and massing, which in the end consists of finding the "nuclear winter" that, when all is said and done, is preferable to the springtime of the Golden Age.

The unique Son of God is unique, if the words still have meaning. This won't keep Augustine of Hippo from admitting that "we shouldn't doubt that Gentiles also have their prophets." And Thomas Aquinas won't hesitate to write what deserves to be read with the utmost attention: "The power of a Divine Person is infinite and cannot be limited to something created. This is why we should not say that a Divine Person has assumed a human nature *in such a way that he could not assume another one."* [5]

*
*   *

Such notable changes of attitude might make one think that we are henceforth heading toward a broader Christianity that, without giving up any of its basic principles, bears witness to its true universality. Some Christians who, only several decades ago, would have been condemned for their boldness, are now opening up to sister religions: a rather hostile curiosity is followed by a sincere interest. This creates hope that perhaps the day will come where, risking a second stage, they will also become interested in the "polytheist paganisms" of which an in-depth study will show that they are neither paganisms nor polytheisms. One will realize that such *open-mindedness* does not pose any threats to the Christian tradition one personally adheres to, that faith in Christ is in no way weakened for all that, that it is even quite revived with the breath of the East, more faithful to the meaning of holiness, more inclined to veneration. Following Clement of Alexandria, Augustine, by considering in *The City of God*

---

[5] *Summa Theologica*, III, a P. 3, 7. Emphasis mine. Even if Aquinas had not admitted the *Avataras*, such a statement remarkably broadens the horizon.

that the gymnosophists of India belonged to the "terrestrial city," felt their ideas about the divinity were correct. Remarkable concession for a man who, given the era in which he lived, could not have the precise idea about the yogis that we have since acquired. It is no longer possible to depict them as they had been in medieval imageries, with ears larger than their body—unless one wants to see the symbol of Knowledge; no longer possible to describe Marco Polo's tales of China as diabolical.

The *Lumen gentium* constitution, promulgated by Vatican II, admits among the just "those who have not yet received the Gospel," and who "under the influence of his grace, try their best to fulfill his will"; these ones "can attain eternal salvation." There is still a bit of condescendence in this judgment, but the angle of tolerance is noteworthy. The publications from the office of secretary for non-Christians multiply the invitations to stop rejecting the other religions, expressions of the "Spirit of Truth" working beyond the visible boundaries of the "mystic Body." It is no longer a question of integrating unfamiliar elements to purify them, or after having purified them, but to think of them as full expressions of the Word, without any afterthought of salvaging.

Pioneers paved the way for the encounter. While, on the Eastern side, Swami Siddheswarananda brought the "face of silence" to the West—Sri Ramakrishna—and explored the *raja-yoga* of John of the Cross, or while D. T. Suzuki revealed Zen to us and saw in Meister Eckhart the closest mystical Christian to the Far East,[6] on the Christian side, men like Thomas Merton explored Buddhism, Olivier Lacombe and Jean Herbert, Hinduism, Louis Massignon and Henri Corbin, Sufism and Iranian Islam. More recently, we could see a Catholic monk who studied the *Advaita-vada* and the Christian tradition for many years equally borrow from Thomas Aquinas and Shankara, Bernard of Clairvaux and Ramana Maharshi. If he is careful to distinguish, in his work *Doctrine de la Non-dualité et Christianisme*, the "hypostatic Union" and the "Supreme Identity," the author concludes no less with these terms: "We have not found anything (in the Hindu doctrine of Non-duality) that strikes us as incompatible with our complete and full faith in the Christian Revelation."

---

[6] Lossky speaks of this as a "Christian non-dualism."

But the most significant example is that of Dom Henri Le Saux (Swami Abhishiktananda), who completed the Himalayan pilgrimage, retreated into the caves of Arunachala, met several sages, studied the Upanishads—referring to them as a "frightening experience of truth." It was not a question of distancing himself from Christianity, even less of him giving it up, but of living it at a much deeper level than the one generally suggested. He judged that the Hindu metaphysics of Non-duality teaches interiorization and unification; it purifies Christianity of the contributions that obscured it. "No one believes more deeply than the Advaitin in the Divinity of Jesus." As Marie-Magdeleine Davy wrote in the essay she devoted to him, "it was through the Upanishads that he was able to capture the true meaning of Christianity, to live it and spread it." Dom Le Saux wrote in *Ermites de Saccidananda*: "Of all the peoples of the earth, it seems that India has received a special mission from the Divine Providence. It seems that a message had been entrusted to her, a message to deliver to the world and to proclaim throughout time.... Testimony and message focused on the primacy of the mystery of God in relationship to the mystery of the created, on the unique value of what does not occur." In his *Journal*, he sees, with the incorporation of Hinduism in Christianity, a highlighting of the apophatic theology. And he writes more: "The advaita is not beyond the Church of Christianity, it is within it...." Lastly, in *Gnanananda*, he says that the moment has come, as much for Christianity as for Eastern wisdom, to reach across their borders, and this, no longer only at the level of the "initiates." One might imagine, consequently, that the "I am that I am" (*Ehyeh Asher Ehyeh*) of the Burning Bush is not very different from the "I do exist" (*Aham Asmi*) of the Vedanta, in the pure transparence of the Absolute Being.

In fact, Christianity in crisis undoubtedly has a duty to work essentially in a double movement. The first consists of *going back* to its deepest roots contained in the Hebrew tradition, to which we have already made several allusions elsewhere. Remember that this tradition is the esoteric explanation of this "transmission," the whole of which constitutes the Torah, and for which Christ declares he never came to abolish; it is thus an *integral part* of the Christian heritage. The second movement consists of *opening* Christianity to the whole of the Eastern traditions, which, far from conflicting with it, confirm its authenticity, and in certain areas, complete it, stimulate it, make it develop.

This double movement of *deepening* and *widening* is not at all contradictory when taken from the point of view of esotericism. It should be simultaneous in its two directions. There is nothing scandalous about it, at least for the minds that are used to it, who hate nothing more than the effort of revision or renovation and the shocks of awakening. The return to Jewish sources in no way signifies the abandon of the evangelical contribution; the reference to Asian sources does not carry the underlying meaning of a submersion of Christianity by foreign alluvion. Both are the enrichment and renewal, Christianity's return to itself.

We won't cover the return to the sources in Hebrew esotericism again, which, in the eyes of many, is taken for granted.[7] The Eastern question is much more difficult. Without a doubt, Thomas Merton was right to warn against hasty assimilations; but this Cistercian monk, with a remarkably open mind, consecrated his last years to the study of Taoism and Zen, adding that "there are certain analogies and a correspondence that are from now on obvious and that may indicate the way towards a better mutual understanding." Thomas Merton's precautions can be explained by a certain sense of discretion dictated by his membership in the Church. This distance fades at the purely intellectual level.

Let's quote the important text from Marie-Magdeleine Davy in *Le désert intérieur*: "It is normal for man to grow, thanks to the different contributions that refer to traditions other than his own.... It is not because of this that he abandons his own path; he will be enriched, and on the contrary, it will be possible for him to better understand it by studying it more deeply...." The one who attends the school for inner life doesn't need to listen to those who attack him with accusations of syncretism. "Envious, jealous, stubborn, devoted to human prudence," unable to broaden their knowledge to that of a universal order, these ones "wouldn't know how to accept that others free themselves from what they are able to overcome. Primitive Christianity knew how to take advantage of Greek and Jewish thinking. Why wouldn't modern man, Christian or not, use the metaphysics from the Far East, which are available to him today?" The length of this quotation will be forgiven by considering the defini-

---

[7] We need to pay tribute here to the essential work of a pioneer such as Claude Tresmontant.

tive nature presented in its very conciseness.[8] But what can be understood from these contributions, if not, in addition to the Hassidic teachings and the Presocratic and Neoplatonic vision of the world, most certainly and at the same time, the poems from the Sufi mystic, the *Bhagavad Gita* and the *Upanishads,* the Taoist treatises, the Zen aphorisms and—their common point of convergence—those alchemic works that only seem foreign to us because our ignorance and infidelity has tossed them behind the bookshelves of oblivion?

It has been largely proven that the areas of the richest fertility are found where different trends meet, born of geographical places and cultural domains that are very distant from one another, from different eras, stemming from equally different traditions. There is good reason to believe that any Christian awakening will remain chimerical without this fertilization and intellectual revival of central truths irrelevant to all hurried syncretism and ignorant confused thinking.

*
* *

The opening up of Christianity to the Hebrew and Eastern traditions has led to ever broader horizons, to the original Knowledge, common to all of humanity, born of an era anterior to the revealed religions, and to which Augustine directly refers in his *Confessions,* when he speaks of "the wisdom that had not been suitable, but is now such as it always was and will forever be." Clement of Alexandria notes on his side, Christianity's elaboration of an extended, strictly initiatory synthesis that does not suppose victory of a particular Church over paganism, but unites with a supra-confessional spirituality that borrows its traits from the Primordial Tradition. The same ultimate reference has continued throughout Christianity, shines in the sixteenth century as a cracked replica of humanist provincialism. Pico della Mirandola, sets out, it may be said, the foundations of comparative esotericism, he for whom

---

[8] This text develops the word of Christ: "Woe to you, jurists, because you have taken away the key to knowledge (gnosis); you have not entered and you have kept out the ones who wanted to enter."

Oratio curiously recalls the Sufi set of themes of the "perfect man." Guillaume Postel, a Catholic priest who covered the Middle East, was interested in Islam whose language he spoke, and in Japanese Buddhism, concluded on a spiritual unity of the world. Nicolas of Cusa not only placed the authority of the ecumenical Council above that of the Popes, but the Roman Cardinal that he was recognized the fundamental unity of the traditions.[9]

This idea of unity, we see, is already familiar to its precursors; but its time had not yet come, although it seemed to have considerably matured in the eschatological *context* that we are aware of. We often hear today that the only international language is contemporary science that, by using the same signs, can be understood by scientists the world over. Where science agrees, religions clash. This obviously forgets *philosophia perennis*, which is found at the heart of these religions, prior to the excesses, the late additions, the diverging literalisms, and offers exactly the same values and same guarantee of universality.

Two characters especially incarnate this Primordial Tradition in Judeo-Christian tradition: Elias (Elijah) and Melchizedek.

Elias has ties with the Revelation God made to the first man: the "unique language" of the origins that will change into a plurality of "languages," that is to say, religions, each one renewing the first Revelation in its own style. While Babel consecrates the blooming of exotericism, Elias clears the way for the Messiah, prepares another cycle, the reign of the New Jerusalem. It is within this same perspective and following the inspiration of this prophet that we should place today's extensive trend of interest in the whole of traditions. Melchizedek is the exteriorization of the Primordial Tradition. It is "without genealogy," that is to say of supra-human origin; it is itself the prototype of man, the image of the Divine Word; the leader of the Three Kings, who personalize the three supreme functions according to Guénon.

The exoteric point of view cannot help protesting against this immersion of Christianity into the whole of traditions stemming from the Primordial Tradition, fearing to see Christian singularity be dissolved in the relativism of false concordances. One might imagine quite the opposite, that this apparent assimilating *ingestion*

---

[9] Especially in his dialogue, *De Pace fidei*, condemning the wars between the believers in the name of the same God they all worshiped.

gives the Christian revelation its true universal character. Indeed, this revelation makes Christ the most direct resurgence of the Primordial Tradition, since, as Saint Paul said, Christ is "the priest according to the order of Melchizedek," he who, like Melchizedek, is "before Abraham," and has neither a beginning nor an end; he who, by establishing the Eucharistic offering, somewhat reiterates and makes official the sacrifice of Melchizedek, the offering of bread and wine.

By breaking the limits of Judaism, the Christlike revelation marks the return to the first Tradition. Since then, "there is no difference between the Jew and the Greek, because they have the same Lord"; "there is only one God who justifies by faith the circumcised and the uncircumcised." Christianity appears from then on as the reactualization of the Primordial Tradition, the return of the Golden Age at the very heart of the time of the end, this Golden Age mysteriously saluted by Virgil in his fourth eclogue; and it is this that legitimizes one more time the need for Christianity to open up to the other traditions. The Light of Pentecost is its answer to the confusion of languages, in anticipation of Heaven where everyone will understand each other.

This reconciliation by the top is placed even above the "ecumenism of flowers"; it would concern a fourth kind of ecumenism that is located at the most subtle level of the Spiritual, the anterior and unanimous Essence, and could be called the "ecumenism of perfumes."

24.   SEEDS OF AWAKENING
(UNPUBLISHED FRAGMENTS)

I Cosmology

- Every bee buzzes a message; every atom murmurs a silence.
- Anxious, the sudden Spirit looks behind one, as if he had forgotten something: Matter.
- While immanence, from the depths of his folds, vociferates his nostalgia for transcendence, from the depths of his crystal palaces, transcendence suggests their lips mingle.
- Matter also has its ecstasy: transparence.
- Press your ear against space: you'll hear the humming of the choir of invisible things and the rustling of energies gliding toward their manifestation.
- All points are points of intersection where space and the Axis of the world link Earth and Heaven. In this sense every point in space is center.
  So, wherever you are, you are at the center, that is to say in God, since God himself is *the* Center.
- The time of the *essential* takes its time: it has the talent for maturing. It is the one made by the sages.
  The time of the *existential* is the one of our clocks; it only makes old men.
- Water transformed into air designs the rainbow, the way of the gods.
  Earth baked by fire condenses the pebbles that pave the path of men.
- The wind blows: God drapes himself in it.
  Serene air: God is nude.
- At the heart of the elements, ether roams, as at the heart of a reflection, light.
- Honey has never known that its mother was a bee; even less that its grandmother was a flower.
- The circulation of air, the humility of the earth, the light of the sun, the immensity of the seas compose the four-point program suggested for man: controlled *breathing*, voluntary *humbleness*, inner *clarity*, boundless *love*.

253

- Every form shows Him because He is in every form.
  None show Him because He is beyond forms.
- The gods hide in the sun so that men can't see them.
  Unable to stare at the radiance of the sun, men say that the gods don't exist.
- The gods will speak to you if you know how to see their silence and hear them smiling over your births.
- The being of the gods is reflected in us under the name of *consciousness.*
- Neuroses and psychoses are the holes left in the soul by the gods, once chased by men.
- By populating nature with gods, polytheism held back the arm bearing the axe, and recited prayers before cutting down the essential.
  By exiling God to the sky, monotheism left to its own a nature devoid of the sacred, and became the carefree accomplice of the demolishers.
- The heart is the place of the greatest wonder: the one where simple mortals bring about the resurrection of the gods.
- There was a time with neither questions nor answers;
  a time where there were only answers without questions;
  a time where there were answers to the questions;
  a time where there were more questions than answers;
  a time where there were only questions without answers.
- In the Golden Age, men speak to the gods face-to-face.
  In the Second Age, they talk to each other through a veil;
  in the Third, through a wall.
  In the Iron Age, men and gods no longer talk to each other.
- God goes on a smile strike: the universe faints.
- Does the flowering of fake prophets plead in favor of an absence of the future?
- The tragedy of an eventual disappearance of humanity would be less in this disappearance than in the fact that, in that case, no particle of matter would be lightened by the actions of the ascetics who, integrating it, sanctify it.

II Presenting Man

- Depositing its thirst there, the caravan kneels before the well, savors the absence of a dune.
  Abandoning his wait, the Divine contemplates himself in the water of Creation, sees man there.
- The universe is simply a comma in the silence of God.
  Man is an entire sentence in the comma of the universe.
- A handful of sand, a swarm of crickets, a flight of pollen suffice for signaling mineral, animal, vegetable.
  It doesn't take less of a glance to say man.
- Man is divine by nature, human by habit, magnificent by glimmers.
- Of all the animals, man is the worst.
  But of them all, he alone can be the contrary of the worst.
- This foliage is your hair, these diamonds, your subtle centers.
  These perfumes speak your essence.
  This air circulates within you in the form of living breaths.
  This fine drop of ether in the cavern of the sky is the fine flame of your spirit in the cavern of your heart.
- Man regards with his eyes, God with his regard.
  Eyes' regard: only one regard;
  regard of God: regard one.
- Thoughts engrave lines, memories sketch reflections.
- All our ideas are dead leaves that maturity transfigured by its autumn.
- Intelligence is diurnal night,
  intuition, lunar day,
  intellection, darkness brighter than the sun.
- The entire history of Western man is a cascade of murders.
  By killing the Non-Being, he deprived himself of the Primordial Ancestor;
  by killing the Being-God, he deprived himself of his Father;
  by killing Nature, of his Mother;
  by killing the Messenger, of his older Brother.
  Patricide, matricide, fratricide, assassin, orphan, Western man has condemned himself to the least curable neurosis.

- Nothing pleases the devil as much as seeing man sad; he sees man in his image.

  But nothing pleases him more than seeing him hateful; then he knows that man is in his likeness.
- Evil is the adolescent crisis of good.
- It is always possible to be more profound than one was before.
- In every sleeping man a death lies awake.
- Dreams are those butterflies whose wings leave divinatory pollen on the fingertips.
- Leave one's faults to the individual, take the qualities of the person.
- For me, God says, every being is the best.
- As Christ is unbearable stone of scandal for humanity, so is humanity for the rest of the universe by everything that helps it escape determinism, and lets it radiate in complete creativity.
- The figure suggests the soul and is expressed in the portrait.
  The visage murmurs the spirit and is fulfilled in the icon.
- The icon: mirror that God leans over to make sure that he has become visage.
- There are ten thousand mistakes, ten thousand awakenings, ten thousand ecstasies.

  But there is only one certainty: that woman's smile floating above the prairie.
- Amid the crowding of celestial virgins and horrible ogresses, between the inaccessible and the unavoidable, the lovely young woman from Ajanta remembers the essential: to put on her lipstick.
- As every mother carries her child inside her, every young girl carries the mother she will someday become. She feels her moving in her womb.
- Woman knows some things she ignores.
- Hazard is the established Order having fun at being subversive.
- Hazard, every time God wants man to doubt Him.
- Who doesn't often feel in Hell in this world, a hell paved with embers—thorns of fire?

  Who doesn't suddenly realize one day that in these embers— thorns of knowledge—diamonds burn?

- We never understand at the time what happens to us: we understand much later why it happened to us.

  More than the momentary incomprehension is the suffering while waiting for the explanation.

- To imagine a future filled with misfortunes that will never occur, is to offend this future and only deserve the occurrence of these misfortunes.

- The most important moments in life are the ones when we receive it—but we don't know that—and the ones when we lose it—but we no longer know that. That is why so many births lead to wasted lives, and so many deaths to lives starting over again.

- If we lived only one of our days to the fullest, we would find the density of an entire lifetime. Man is so dispersed that life must allow him tens of thousands of days so that he will finally *understand*.

  And one day, weary of war, it no longer provides for him: man ceases to live without ever having lived.

- Contemplating the fleeting, one becomes fleeting.

- Each bat of an eyelash eye is like the stroke of a pick in the clay of time still left to us.

- To identify oneself with the Whole is to *disidentify* oneself from the whole.

- The West has only anguish and repulsion for the idea of returning to what it considers to be only nothingness, son of nothingness.

  The East joyfully soars toward this nothingness where it recognizes Divine Vacuity.

- A man who is dead inside is a man who has vomited his essence.

  If, however, he is dead, he doesn't yet know it: all hope is not lost. For as long as he doesn't know that he is dead, returning to life is possible.

- The real victory over death is to conquer the evil within us.

  For evil is death within us.

- The quality of the final hour determines life after death; attaining this quality takes a lifetime of effort.

- Life and death are two sides of this coin placed long ago in the mouth of the deceased.

- Finish one's life with a spelling mistake, and say "I dies."

III   On Religions

- Religions don't necessarily answer the questions we ask; they prefer to answer the ones we don't ask, and which are the real questions.
- Judaism and Islam speak the abrupt language of the desert, which is the blow of the club of the One.

  Panicked by paradoxes, Christianity cries over the death of the Immortal, exults the resurrection of Death.

  Hinduism multiplies names and forms, with which it takes as many steps to the pyre of the Absolute.

  Buddhism melts the dualities in the crucible of a smile, makes emptiness its plate, reaches the Truth by eliminating God.

  Taoism has scruples about not being lighter than air, of which it quietly whispers the transmutations.
- Sects throw the confetti of illusion at *nirvana*.
- The disagreements between religions are quarrels of words, like the one that confronted the "circulators" and Harvey's adversaries. Yes, blood does circulate!

  But so slowly…
- Before all the pigments, the same genes; all the cultures, the same thinking; all the lives, the same breath; all the languages, the same silence; all the nights, the same light.

  Before all the Words, the same Logos.
- Symbols and universal myths form the structures of all tradition, its *consonants*.

  Specific dogmas and rituals are the variants, the *vowels*.
- Kataphasis, which proceeds by additions, adds pearls to pearls; apophasis, which proceeds by subtractions, only keeps the string.

  Silence no longer offers but the *orient* to its jewel box of Unawareness.
- Man's downfall looked at itself in the mirror of the Absolute.

  Seeing itself reflected backwards, it called itself the Divine Descent.

- With Incarnation, God spares man the sin of anthropomorphism.
- God is to his image and to his likeness.

  To his image in that He is conciliation of the contraries; to his likeness in that He is beyond this conciliation.
- The miracle is a paradox that has reached maturity.
- Every point in space being the spot where a vertical and a horizontal intersect, every point in space is a cross, therefore altar and sanctuary.
- The providential aspect of the Christlike message is that it favored Mercy over Strictness, at the cyclical moment where the latter, at its peak, would go wild.
- By suffering with us in the flesh, Christ helped us in advance to suffer with someone—and in that way, to suffer less.
- Weary of having had breath covered with clay, the Word, back in the peace above, shakes the dust of projections from its coat, takes leave of controversy, dusts off the insults, puts up its objurgations, wipes the foam of cries on the silence it becomes once again.
- Every one of the others is a facet of the mirror in which we look at ourselves; in this way, everyone teaches how to better know ourselves.
- Another has the right to be unlike what one would like him to be, the duty to become what he is, and the vocation of being.
- Having to do with whomever means never having to do with anyone.
- You can only help yourself, but you can only help yourself by helping another.
- The shortest road between myself and the others is the Self.

  Neither myself first: that's egoism; nor the others first: that's utopia; but the Self in me, which is also in them.
- "The other" is always more than "another."
- We only take with us what we have given; and all we can give is the sacrifice of ourselves.
- God asks us to love Him; and we ask Him if He exists!
- The Sustaining Power of God: in the thunder of his anger, in the night of his scowling brow, in the harshness of his punishment:

defective trials of a God not yet succeeding at himself.

In its maturity, it only explodes in the fire of forgiveness.

- The secret suffering of Love is to dream that he isn't loved.
- Man loves—or doesn't love—,God letting him love Him or not.
- By pretending to love God, isn't it still me that I love under the pretext that I am Him?
- All of humanity refracting in every being, truly loving a being is loving all of humanity.
- Because love constitutes the very essence of the being, the only way to find the being is to love.
- The flame of things burns on the pyre of fervor.
- The flames of Love are the mirrors where I see Thou.

IV The Spiritual Quest

- We shall remain orphans from our birth for all of our life, if, during our lifetime, we don't know how to make another life.
- One has to have already been *born* to want to be reborn.
- After having lost their way in the forest of appearances, the eyes return to their regard.
- The caterpillar weaves a tomb of saliva, encloses itself there, wilts there.
  From the cadaver, a whole flight of colors unfolds.
  Who would have also thought of it as such a present to oneself without even recognizing it?
- There is no crossing the desert; there is only a march to the oasis.
- The sorrow of the human condition is that man basically aspires to absolute happiness, and that this absolute happiness is impossible because of the relative nature of this condition.
- Caught between the frantic desire for the creature and his loyalty to his own Essence, God suffers.
  Man suffers, caught between his attachment to himself and his aspiration for the divine.
- In no way hazard, if the Infinite being forever infinitely closer to man, since it is omnipresent, man feels infinitely far from him.
  Because from the Infinite that he once was, he became indefi-

nite, from the indefinite, the finite, from the finite, fragmentary. From this fragment he has to start afresh by taking inventory and the reconstitution, as from an infinity of tiny chips, will design an entire mosaic.

- Sometimes we are convalescents of illnesses that we haven't had. Thus, the night of dereliction, even though the Loved has never abandoned his own.

- Modern man: "At last some silence!"
Ancient man: "You destroy it by saying it."

- The best way to talk about silence is to say nothing; the best tribute one can pay it is by listening to it.

- As the shepherd stirs the embers with the end of his staff, God triturates noise with silence.

- Silence merely whispers at the edge of speech, like a light fringe of foam at the lip of the wave.

- Meditation is a certain way of putting oneself on the edge to be more in the center.

- Two ways of facing a wall: the first is that of the desperate banging their heads against the lack of an issue; the other, that of a monk sitting in front of the wall, which disappears by his power of concentration.

- Faith is knowing that what one doesn't see is truer than what one sees.

- It's a good idea to be even more humble when we think we are being humble, for those times when we don't think about it.

- Wanting to do better than everyday life might first consist of doing better at everyday life.

- When the crimson coat takes the vows of poverty, when the din pledges allegiance to silence, when the groans of the orgy become sighs of chastity, when disheveled folly sides with the comb of the reasonable, the billow of bewilderment that rises to the height of the sky falls down again as dew on the earth.

- Giving up a possession that is obviously an illusion means giving up an illusion.
Illusion is a nothing. Therefore, it means giving up a nothing.

- In this illusory world, every creature is illusion. Except when one of them sacrifices itself for another. An illusion that dies for another makes a reality, as a negative multiplied by a negative produces a positive.

- Make everything lighter, imitate the feather: the only way to weigh less on the scale of Judgment.
- Drunk with lucidity, the awakened, fully measuring what he is, understands that this very little that he is can only truly be by his renouncing it.
- The Commencement is in every moment. Living in the present moment is, moment by moment, living in the Commencement.
- By adding the stitch to another, the step to another, the note to another, the drop to another, the tapestry unrolls on the loom, the caravan crosses the desert, music springs into the sky, embraces it, the source swells its front, wellspring surges.

V Approaches to Mystery

- Archetypes, orchids from the garden of the Essence.
- The peaceful rivers, and the wide prairies, and the lovely gardens are very much the memorial signs of the *other country,* where the rivers are eternity flowing, the prairies, infinity perpetuating, and the gardens, light spreading indefinitely like bushes.
- Mystery is an extract from the invisible *immensified.*
- Naming the Unnamed, forces him to take name.
- God is the sum of the Names He calls himself when we name Him by them.
- The remembrance of God commemorates the memory and "rememorates" the immemorial himself.
- We don't have to get into Heaven: we are there.
  We just have to remember where we are.
  And we remember by invoking the Name. Because Name and Heaven are one.
- Man's most important job is to comfort God in those vacillating hours of his faith in man. And there is no surer way of giving life to God than to revive the Name deposited in the heart of man.
  To nourish God of our being is to nourish Him, in reality, of his Being, from which we are most intimately made. This works by the memorizing commemoration, the prayer of the Name.

- What we say about God isn't what counts, but what we let God say in us; this right that we grant Him to say Himself—instead of us.
- Dew to refresh.

  Drops of blood to be born again.

  Tears of joy to grant mercy.
- There are men-answers. Their answer is in their presence.
- The demiurge informs the world: by giving it "scale, number and weight."

  Man transforms it: either in favor of beauty or to the detriment of nature.

  The saint transfigures it: by expressing its essence through its own light and lightness.
- In the secret of the top room, the saint consoles his Beloved, whose faith in man vacillates, for all the infidelities that men have committed and commit.
- Universal compassion and passion for the person make a saint.

  Personal impassiveness and universal compassion make a sage.
- Wherever he goes, the steps of the sage leave no footprints because the coming snows have erased them in anticipation.
- The liberated knows that at the hour of Liberation, it isn't death that kills, but the illusion that dies.
- What opposes darkness is not light; it is Vacuity.

  But Vacuity is light.

CHRONOLOGY OF THE LIFE OF JEAN BIÈS

1933   Born in Bordeaux, France.

        Childhood and adolescence spent in Algeria where he receives his first influences from the East.

1951   While studying philosophy, he discovers the work of René Guénon, who will be his inspiration for the rest of his own work.

1952   Meets Sheikh Adda Bentounès at the Sufi tariqa al-Alawiyya in Tigditt, Mostaganem, Algeria.

        Studies classics at the University of Algiers and at the Sorbonne, Paris.

1953   Meets Swami Siddheswaranda at the Vedantic Center Sri Ramakrishna in Gretz- Armainvilliers, France.

1958   Travels to Greece and Mount Athos, which will be the subject of his first book.

1962   Teacher of Classics in the southwest of France where he settles with his wife. Begins a studious retreat in the heart of the Pyrenees.

1965   Earns a graduate degree with a thesis devoted to the poet René Daumal.

1967   Meets several times with Frithjof Schuon in Lausanne, Switzerland.

1969   Meets Jean Herbert, translator for the sages of contemporary India.

1970   Grand Prix from the Society of French Poets.

1971   Discovers the alchemic work of C.G. Jung.

1973   Earns his Doctorate with a dissertation on French Literature and Hindu Thinking (Prix de l'Asie from the Overseas Academy of Science). Visits India (Ashram of Sri Ramana Maharshi).

1974   Professor of Greek Literature at the University of Pau, France.

1981   Meets Marie-Magdeleine Davy, specialist of Medieval Christianity.

1985   Invited by the University of Caracas, Venezuela, as a conference speaker.

1987   Meets Francois Chenet, specialist of India.

1997   Named Chevalier of the French Legion of Honor.

1999   Meets Patrick Laude, Ph.D., Professor of French at Georgetown University.

LIST OF EXTRACTS*

- *Tarini, Pioneer of Awakening.* Originally published as *L'Initiatrice*. Paris: Éditions Jacqueline Renard, 1990.

- *The Door to the Women's Apartment.* Originally published as *La Porte de l'appartement des femmes*. Paris: Éditions Jacqueline Renard, 1991.

- *Return to the Essential.* Originally published as *Retour à l'Essentiel*. Paris: Dervy Livres, 1986.

- *Athos, the Transfigured Mountain.* Originally published as *Athos, la Montagne Transfigurée*. Paris: Éditions Les Deux Océans, 1997.

- *The Pathways of Passion.* Originally published as *Les Chemins de la ferveur: Voyage en Inde*. Lyon: Éditions Terre du Ciel, 1995.

- *Art, Gnosis, and Alchemy.* Originally published as *Art, Gnose et Alchimie*. Paris: Éditions Le Courrier du Livre, 1987.

- *Passports for New Times.* Originally published as *Passeports pour des temps nouveaux*. Paris: Éditions Dervy Livres, 1982.

---

* The author would like to thank the various publishers for authorizing the translation of selected extracts from his collection of titles.

Titles by the Same Author

- *Mont Athos.* Paris: Albin Michel, 1963.
- *René Daumal.* Paris: Pierre Seghers, 1967, 1973.
- *Empédocle d'Agrigente.* Paris: Editions Traditionnelles, 1969.
- *Littérature francaise et Pensée hindoue.* Paris: C. Klincksieck, 1973, 1992.
- *Passeports pour des temps nouveaux.* Paris: Dervy, 1982, and Lausanne: L'Age d'Homme, 2004.
- *Retour à l'Essentiel.* Paris: Dervy, 1986, and Lausanne: L'Age d'Homme, 2004.
- *Art, Gnose et Alchimie.* Paris: Le Courrier du Livre, 1987.
- *L'Initiatrice.* Paris: Jacqueline Renard, 1990.
- *La Porte de l'appartement des femmes.* Paris: Jacqueline Renard, 1991.
- *Miroir de Poésie.* Paris: Groupe de Recherches Polypoétiques, 1994.
- *Les Chemins de la ferveur: Voyage en Inde.* Lyon: Terre de Ciel, 1995.
- *Paroles d'urgence.* Lyon: Terre de Ciel, 1996.
- *Voies de sages.* Paris: Editions du Félin, 1996.
- *Athos, la Montagne transfigurée.* Paris: Les Deux Océans, 1997.
- *Sagesses de la Terre.* Paris: Les Deux Océans, 1997.
- *Grands Initiés du XX Siècle.* Paris: Editions du Félin, 1998.
- *Les Alchimistes.* Paris: Editions du Félin, 2000.
- *Par les chemins de vie et d'oeuvre.* Paris: Les Deux Océans, 2001.
- *Semences d'éveil.* Paris: Dervy, 2004.

FORTHCOMING TITLES

- *Des Poètes et des Dieux. Métaphysique et Littérature.* Lausanne: L'Age d'Homme.
- *Paysages de l'Esprit.* Paris: Editions du Rocher.

BOOKS TRANSLATED INTO OTHER LANGUAGES

- *Passeports pour des temps nouveaux.* Translated into Spanish. Caracas: Mandorla, 1985.
- *Voies de sages.* Translated into Portuguese. Sao Paulo: Triom, 2001.
- *Paroles d'urgence.* Translated into Romanian. Bucharest: Mirabilis, 2001.

JOURNAL ARTICLES
(numerous articles have appeared in the following journals)

- *Aurores*
- *Troisième Millénaire*
- *Vers la Tradition*
- *Connaissance des Religions*
- *Terre du Ciel*

BIOGRAPHICAL NOTES

JEAN BIÈS was born in Bordeaux, France, in 1933. He studied Classics at the University of Algiers and later at the Sorbonne. He was first influenced by the East during his childhood and adolescence spent in Algeria. The discovery of René Guénon's writings in 1951 was to become a determining influence by revealing to him the existence of initiatory teachings. He later met several representatives of traditional wisdom including the Sufi sheikh Adda Bentounès in 1952, Swami Siddheswarananda in 1954 and 1956, and Frithjof Schuon in 1967, 1968, and 1971. In 1973, he defended his doctoral dissertation in which he studied the relationship between French literature and Hindu thinking (*Littérature française et Pensée Hindoue*). This work was awarded the Prix d'Asie by the Académie des Sciences d'Outre-mer. The same year, he traveled extensively throughout India.

During his career as a teacher of French at the High School in Nay and as a Professor of Greek Literature at the University of Pau, he also gave several conferences in France and in Switzerland, Belgium, and Venezuela. He wrote numerous articles which appeared in a range of reviews, while at the same time obstinately pursuing his work as a writer. He retired in 1993 in order to devote his time entirely to his works. In 1997, he was named Chevalier of the French Legion of Honor.

Jean Biès' works are divided into theoretical essays: presentations of traditional teachings, travel and personal accounts, testimonies, and collections of poetry—some 10,000 pages of published and unpublished texts. Situated at the confluence of East and West, and in the constant light of the *philosophia perennis* at an especially critical time of the *Kali Yuga*, his work offers spiritual "keys" and suggestions for the urgent preparation of the future.

Since 1962, he and his wife have lived in a country home, "Saint-Michel-la-Grange," at the foot of the Pyrénées.

DEBORAH WEISS-DUTILH, of Hungarian origin, was born in Los Angeles, California. She holds a Bachelor of Arts degree in French from the University of California, Irvine and a teaching credential in English. Her studies led her to the Sorbonne and to Pau, France, near the Pyrénées, where she lives with her husband and two sons. Studies in psychotherapy, with a keen interest in the link between psychology, spirituality, and philosophy sparked her friendship with Jean Biès and their subsequent collaboration.

PATRICK LAUDE is Professor of French at Georgetown University. Born of Gascon and Basque stock in 1958 in Lannemezan, Hautes Pyrénées, France, he later studied history and philosophy at Paris-Sorbonne and was a Fellow at the Ecole Normale Supérieure in Paris (1979-1982). His academic career took him to the United States where he obtained a Ph.D. in French literature, specializing in poetry and mystical literature. He is the author of numerous works dealing with the relationship between mysticism, symbolism, and literature, including *Music of the Sky: An Anthology of Spiritual Poetry* (co-edited with Barry McDonald, World Wisdom, 2004) and *Singing the Way: Insights in Poetry and Spiritual Transformation* (forthcoming World Wisdom, 2005). Dr. Laude is also the author of several studies on important contemporary spiritual figures such as Jeanne Guyon, Simone Weil, and Louis Massignon. He recently co-edited a work (with Jean-Baptiste Aymard) on Frithjof Schuon, the renowned Swiss metaphysician and expositor of the Perennial Philosophy, entitled *Frithjof Schuon: Life and Teachings* (SUNY Press, 2004). He is presently preparing *Cracks of Light: Demiurgic Gods and Tricksters, Sacred Clowns and Holy Fools* for publication.

INDEX

For a glossary of all key foreign words used in books published by World Wisdom, including metaphysical terms in English, consult:
www.DictionaryofSpiritualTerms.org.
This on-line Dictionary of Spiritual Terms provides extensive definitions, examples and related terms in other languages

Titles in the Perennial Philosophy series by World Wisdom

The Betrayal of Tradition: Essays on the Spiritual Crisis of Modernity,
edited by Harry Oldmeadow, 2005

Borderlands of the Spirit: Reflections on a Sacred Science of Mind
by John Herlihy, 2005

A Buddhist Spectrum by Marco Pallis, 2003

The Essential Ananda K. Coomaraswamy, edited
by Rama P. Coomaraswamy, 2004

*The Essential Titus Burckhardt: Reflections on Sacred Art, Faiths, and
Civilizations,* edited by William Stoddart, 2003

Every Branch in Me: Essays on the Meaning of Man,
edited by Barry McDonald, 2002

Every Man an Artist: Readings in the Traditional Philosophy of Art,
edited by Brian Keeble, 2005

Hinduism and Buddhism by Ananda K. Coomaraswamy, 2005

*Islam, Fundamentalism, and the Betrayal of Tradition: Essays by Western
Muslim Scholars,* edited by Joseph E. B. Lumbard, 2004

*Journeys East: 20th Century Western Encounters with Eastern Religious
Traditions* by Harry Oldmeadow, 2004

Living in Amida's Universal Vow: Essays in Shin Buddhism,
edited by Alfred Bloom, 2004

Paths to the Heart: Sufism and the Christian East,
edited by James S. Cutsinger, 2002

Returning to the Essential: Selected Writings of Jean Biès,
translated by Deborah Weiss-Dutilh, 2004

Science and the Myth of Progress, edited by Mehrdad M. Zarandi, 2003

Seeing God Everywhere: Essays on Nature and the Sacred,
edited by Barry McDonald, 2003

Singing the Way: Insights in Poetry and Spiritual Transformation
by Patrick Laude, 2005

Ye Shall Know the Truth: Christianity and the Perennial Philosophy,
edited by Mateus Soares de Azevedo, 2005